D1518537

Roy Rogers
and
Dale Evans

It Was Always the Music

A celebration of
Roy and Dale's singing cowboy B-Western era of
country-western music.

by

Eric van Hamersveld

Authorized by
Dale Evans Rogers,
Roy "Dusty" Rogers, Jr., and
the Roy Rogers-Dale Evans Museum

Roy and Dale rehearsing a new song.

Roy Rogers and Dale Evans

It Was Always the Music

A celebration of
Roy and Dale's singing cowboy B-Western era of
country-western music.

by

Eric van Hamersveld

Authorized by
Dale Evans Rogers,
Roy "Dusty" Rogers, Jr., and
the Roy Rogers-Dale Evans Museum

Published by:
R&R Publications Marketing Pty., Ltd
ACN 27 083 612 579
12 Edward Street, Brunswick, Victoria, 3056
Australia

Publisher: Richard Carroll
Author: Eric van Hamersveld
Project Management: Eric van Hamersveld

All the songs in this publication were transcribed from the original soundtracks by the author.

Includes Index
ISBN 1 740221 45 1
EAN 9 781740 221 450

First Edition Printed October 2003

R&R Publications Marketing Pty., Ltd
12 Edward Street, Brunswick
Victoria, 3054, Australia
Phone (61 3) 9381 2199 Fax (61 3) 9381 2689
E-mail: info@randrpublications.com.au
Web: www.randrpublications.com.au
Printed in China

**Roy's favorite guitar was the Gibson Super 400
featured on the book's end papers.**

DEDICATION

To my wife, Sue, who deserves a special award for
putting up with this project for almost 5 years.
She gladly participated in visiting with people all over the country,
dressing up in cowgirl outfits and going to film festivals, and
waking up every morning in an empty bed (I work best starting at 5:00 am).
Her only comment is that I'll really enjoy the quilting conventions
that I'll be going to with her as payback.

TABLE OF CONTENTS

** Author's Note:
These songs are from uncut films that we could not find.
They are placed in the Table of Contents to show where they appeared in the film.
If you have a uncut copy of any one of these films, or know where we can obtain an uncut copy, please contact us through the publisher or email: esvh@connectnet.com.

ACKNOWLEDGEMENTS

I sit here in front of the computer, sipping hot mocha from a Roy Rogers mug. I look at shelves and file cabinets full of sheet music, correspondence, video tapes, photos, and books that represent a large portion of my life for the past five years. The letter writing, the phone calls, the traveling and visiting, the emailing, the creating of the book pages, the film viewing, the audio editing, the hammering on song publishers, the waiting for a key piece of information. . . all of this would not have happened without the support and assistance of the following kind folks:

...Roy, Dale, and Herb Yates, head of Republic Studios, for making the pictures (Roy always called them "pictures" not films) and the memories that sparked the idea for this book.

...Roy "Dusty" Rogers, Jr., President of the Roy Rogers-Dale Evans Museum, without whose approval for this project from the very beginning I would not have proceeded. From the very beginning I knew that it was not the "cowboy way" and certainly not "Roy's way" to produce anything about a person's life's work without permission. Dusty is just like his dad; what you see is what you get. He took one look at my book proposal and not only gave me permission but allowed me access to priceless materials in the museum's backroom. He also provided names and phone numbers of folks who might help with my research, and he wrote a letter of introduction on my behalf that cleared the path on many occasions to get information that I needed.

...Joel "Dutch" Dortch, Executive Director of the Happy Trails Children's Foundation, whom I first met at a film festival in Lone Pine, California. Standing there behind a table in full western dress, including six-guns, Dutch looked like the kindly sheriff of a small western town. He was ready to greet visitors with a smile and a "Howdy, Partner." I showed him a sample of my project and he enthusiastically agreed to introduce me to Dusty anytime I was ready. I was so taken with Dutch and the work he is doing for abused kids and so grateful for his assistance in any way he could, that I decided then and there to donate a portion of this project to help the Foundation.

...Scott Homan, an extraordinary musician, who transcribed 138 audio tracks into song sheets. I would not have been able to have all the audio tracks transcribed into song sheets within the timeframe needed with without Scott's dedication to the project. He made the process seem effortless. I would deliver an audio CD of the tracks, along with the lyrics, to him in groups of 10 and he would soon return the handwritten song sheets that made this project possible.

...Larry Zwisohn, writer and music historian, who has worked in the business side of music of the motion picture industry for years and has at his fingertips (actually buried in his head) more information about the songs and songwriters of yesteryear than can be imagined. During the many conversations we had, Larry would patiently discuss minute details about the writers lives and their work. He was an invaluable resource, for he not only knew about the genre but, because of his close friendship with Dale, Roy, Dusty, Ken Carson, Bob Nolan and others, he knew about many of the other people involved in the productions.

...Cheryl (Rogers) Barnett, Director of Education at the Roy Rogers-Dale Evans Museum and Dusty's older sister, who gave time from her busy schedule to find contacts for me to pursue when I became stuck or had a question about a particular film. I'll always remember the day that my wife and I had just come from a visit with her mother, Dale, and were at the museum waiting to ask Cheryl about something or other. It was around lunchtime, and Cheryl came rushing out of her office and suggested that we go to lunch at a restaurant that her mom and dad loved. Sitting around the table and chatting about her life at home with Roy, Dale, Dusty, and the rest of the kids, was truly a heartwarming and informative experience that I will treasure for a long, long time.

...the Roy Rogers-Dale Evans Museum Staff, especially Dave Kock and Dustin Rogers, for providing guidance during my backroom museum research activities, making copies of materials I discovered, and fielding my constant calls for bits of information or the copy of a stray photo.

...Elizabeth McDonald, who has collected and collated all of Bob Nolan's works. Although we've never seen each other in person, through the internet Elizabeth and I have become friends and exchanged enough information to publish several volumes. She was always there when I needed clarification of a word or phrase on old film soundtracks, or a specific date when something happened, or some other detail that had me stumped.

...James D'Arc, Curator of Arts and Communication Archives at Brigham Young University, whom I contacted when I found that Republic Studios had given their entire music collection to the university. Through Jim's efforts I was able to uncover several original song sheets that were used on the actual movie set but never published for the public.

...Hal Spencer, son of Tim Spencer of the original *Sons of the Pioneers* and owner of several music publishing companies, whom I met through a referral by Dusty and an introduction by his friend, Stan Corliss (mentioned below). When I discussed my project with Hal, he was delighted and sent me several songs of his dad's that I needed but had never been published. I thank him for his continuing interest and support.

...Michelle Sudin, past Executive Director of the Western Music Association, who was immediately taken with the project. She gave me several names to contact and wrote a letter of support on my behalf that opened many doors that would otherwise have remained tightly shut.

...Dr. Elizabeth van Hamersveld, yes, my mother, but one heck of an editor. She has a doctorate in English Literature, was a teacher, and even helped compile the *World Publishing Company, College Edition, New World Dictionary*. I couldn't have given what little writing there is in this book to a more qualified wordsmith. I am probably the world's worse speller so, with a mother who was a lexicographer, I have always been in fear of the red pencil. I told her once that it anyone could spell a word like everybody else. I told her that it took a truly creative mind to come up with alternative spellings. Thankfully, today we have "spell check" on our word processors... and I still have Mom.

...Stan Corliss, western music entertainer, whom I first saw at Roy's memorial service. He was wearing a Roy Rogers' creased hat. Later, I traced his phone number and gave him a call to see where I could get one like it. Typical of "the cowboy way," Stan said that Roy showed him how to crease the hat and would gladly do one for me. Just give him my hat size. He'd buy the hat, crease it, ship it to me and, if I liked it, then I could send him a check. Now, we had never seen each other and yet Stan spend money and time for a stranger. I was awed by Stan's generosity and trust. By the way, the creasing process is an all-day affair. Because of the sharp creases the hat must be soaked and slowly shaped and dried. The best way to do this is to wear the hat while taking your morning shower. So, can you imagine your cowboy hero, Roy, standing in the shower, stark naked, with his cowboy hat on? Anyway, since meeting Stan, my wife and I have been his guests at the Golden Boot Awards Round-Up party, that made it possible to rub elbows and chat with the current and past greats in the western film arena.

...Mindy Petersen, Candie Halberg, and **Julie Ashley,** Roy and Dale's grand-daughters, of *The Rogers Legacy* who met with me during their performance in Tucson with the *Sons of the Pioneers*. At that time I showed them the beginnings of the book. They were excited to see the possibility of new material to sing, especially songs from their grandparents, and, just like the others, they gave me the names of several key folks to contact.

...Many thanks go to: **John Elliott, Jr.** and **Vicki Benet Elliott,** the son and widow of songwriter Jack Elliott; **Sally Henderson Maxwell,** daughter of songwriter Charles E. Henderson; **Bobbie (Nolan) Mileusnich** and **Calin Coburn,** daughter and grandson of Bob Nolan who was a songwriter and one of the original *Sons of the Pioneers*; and **Gretchen Carson,** widow of songwriter Ken Carson who was also a member of the *Sons of the Pioneers*. They all gladly gave me permission to search any archives for their loved ones' works, and to publish the finished song sheets.

...Dr. Will Cratty, San Diego State University Music Department, who transcribed the first song sheet for the book, *The Cowboy and the Senorita*.

...Jane Leigh, music teacher and mother of my son's wife, who created the song sheet for Tim Spencer's *The Bunkhouse Bugle Boy*.

...Tom and **Kate Harnish** who, although they now own and operate Barnstorming Adventures, (visit www.barnstorming.com), are published authors offering financial advice and guidance to entrepreneurs (visit www.findingmoney.com). They are devoted friends and helped direct me through the business side of writing and publishing.

...Fenton Rosewarne, President of Digital Imagination, who took one look at my project and immediately pitched the book proposal to his friend, Richard, the owner of R & R Publishing.

...Richard Carroll, my publisher, who was raised on a station (ranch) in Australia and has always been a Roy Rogers fan. I'll aways remember the time when, on a trip to my home to discuss the book and meet with Dusty, I dressed him up with a cowboy hat, vest, and six-gun and took a picture of "Ricky the Kid."

...Louie Stevens, an extraordinary audio engineer, who brought the original fifty-year old soundtracks back to life.

...Others that also deserve many thanks are: **Lilian Turner,** Archivist at the Cody Museum; **James Austin,** head of Rhino Records; **Mike Johnson,** a Rogers family friend; **Marcello Radulovich,** musician; **Elizabeth Reyes Vidrio,** Spanish translator; **Fred Goodwin,** owner of Concept Productions; **Truman Lee Evett,** avid western collector; **Packy Smith,** film collector and producer; **Bob Carman,** author; and the many members of the **Single Action Shooting Society** and the **Western Music Association.**

...Also, a very special thanks to my close family and friends who have put up with my sometimes insane exuberance for this project: my two sons **Chris** and **Mark**; my brother **Craig** and brother-in-law **Bill Twitty**; **Bill** and **Kathleen Dabbs**; **Mike** and **Karen McNamara**; **Al** and **Joan Cox**; **Nancy** and **Earl Viets**; and **Jack** and **June Toplift**.

Bless you all.

DALE'S FOREWORD

Music has always meant a great deal to me. It helped me celebrate the good times, and it helped me get through the bad times.

While a small child, my ambition was to grow up, marry Tom Mix and have six children. Well, I grew up to marry Roy Rogers and raise nine children.

In my teens and early twenties, my ambition was to star in Broadway musicals.

I was a singer on radio and with the big bands of the 1930s and 1940s. While singing on CBS's "The Chase & Sanborn Hour," I attracted the attention of Hollywood. Republic Pictures signed me to a one-picture contract, with a one-year option, if the studio liked how I looked and sounded on film.

The picture I made was called "Swing Your Partner." The film co-starred me with two stars from the WLS "National Barn Dance" radio program, Lulubelle and Scotty. The movie wasn't a huge success but it was great timing for me.

Herbert J. Yates, who was president of Republic Pictures, had recently seen "Oklahoma" on the New York stage. He was so impressed that he wanted to create a Western movie musical for the studio's number one box office star, Roy Rogers.

When Republic cast me with Roy, most of the music in our films was written specifically for that film and specifically for our characters or our co-stars.

Most of the 28 movies we made together at Republic are mini-Broadway productions and the term "Horse Opera" was truly appropriate. The music was designed to move the plot along and the songs were a very integral part of the story.

To produce quality sound for the music and songs, the music track was recorded first in Republic's recording studio usually with an orchestra. Then, some days later, Roy and I would film the scene - sometimes on a sound stage along with dancers and visible musicians, or sometimes outdoors, riding on our horses accompanied by an invisible orchestra.

In between the recording of the sound and the filming of the scene were hours of practicing our lip movements to a record of the song so that, when we were filming, it would look like we were actually singing live on the film. This is called lip-syncing and is VERY difficult.

The songwriters and musicians we worked with at Republic were wonderful. Writers like Jack Elliott, Ned Washington, Charles Henderson, Tim Spencer, Bob Nolan, and others give us beautiful songs to sing. And don't forget the Sons of the Pioneers providing their own brand of harmony with and without us. No wonder our movies were so well received!

I do hope that you enjoy the songs that Eric has managed to recreate in this collection as much as we did when we originally recorded them.

Dale Evans Rogers

DUSTY'S FOREWORD

I guess when you grow up in a musical family, some of that music has to rub off on you. I mean, it only stands to reason when your father was "King of the Cowboys," and your mother was "Queen of the West", that you will either love music, or hate it.

Thankfully, I LOVE music, and always have! I can't read musical notes very well, but I can pick a tune up by ear, hear it once, and sing it right back at you.

My earliest recollections of hearing music was my father playing the guitar and singing to me "My Little Buckaroo." As I was growing up, mom would sing religious songs around the house, and who could forget Christmas holiday songs around the piano. All of us kids, 9 in all, would sing or play some kind of instrument. From trombone (Sandy), to piano (the piano), guitar (Dad), and kitchen pans (me). Music was a huge part of our family's life.

I remember our family's first recording session - what a fiasco! Trying to get everyone on key was an all day, frustrating experience! I guess that's why the Rogers family only did one family album. The Von Trapps we were not, but we did love the "Sound of Music."

I always sang in the church choir during high school, and I joined a barber shop and gospel quartet singing bass. The group was called the "Fuzzy Wuzzies," because we wore alpaca sweaters. I did not start my solo career until I was 21.
I was married and lived in Ohio with my wife Linda. I started singing with a small country group, and within 3 months I had my own TV show on WEWS-TV in Cleveland, Ohio. The program was called "The Roy Rogers Jr. Show," and was a musical/variety format.

My love for music continued to grow. I performed with mom and dad and the Sons of the Pioneers at many state fairs and rodeos. When I moved back to California in the mid-1970's, I found I needed my own band, so I started looking for members of the band that would eventually be known as the "High Riders."

Our love for western music was sparked by working side by side with the Sons of the Pioneers. I guess my soul always needed to pay respect to the musical phenomenon that my father started so many years before.

Now that my father and mother have graduated to their new life, the baton has been handed off to me, and I will be proud to run with it. The "High Riders" and I are singing a lot of the songs you will find in this wonderful musical retrospective that Eric has put together. I know you too will find yourself humming along!

Trails Of Happiness To You All!

INTRODUCTION

It was a hot July day in 1998. Over 2,500 folks from all walks of life, some from as far away as Australia, India, South Africa, Malaysia, Portugal, and Canada have gathered in a small desert town northwest of Los Angeles. CNN, ABC, NBC, CBS, and FOX news services have set up direct satellite feeds. The California State Senate and Assembly have adjourned to honor the occasion. Additional telephone operators have been hired to handle the thousands of incoming calls and the over 700 individual charity contributions, in lieu of sending flowers. Why? The King of the Cowboys has passed away and his memorial service is underway.

For over 60 years Roy Rogers and Dale Evans had been a part of the lives of everyone who showed up that day. Each in his or her own way was paying tribute to their childhood hero and remembering the "good old days" . . . and those "kids" certainly had something to remember.

They remembered being one of the 80-million people a year seeing Roy, Trigger, Dale, and Gabby catch the "bad guys" in the 188 action films and television programs that put Roy as the Number One western star for 12 consecutive years; or one of the 65-million readers of Roy Rogers newspaper comic strips; or spending 10-cents for one of the 1.3 million Roy Rogers and Dale Evans comics sold per year; or eating cereal out of one of the 2.5-million boxes with Roy's picture on it; or adding allowance money to the $1-billion spent on over 400 licensed, and personally guaranteed, Roy Rogers' products; or listening along with 20-million others to Roy's radio show broadcast from 500 stations coast-to-coast; or writing one or more of the over 900,000 fan letters Roy received in 1947 alone; or belonging to one of the 2,000 international fan clubs, one of which totaled 50,000 members.

They also remembered listening to the more than 400 songs Roy and Dale recorded. Most of these songs were threaded through their film and television program story lines and are one of the richest sources of our country-western music heritage.

This area of our musical legacy began as a genre dubbed "the B-Western with singing cowboys." Invented and exploited by Herbert Yates, head of the Republic Studios, it used the talents of young song writers for the short musical numbers performed in the films.

Many of these prolific writers went on to become famous in their own right: Ned Washington, wrote the Academy Award winning song *"When You Wish Upon A Star"* for Disney, and the *"High Noon"* movie theme; Jack Elliott, also an Academy winner, wrote Disney's *"Toot Whistle Plunk and Boom;"* Bob Nolan, who along with Tim Spencer and Roy Rogers, started the *Sons of the Pioneers*, and wrote the western classics *"Tumbling Tumbleweeds"* and *"Cool Water;"* Billy Hill, wrote *"That's When Your Heartaches Begin"* for Elvis Presley; Charles Tobias wrote *"Those Lazy Hazy Crazy Days of Summer"* for Nat King Cole; Charles Henderson wrote *"Give My Regards to Broadway"* and the musical cues to many films including Henry Fonda's *"My Darling Clementine"* and Marilyn Monroe's *"Gentlemen Prefer Blonds."* Some of their songs are better than others. . . some are great. . . but, sadly, because some songs were never published and Mr. Yates had the original films cut to 54-minutes for Saturday morning television, many have been lost in time.

Watching an uncut Roger's film one day and trying to play my guitar along with Roy, it occurred to me that these B-western films contained a monumental amount of classic country-western music waiting to be rediscovered and enjoyed.

I talked with many people in and out of the music industry about this music and several of them said that, if I found or reconstructed the music, they would be interested in buying a copy. This sparked the idea to publish a book of sheet music from this long overlooked period of our musical heritage.

The most popular singing cowboy and my all-time childhood hero was Roy Rogers. I decided to tackle the songs in his films. I quickly discovered, however, that he and his costars sang hundreds of songs in his 88 films. I chose to focus on the 28 films that Roy and Dale did together. I even composed a title for the book, *Roy Rogers and Dale Evans: It Was Always the Music*.

Before proceeding further, I wanted to contact Roy "Dusty" Rogers, Jr. to see if he would grant me permission to publish my effort. With an introduction from Joel Dortch of the Happy Trails Children's Foundation, I met with Dusty and was given more support than I could have imagined: a letter of introduction for me to use if I needed credibility; access to the backroom of the Roy Rogers-Dale Evans Museum to look for materials they might have that I could use; and names of people to contact. Dusty also arranged a meeting with his mother, Dale, at her home so that I could show her the manuscript. The meeting with Dale was so cordial that I even got up the nerve to ask her to write the foreword to the book. She graciously consented.

Little did I know that I was going on a two-year hunt much like a detective looking for missing persons. I first obtained music cue sheet lists from the 28 films, and counted almost 170 songs! Some of them were show tunes and popular songs of the era, and the rest were western songs or songs with a western flavor.

Armed with this list I set out to find as much old printed music as I could. I bid and won music sheets on eBay; I found several sheets at the Roy Rogers-Dale Evans Museum; I found some in music books; and found a few in the Library of Congress. I received only three music sheets from music publishers. I also contacted the relatives of the original song writers. Surprisingly, they had very little of their father's or grandfather's work.

In the end, I uncovered printed sheet music to only 30 of the 170 songs. This meant that I would have to transcribe the remaining 140 songs directly from the film's audio track. I can read music but I can't write it; I hired a songwriter to transcribe a song for me. I sat in on the process and it was a wonderful experience seeing music decoded. The song I chose was the theme to *"The Cowboy and the Senorita,"* Roy and Dale's first film together. It was amazing to see a song that has not been heard for over 50 years come back to life.

Now I had to find the films. Remember that Mr. Yates cut the films to 54 minutes for TV. As the story goes, he keep the cut portions in separate film boxes but in a cleanup effort these boxes were thrown away. The cut portions usually contained the musical selections because the kids watching the films on Saturday morning TV only wanted the action. (Can you believe that there was only 6-minutes of commercials in a one-hour TV show in 1950? Today it's about 23-minutes.) I searched all over the world via phone calls, faxes, and the internet and found, on video tape, all but three of the films uncut. The missing uncut films are *"Song of Nevada," "The Man From Oklahoma,"* and *"Sunset in El Dorado."* I know the titles of the songs from cue sheet lists, but these songs are gone forever unless one of you becomes a hero and contacts us with an uncut copy (esvh@connectnet.com).

The book is divided into 28 chapters. These chapters represent the 28 films Roy and Dale made together. The opening page to each film presents credits, a story line, and stills that represent the action story points. The following pages are the songs within the film in the order in which they were sung. Each song has stills associated with it that depict what was happening while the song was being sung and a description of why the song was in the film.

Since perhaps some of you can't read music, or want to know how the song was sung in the film, I've included a sample audio CD of 18 selected songs taken directly from the soundtrack. A set of 4 CDs of all the songs can be obtained separately.

Now the work is done and we can sit around the campfire with our song book in front of us, the CD in the boombox, and sing along again with Roy, Dale, Pat Brady, Bob Nolan and the Sons of the Pioneers, Estilita Rodriguez, and Foy Willing and the Riders of the Purple Sage. Truly a nostalgic experience, remembering those innocent, simpler days of our youth, but isn't it fun!

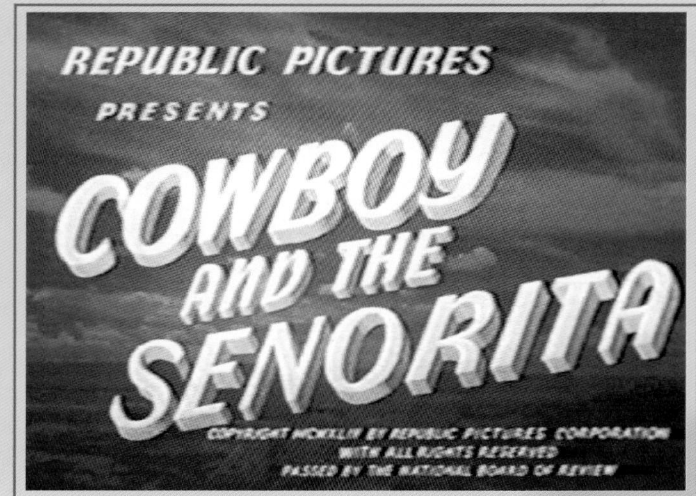

Produced By
Harry Grey

Directed by
Joseph Kane

Screenplay by
Gordon Kahn

Starring
Roy Rogers, Dale Evans, Mary Lee, Bob Nolan, The Sons of the Pioneers, Trigger

with
John Hubbard, Guinn Williams, Fuzzy Knight, Dorothy Christy, Lucien Littlefield, Hal Tailaferro, Jack Kirk, Jack O'Shea, Rex Lease, Lynton Brent, Julian Rivero, Bob Wilke, Wally West, Dancers: Capella and Patricia, Jane Beebe, Ben Rochelle, Tito and Corinne Valdez

Prod: #1321 Released: 12 May 1944
Black/White - 77min.

Dale's first film with Roy. As Ysobel she is selling a worthless gold mine inherited by her half-sister, Chip (Lee). Chip becomes upset at Ysobel and runs away. Roy and Teddy Bear (Williams), drifters looking for jobs, are mistakenly accused of kidnapping Chip. There is a treasure in the mine and the villainous potential buyers are out to get it any way they can.

RB

1. Roy and Teddy Bear learn that Chip is lost.

2. Ysobel meets the "kidnappers" for the first time but doesn't believe they did it.

3. Swinging on a chandelier, Roy and Teddy Bear escape the authorities.

4. Chip, the runaway, is discovered and explains the mine situation.

5. The mine's "treasure" is a note to Chip from her dead father telling about GOLD!

6. Roy and the Pioneers load gold from the mine on to wagons.

7. Roy and the Pioneers race to stop the sale of the mine to the villains.

8. They arrive just in time to thwart the sale and have the bad guys arrested.

9. Chip, Roy, and Ysobel sing the title song in the film's finale.

COWBOY AND THE SENORITA

(As sung by Roy Rogers in the Mexican restaurant)

transcribed by
WILL CRATTY
ERIC VAN HAMERSVELD

words & music by
NED WASHINGTON
PHIL OHMAN

(Roy and Dale verses at end of film)

(Both) The Cowboy and the Senorita,
Met in Rosarita, one night not so long ago.
(Roy) I kissed her and she whispered,
(Dale) "Mister, Take me to your airy old
prairie, I love it so."
(Both) Their life is sunshine and
full of laughter.
They'll be happy for ever after.

Why don't you come along,
where the air is sweeter,
With the Cowboy and the pretty Senorita.

Republic Pictures Page 3
"Cowboy and the Senorita" Script Revision: #5

CROSS DISSOLVE FROM OPENING TITLE TO LONG SHOT PAN OF OUTDOOR RESTAURANT. STOP AT ROY AND WILLIAMS. NOONTIME.

Roy and Williams have jobs in a restaurant. Williams is busboy, Roy the singer. While Roy sings "The Cowboy and the Senorita," Williams is harassed by a smart aleck kid (Spanky from the "Our Gang" comedies) who winds up tripping him, spilling a tray full of food all over the seated guests.

THE BUNKHOUSE BUGLE BOY

(As sung by Roy Rogers and the Sons of the Pioneers at the ranch)

transcribed by
JANE LEIGH
ERIC VAN HAMERSVELD

words & music by
TIM SPENCER

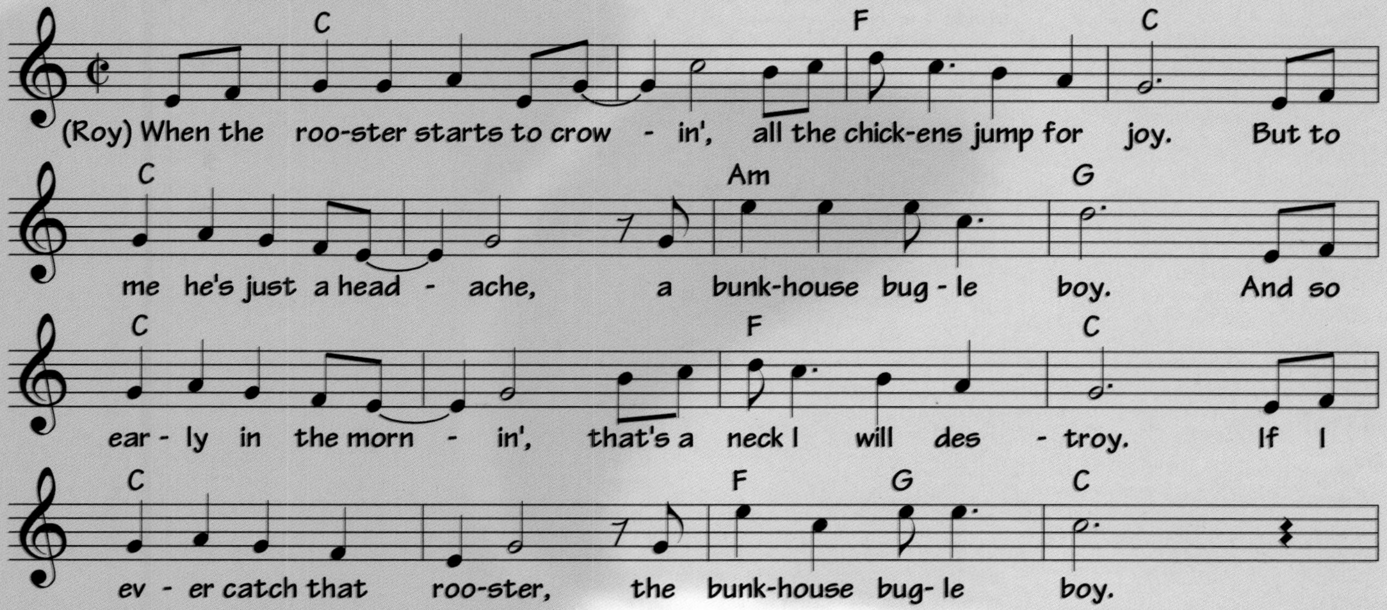

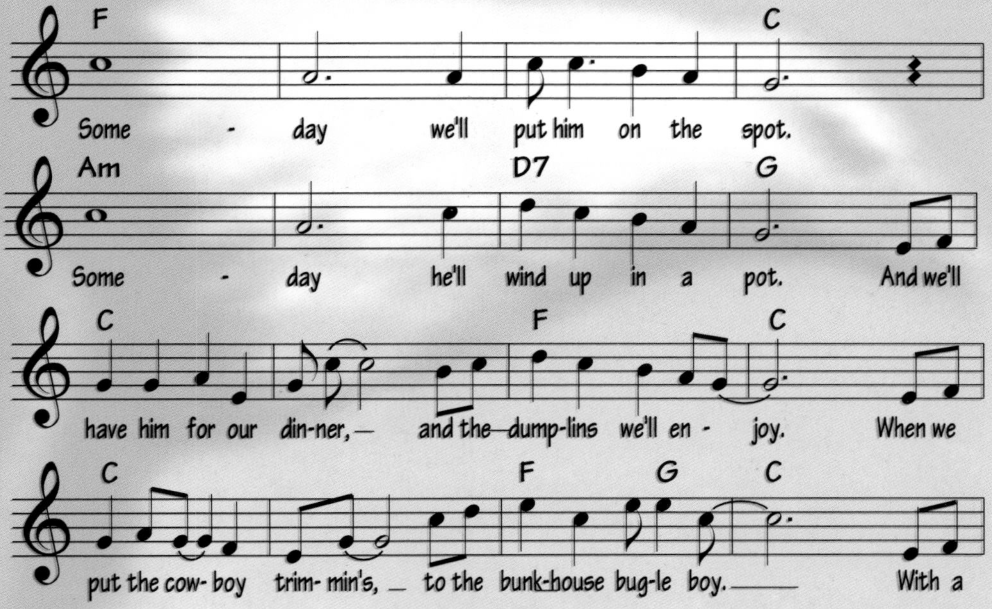

C F C
(Roy) When the roo-ster starts to crow - in', all the chick-ens jump for joy. But to

C Am G
me he's just a head - ache, a bunk-house bug - le boy. And so

C F C
ear - ly in the morn - in', that's a neck I will des - troy. If I

C F G C
ev - er catch that roo-ster, the bunk-house bug- le boy.

F C
Some - day we'll put him on the spot.

Am D7 G
Some - day he'll wind up in a pot. And we'll

C F C
have him for our din-ner,— and the—dump-lins we'll en - joy. When we

C F G C
put the cow- boy trim- min's, — to the bunk-house bug-le boy.—— With a

C F C
cock- a - doo- dal - doo-dal-doo,— you can tell he's do- in' fine, When the

C F G
day is break-in' on the prai - rie.———— Ev - ery

C Am
cow-boy in his bunk-house bed,— Is wait-in' for the time that our

Republic Pictures Page 73
"Cowboy and the Senorita" Script Revision: #4

FADE UP LONG SHOT MARY LEE IN BED. MORNING.

Chip awakens to the ranch hands, including Roy and the Pioneers, getting ready for the day (washing, dressing, sitting down to breakfast) while singing "The Bunkhouse Bugle Boy."

WHAT'LL I USE FOR MONEY

(As sung by Roy Rogers, Dale Evans, Mary Lee and
the Sons of Pioneers on the trail)

words & music by
NED WASHINGTON
PHIL OHMAN

What'll I Use for Money-2
Eb Fm Bb7 Eb
vein of gold. (Sons) All you have to do is look a - round.
D7 Gm F7
(Roy) But when I think of all that gold, think of the troub- le it's gonna be
Bb7 Eb
gettin' it out of the ground. (Dale) You're a - bout to con - fess that you'll
C7
set - tle for less. (Mary) Guess you're just a plain dumb
Fm Bb7 Fm Bb7
bun - ny. (Roy) But I get so up - set. But I al - ways for - get.
Eb D7
What - 'll I use for mon - ey? (Sons: How 'bout, marbles?
Db7 C7 Fm Bb
Old toothpicts? Did ja ever try usin' money?) (Dale/Mary) May - be he'll find a
Eb Fm Bb7 Eb
vein of gold, just like a luck - y pup. (Sons: Oh! Sure.)

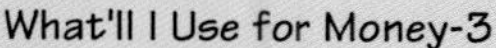

D7 Gm F7
But when I think of all that gold, I'd get kind - a tir - ed

Bb7 Eb
dig - gin' it up (All) Well, you can't buy the moon, or a

C7
wed - ing in June, or a sky that's blue and

Fm Bb7 Fm Bb7
sun - ny. If you drop all your care, you're a rich mil - ion - aire.

Eb
(Roy) But what - 'll I use for mon - ey?

Republic Pictures Page 85
"Cowboy and the Senorita" Script Revision: #3

CROSS DISSOLVE FROM EXTERIOR RANCH CORRAL TO LONG SHOT. CAMERA MOUNTED ON TRUCK RUNNING IN FRONT OF RIDERS. DAY.

On the morning of Chip's birthday, Roy, Ysobel, Chip, the Sons of the Pioneers, Williams, and Knight decide to take a leisurely morning trail ride to take the pressure off the gold mine situation. Along the way they sing "What'll I Do For Money."

BÉSAME MUCHO

(As sung in Spanish by Dale Evans at Chip's Birthday Party)

words & music by
SUNNY SKYLAR
CONSUELO VELAZQUEZ

Republic Pictures Page 132
"Cowboy and the Senorita" Script Revision: #3

FADE IN ON CLOSE UP OF GUITAR. TILT UP TO MEDIUM SHOT OF DALE ENTERING. TRUCK BACK TO LONG SHOT OF ROOM. EVENING.

Ysobel entertains guests at Chip's birthday party by dancing and singing to "Bésame Mucho" in Spanish, accompanied by the Sons of the Pioneers.

'ROUND HER NECK SHE WORE A YELLOW RIBBON

(As sung by Mary Lee to the guests at the 16th birthday party)

words & music by
TRADITIONAL

(Opening Verse)

I don't know how to thank you.
I don't know what to say.
If my great grandma could be here,
she'd really save the day.

She'd do a little curtsy
in hoops of crepe de chine.
Great grandma knew her etiquette,
when she was sweet sixteen.

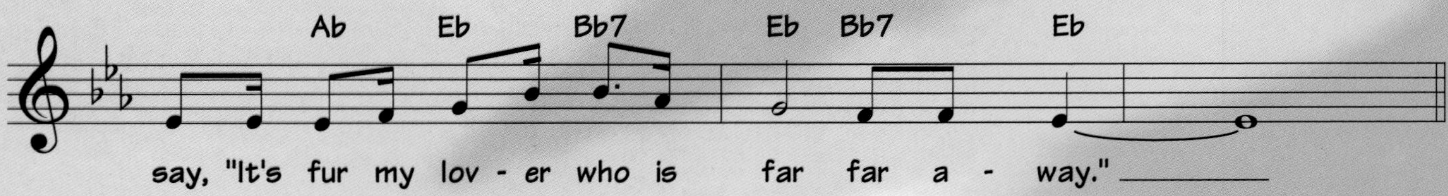

(Interlude Verse)

My grandma on my father's side was . . .
. . . tough.
She never knew the meaning of fear.
She liked her cider hard, her men folks . . .
. . . rough.
For at sixteen she was a hardy pioneer.

Ho - da - lay - ee . . . Ho - da - lay - ee . . .
(Pioneers) Get along . . . Get along . . .

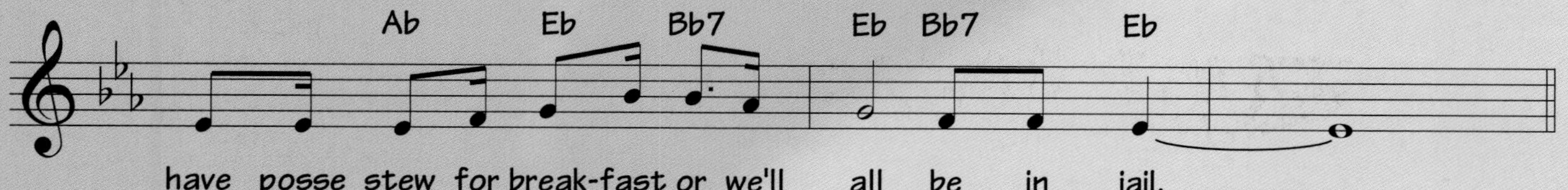

Republic Pictures Page 136
"The Cowboy and the Senorita" Script Revision: #4

CUT TO INTERIOR OF RANCHO. CENTER FRAMED LONG SHOT OF ROY ENTERING FROM COURTYARD HOLDING LARGE CAKE. WALKS TOWARDS CAMERA. TILT AND CRANE UP TO TOP OF STAIRCASE FOR LONG SHOT OF LEE. CRANE DOWN AND TRUCK BACK FOLLOWING LEE DOWN THE STAIRS AND INTO HER PRODUCTION NUMBER. LATE EVENING.

Continuing the birthday celebration, Roy is bringing in the birthday cake. Chip yells, "Oh, Roy!" He looks up, and she makes a formal entry down the staircase. After a quick greeting to Ysobel, her half-sister, she takes a bow and, to thank her guests, she begins an extended production sequence . Through song and costumes, beginning with "'Around Her Neck She Wore A Yellow Ribbon," she sings about the life of her grandmother, mother, and herself.

ENCHILADA MAN

(As sung by Roy Rogers, Dale Evans, Mary Lee, and the Sons of the Pioneers at the celebration party)

words & music by
NED WASHINGTON
PHIL OHMAN

The Enchilada Man-2
Em Dm G7 C
spread- ing in - di - gest - tion? It's the en - chi - la - da man.
D7 G D7 G
(Mary) I've got a pen -ny. You've got a pen - ny. (Roy/Mary) May- be we can share one.
D7 G D7 G
(Sons) He's got a pen - ny. She has -n't an - y. (All) May - be we've a spare one.
D7 G D7 G
(Dale) One lit-tle fel- low starts in to bel- low. He would like to tear one.
C G D7
(Dale/Mary) So the lit-tle pea-sent gets one as a pre- sent from the en- chi- la- da
G C G7 C
man. (Ken) En-chi - la - da. (Sons) One two three. (FX: Whap!)
C G7
(Dale) Now he's gone a - way come a-noth-er day, ev- ery bod-y's got one.
G7 C
(Roy) See the peo-ple laugh. See them bent in half. Pan-cho got a hot one.
C G7
(Mary) What's he leav-in' for? He could sell some more. Well. you see there's not one.
F Em Dm G7
(All) Ev -'ry bod - y took-'em. He'll get more and cook 'em. He's the en - chi - la - da

The Enchilada Man-3
C G D7
man. (Mary) He ought to be in the ope - ra sing - ing
G
tra-la-la lay-dee-oh (Sons) tra-la-la (Mary) tra-la-la-lay-dee-oh (Sons) la-la-la. (Dale) He's much too
D7 A7
good for the o' - pra, with his "Get 'em while they're fresh."
D7 G C
en- chi- la- da rhap-so - dy (Sons) tra - la - la - la (Dale/Mary) He's not what I'd
G C
call a ten -or (Ken) CEE - PUO! (Dale/Mary) And he's not a great bar - i -
G C G
tone. (Roy) Me, Me, Me. He's tir -ed and old, but his
Am G Am D7 G
heart's made of gold with a new kind of voice all his own.
C
(Ken) En- chi - la - da. (horse whinnies)
C G7
(Dale) Hear him come a -long. Hear his lit- tle song, "Buy an en- chi - la - da."
C
Pat -ches on his seat, noth-ing on his feet. Try an en - chi - la - da.

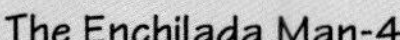

C Dbdim G7
It's a sil - ly whim pat - ro - niz - ing him, but you've real - ly got - ta.

F Em Dm G7 C
(Dale/Mary) Who's the man in quest-ion spread-ing in - di -gest- ion? He's the en- chi - la - da man.

F Em
(Dale) When he sells beeg ones, he shouts, (All) "En-chi - la-das!" (Dale) But

D7 G7 F
when he sells lit-tle ones, he whis-pers, (Roy) "En-chi - la-das," (Mary) "En-chi -

Em Dm C
la - das (Sons) En-chi- la-das. (Dale) Oh, what's he leav - ing for,

F
He could sell some more. Well, you see there's not one

F Em Dm C
(All) Ev - 'ry bod -y took 'em. He'll get more and cook 'em. He's the en -chi - la - da man.

Republic Pictures Page 217
"The Cowboy and the Senorita" Script Revision: #5

FADE UP TO TOP OF LARGE SOMBRERO PROP IN THE MIDDLE OF RANCO COURTYARD. TRUCK BACK TO REVEAL GUESTS WATCHING DANCERS. ROY, DALE, MARY LEE, AND PIONEERS ARE BEHIND BUFFET TABLE IN BACKGROUND. EVENING.

Roy, Williams, and the Pioneers found the gold, captured one of the villains, made him talk, and raced to the judge's office to prove that Mr. Allen was trying to steal the mine from Ysobel. Allen is arrested and everyone decides to have a celebration. That evening during the festivities, Roy, Ysobel, Chip, and the Pioneers sing "Enchilada Man" while serving the buffet. Ken Carson of the Pioneers sings tenor accents.

Produced By
Harry Grey

Directed by
Joseph Kane

Screenplay by
Jack Townley

Starring
Roy Rogers, Dale Evans, Grant Withers, Bob Nolan, The Sons of the Pioneers, Trigger

with
Harry Shannon, George Cleveland, William Haade, Weldon Heyburn, Hal Teliaferro, Tom London, Dick Botiler, Janet Martin, Brown Jug Reynolds, Bob Wilke, Jack O'Shea, Rex Lease, Emmet Vogan, John Dilson, Fred Toones

Prod: #1322 Released: 24 June 1944
Black/White - 69min.

Betty's (Dale) father, Sam Weston (Shannon), who was wrongly convicted of stealing money five years earlier, has broken out of jail. Roy, an undercover insurance investigator trying to recover the stolen money, gets a job as a singer on Captain Joe's (Cleveland) boat the "Yellow Rose Of Texas" showboat, where Betty works, hoping that her father will show up.

RB

1. The showboat's Captain tells Betty that her father has escaped from prison.

2.Told to "Get out of town," Roy punches out one of the bad guys.

3. A classic Roy and Trigger chase.

4. Weston arrives just in time to see the "Yellow Rose of Texas" steam by.

5. Roy confronts Weston and is told of his innocence.

6. Roy and the Pioneers find evidence to clear Weston.

7. Roy, as a showboat entertainer, sings "The Yellow Rose of Texas" with Betty.

8. In a freak accident, Roy rescues a little boy from a runaway wagon.

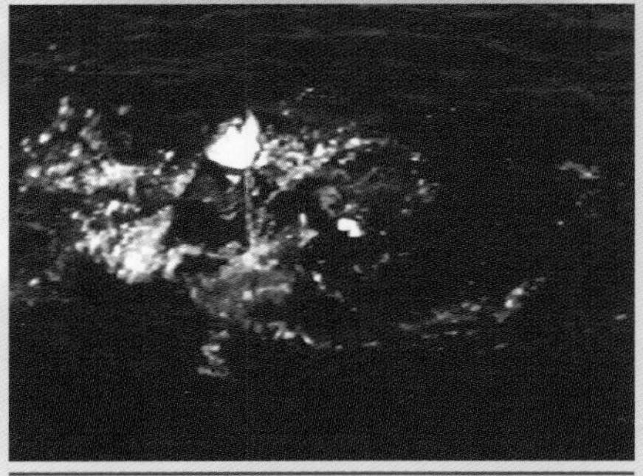
9. Roy dives in the river and captures the escaping leader of outlaws.

LUCKY ME, UNLUCKY YOU

(As sung by Roy Rogers on the showboat stage)

words & music by
CHARLES HENDERSON

Em7 E9 A+7

way. And just be con- tent with things as they are.

D B7 Em7 A+7

Folks who get rich spend their time com-plain - in'.

D9sus D7 G Gm D C9

That's a pret - ty, "How - do - ya - do!" I sing a song when it's rain -

B9 Em7 n.c

in'. Luck - y me, look in the mir - ror and you'll

E9 A13 D6/9

see, un - luck - y you.

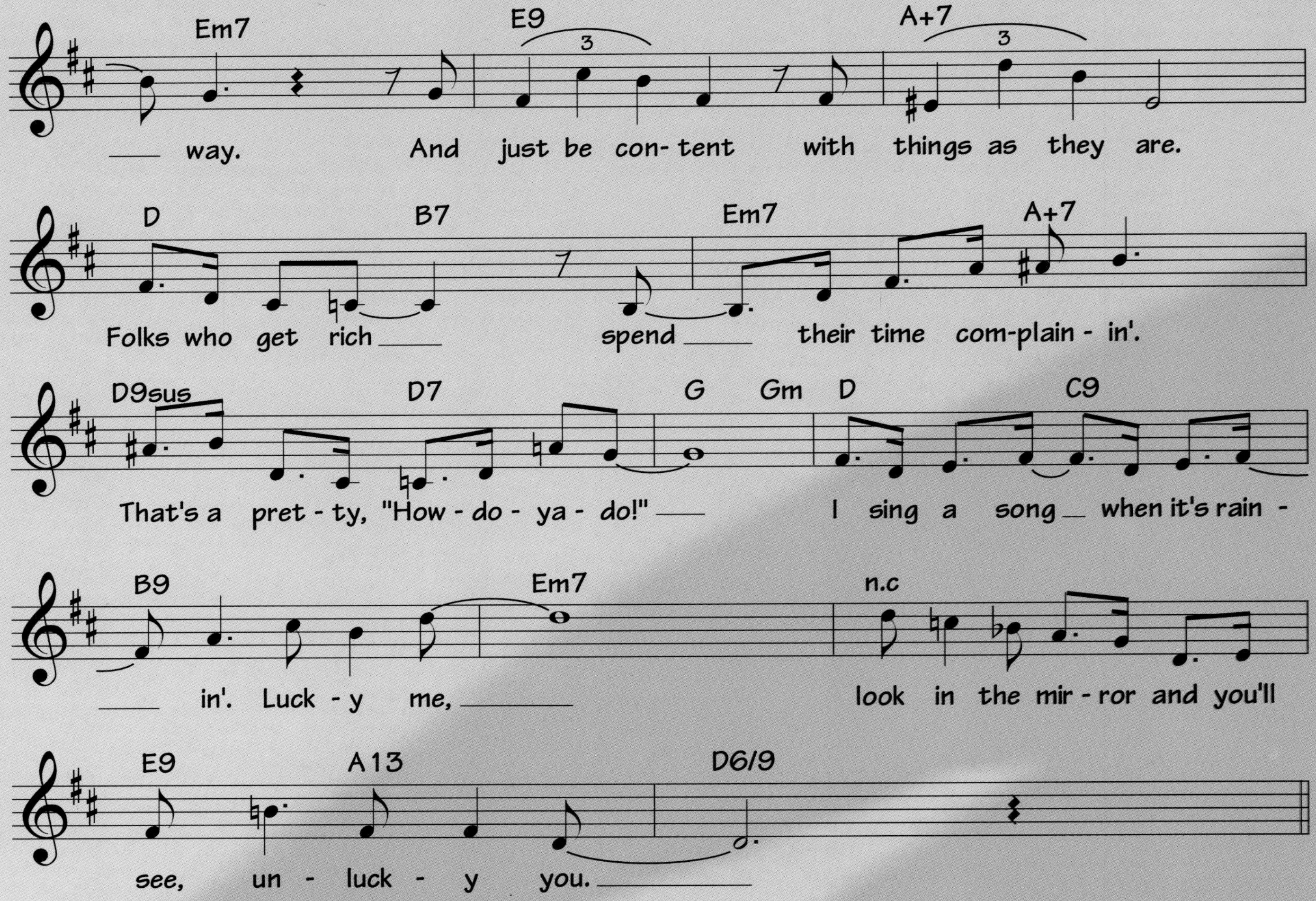

Republic Pictures Page 32
"Yellow Rose of Texas" Script Revision: #5

CUT TO LONG SHOT OF SHOWBOAT STAGE SET DRESSED WITH HAY BAILS, WAGON WHEEL, ETC. ORCHESTRA IN PIT, ROY, DALE, AND VARIOUS ENTERTAINERS ON STAGE.

Roy is on stage singing the opening verse to "Lucky Me, Unlucky You" for Betty when Captain Joe, the showboat captain, rushes in demanding what's going on. Betty explains that she has hired Roy for the show. Cap wants to hear him sing before he approves. Roy continues the song where he left off (at the chorus). At the end of the song Cap is convinced that Roy has talent and shakes his hand to welcome him aboard.

THE YELLOW ROSE OF TEXAS

(As sung by Roy Rogers and Dale Evans in a showboat production)

words & music by
TRADITIONAL

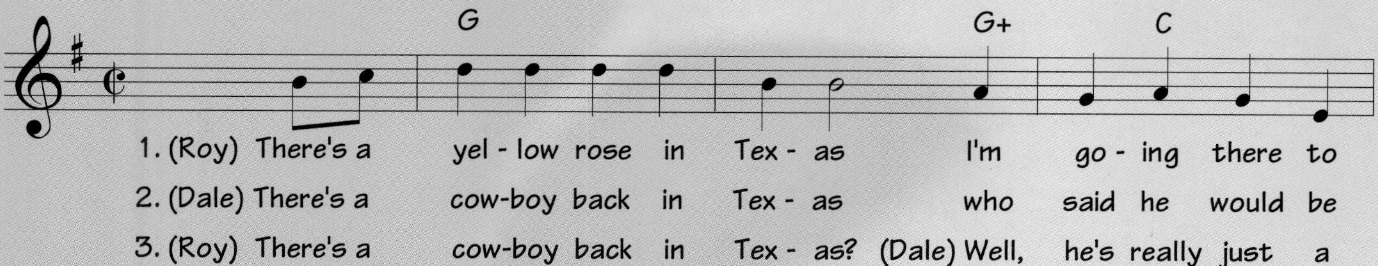

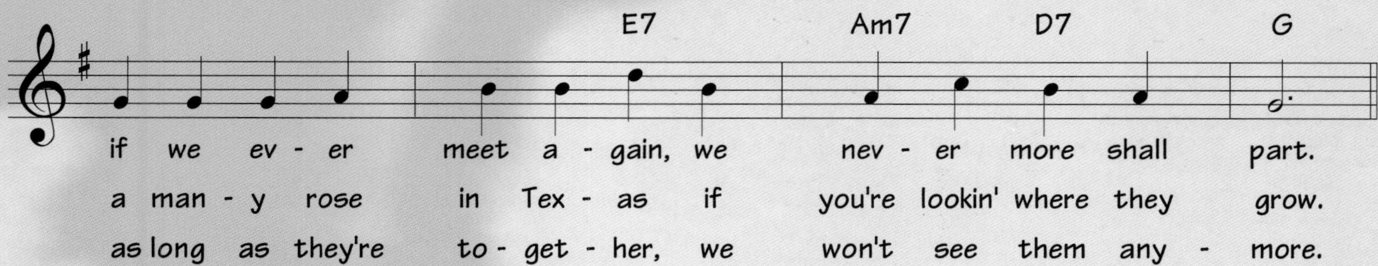

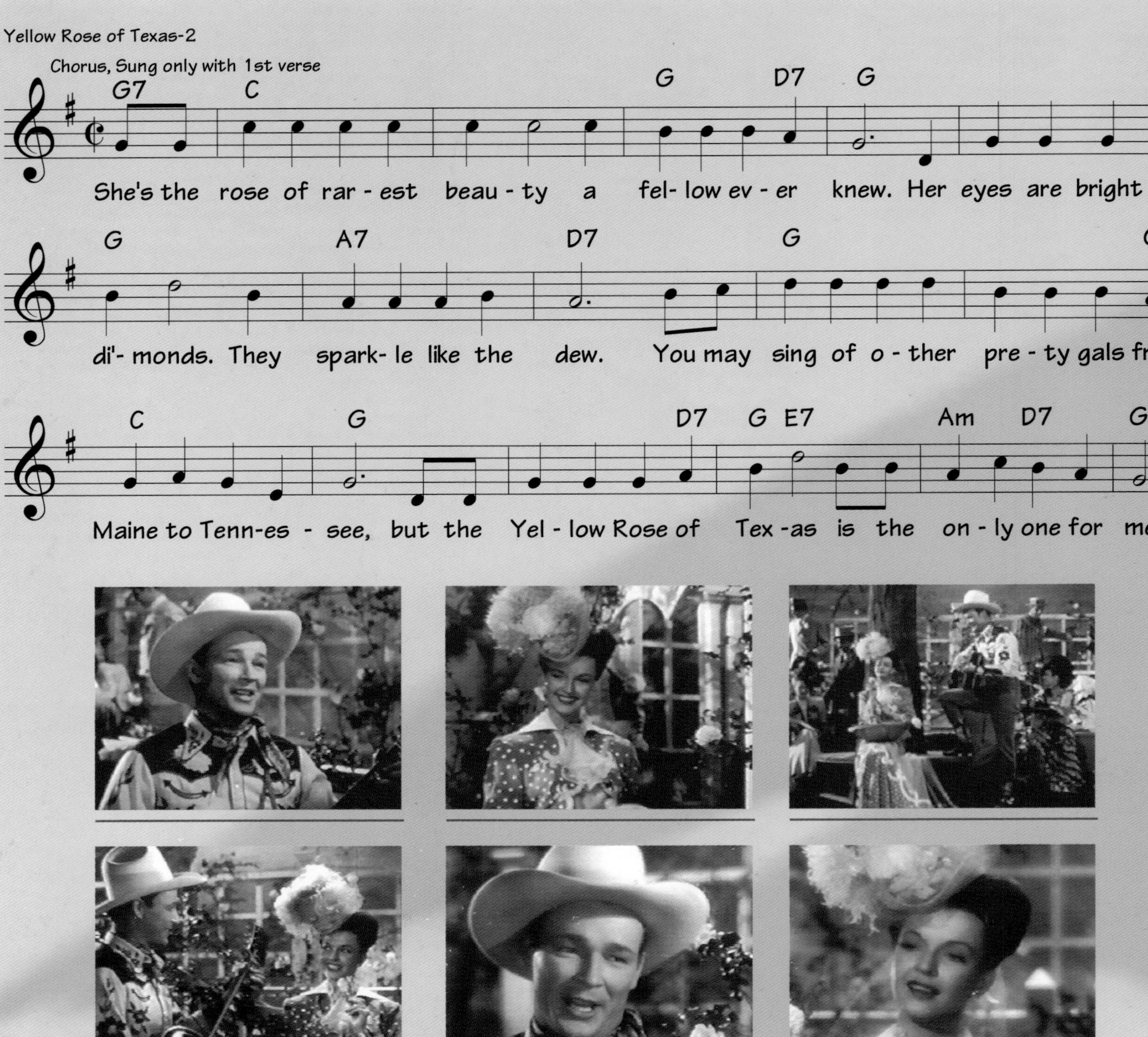

Republic Pictures Page 52
"The Yellow Rose of Texas" Script Revision: #3

LONGSHOT FROM AUDIENCE POINT-OF-VIEW TOWARDS SHOWBOAT STAGE. CURTAIN RISES TO REVEAL OUTDOOR SCENE. CHORUS IS MILLING AROUND. ROY IS STRUMMING GUITAR TO OPEN MUSIC. ENTER DALE FROM STAGE RIGHT AND WALKS UP GAZEBO STAIRS. EVENING.

A typical show number aboard the "Yellow Rose of Texas" showboat. This number is preceded by a dance production followed by a solo dance routine which brings down the curtain. During the song, Betty periodically glances toward the sheriff who is standing at the back of the audience.

SONG OF THE ROVER

(As sung by the Sons of the Pioneers in the Express Office)

transcribed by
SCOTT HOMAN
ERIC VAN HAMERSVELD

words & music by
BOB NOLAN

Song of the Rover-2
Db
stand there wait - in'. (All) Smile as I come by. I'm com - in'.
Db Gb Db Ab Db
Here comes your ro - ver com - in' home. I'm com - in'.
Db Dbm Db Edim Ebdim
Woo, Woo.
Db
(Dissolve to stage set) I'm com - in'. (Bob) I've got a yearn - in',
Db
home fires burn - in'. Dar - lin' don't you cry. I'm com - in'.
Db Gb Db Ab Db
(All) Here comes your ro - ver com - in' home. I'm com - in'.
Db
(Bob) I see the light of your eyes so bright and
Db
(All) I see a clear blue sky. I'm com - in'. Here comes your
Gb Db Ab Db
ro - ver com - in' home. (Hugh) I'm com - in'.
A
(Ken) Out of a storm cloud in - to a warm cloud,

Republic Pictures Page 44
"The Yellow Rose of Texas" Script Revision: #3

LONG SHOT INSIDE EXPRESS OFFICE. DAY

After a fight with the bad guys, Roy and the Sons of the Pioneers pick up their instruments at the Express Office. Roy wanders outside, sees Cap walking down the street, and has an idea of how to get the Pioneers hired on the showboat with him. He tells the Pioneers to start singing something NOW, and they sing "Song of the Rover." Cap hears them and comes in to watch. A small crowd gathers and Roy says that the Pioneers would be a good addition to the showboat's cast. Cap looks around at the crowd and agrees.

SEAMLESS AUDIO CROSS DISSOLVE WITH VISUAL DISSOLVE TO LONG SHOT OF THE PIONEERS SINGING ON THE SHOWBOAT STAGE.

DOWN AT THE OLD TOWN HALL

(As sung by Roy Rogers and Dale Evans on the showboat stage)

words & music by
CHARLES HENDERSON

Down At the Old Town Hall-2
C G7 C G7 C G7
(Dale) I would real-ly love to go. Guess I'll wear my cal - i - co. Hope I know a lot - ta folks
C Cm7 Bb7 Cm7 Bb7
there. (Roy) You'll know each an' ev - 'ry one least be -fore the night is done
Cm7 C G7
'cause it's a so- cial af - fair. (Dale) Bet I see my cou - sin Sue,
C G7 C G7 C D#7
mmay - be Mrs. __ Pet - ti - grew. She's been bak - in' cook - ies and pies.
Ab C G7
(Roy says: Did you hear a - bout the judge. Well, they've got him sell - in' fudge, and there's a luck -y
Gm7
sur-prise!) (Dale) I sup- pose the la - dies aid will pro- vide the lem - on - ade.
C7
(Roy) Yes and Mrs. __ E - ben - e - zer lent her ice cream free - zer.
F Dm Gm C7 F Dm Gm C7
(Roy) I'd like to take you to town with me, I'm in - vit - in' you once for all. 'Cause to-
F Bb Bbm F G7 F F7
night we're gon- na have a par -ty down at the old Town Hall. (Dale) Will there be
Bb Cm7 Bb Cm7 Bb F7 Bb G7
mu-sic by a four-piece or-ches-try and all the cake that you can eat? (Roy) You Bet! And when I

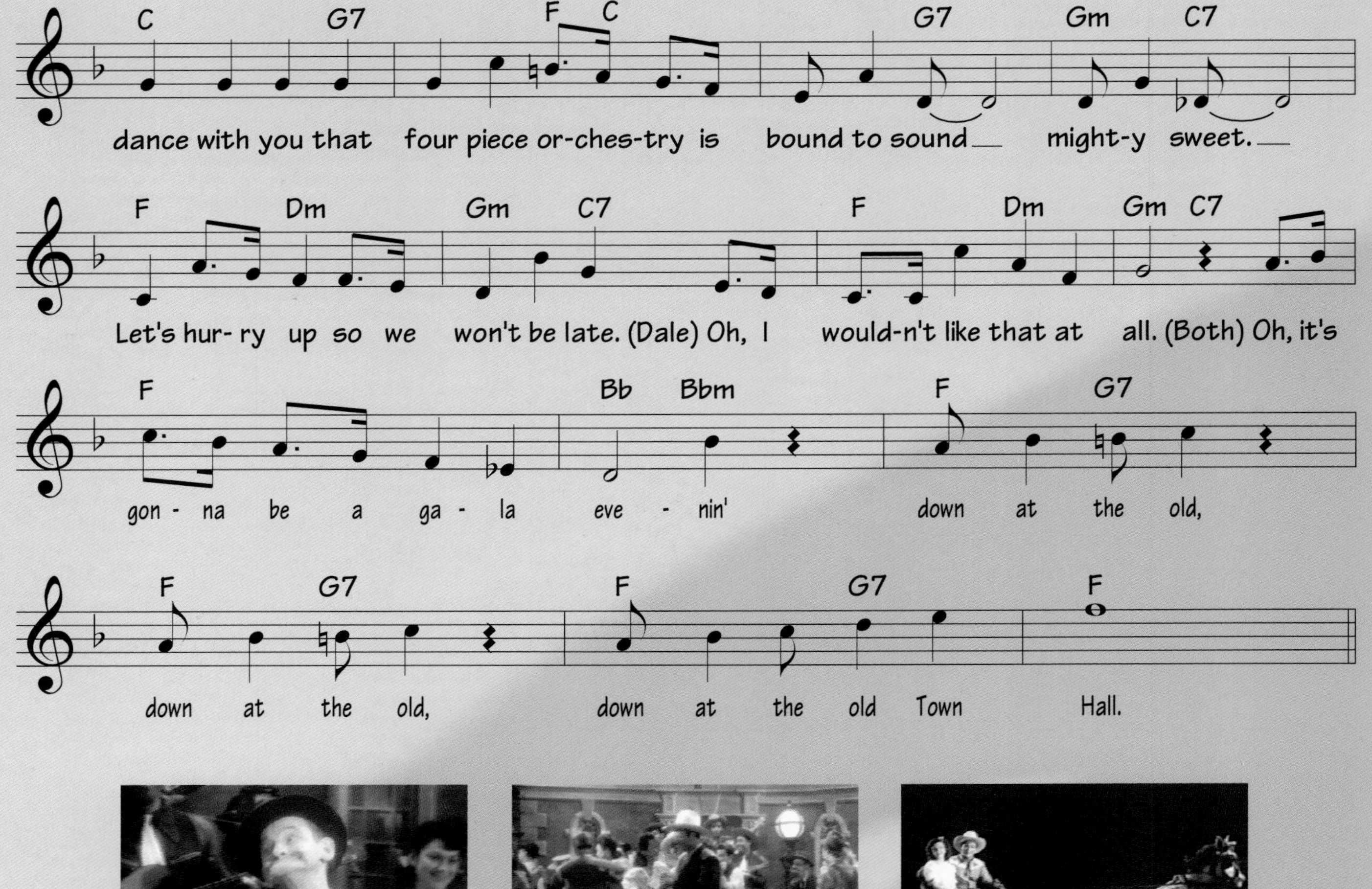

Republic Pictures Page 52

"Yellow Rose of Texas" Script Revision: #3

CUT TO LONG SHOT STAGE. CURTAIN OPENS ON SET DRESSED WITH A FENCE ON EACH SIDE AND A PAINTED GAUZE BACKGROUND GRAPHIC SCREEN DEPICTING A FARM HOUSE.

The Sons of the Pioneers have just finished singing "Song of the Rover." Insert a cutaway shot to one of the bad guys buying a ticket for the show. Cut back to the showboat stage. As the curtain opens, Roy enters on a wagon drawn by a horse (two actors in a costume) which begins a major showboat production number. Betty enters and they sing "Down At the Old Town Hall." Part way into the song they ride off on the wagon and the gauze background becomes backlit revealing an outdoor garden party scene behind. Roy and Betty enter the party and continue the song while greeting everyone, joining the buffet, and dancing. They stroll off and the gauze background is relit with the farm house graphic. Roy and Betty drive through on the wagon singing the last few bars of the song, and the curtains close.

WESTERN WONDERLAND

(As sung by Roy Rogers and the Sons of the Pioneers around the campfire)

words & music by
GUY SAVAGE
KEN CARSON

Republic Pictures — Page 62
"The Yellow Rose Of Texas" — Script Revision: #3

FADE UP CLOSE UP HUGH STRUMMING GUITAR AT CAMPFIRE. PAN RIGHT TO MEDIUM TWO SHOT OF ROY AND DALE. NIGHT.

On the way to look for the lost payroll box that will free her father, Roy, Betty, Weston and the Pioneers camp out for the night. Around the campfire Roy and the pioneers sing "Western Wonderland."

THE TIMBER TRAIL
(As sung by the Pioneers on the showboat stage)
words & music by
TIM SPENCER
O - ver moun-tains high, down the can-yons wide, let me roam and ride, ride through tim-ber!
When the day is done, by the camp-fire's-gleam, let me lie and dream, dream of tim-ber.
Chorus
Tall tim-ber's call - ing and the ech - o rings. For all na-ture sings a song a - long the tim-ber trail!
Blue shad-ows fall - ing down the can-yon vale, where the whis-p'rin' pines en-twine a - long the tim-ber trail.
High in the sky, a - bove, the love song of the trees, will blend and wend its way out on the breeze.
Tall tim-ber's call - ing and the ech-oes ring. For all na-ture sings a song a- long the tim-ber trail.
Tall tim-ber's trail
Republic Pictures
"The Yellow Rose Of Texas"
Page 23
Script Revision: #3
CUT FROM SHOWBOAT STATEROOM TO LONG SHOT OF STAGE.
Roy has just explained to Cap that he is leaving the Showboat, but the Pioneers are still employed and they sing "The Timber Trail." At the end of the song, a prop tree crashes on to Shug, bringing laughter and applause from the audience.

A TWO SEATED SADDLE AND A ONE GAITED HORSE
(As sung by Dale Evans in a showboat production)
transcribed by
SCOTT HOMAN
ERIC VAN HAMERSVELD
words & music by
TIM SPENCER
Freely
(Dale) Broad - way and bright lights and gay ci - ty night life are
still in my mem-or - y. But quo-ting from Gree- ly
I can speak free-ly. It's the west, young man, for me. I'm
look-in' for a cow - boy and a hand-some one of course. Ah, with a
two seat-ed sad - dle and a one gait-ed horse. I'm
yearn-in' for a blue - sky and a great big yel- low moon, and a
eas- y rid -in' cow - boy who -'ll croon me a tune. A song of the
sage bru - sh and cat-tle who will
sing me to sleep in a re-peat seat-ed sad - le. Until I find that cow - boy, I'll live in deep re -morse. Ah, for a

A Two Seated Saddle and a One Gaited Horse-2
two seat-ed sad - dle and a one gait-ed horse. (horse dances
) (Dale) Hey,
I will e - ven learn to yo - del, (horse yodels)
and a gui - tar I will buy.
I'd
ev- en change my name to "Dog-gie," there is
noth - in' I won't try, try, try. (All) Un-
til I find that cow - boy, I'll live in deep re-morse. Ah, for a

Bbm Eb7 Ab Bb7 Eb7 Ab n.c.

two seat-ed sad - dle and a one gait- ed horse. (horse

Bbm Eb7 Ab Bb7 Eb7

clomps) (Dale) No, a two seat- ed sad - dle and a one gait - ed horse.

n.c. Bbm Eb7 Ab

(horse clomps) (Dale) No! A two seat- ed sad - dle and a

Bb7 Eb7 Ab n.c. Bbm Eb7

one gait - ed horse. (horse clomps) (Dale) Yes, a dou - ble seat-ed sad-

Ab F7 Bbm Eb7 Ab

le, (All) and a sin - gle gait - ed horse.

Republic Pictures Page 209

"The Yellow Rose of Texas" Script Revision: #4

CUT FROM ROY TALKING WITH DALE'S FATHER IN A HAYLOFT TO A LONG SHOT OF THE SHOWBOAT STAGE. INDOORS. EVENING.

It's Betty's turn to entertain the showboat's guests. The stage is set with a wagon and corral. Betty and a group of four gals sing "A Two Seated Saddle and a One Gaited Horse." During the number a comical tap dancing horse (two dancers in a costume) joins in.

DOWN MEXICO WAY

(As sung by Janet Martin in the villains nightclub)

words & music by
JULE STYNE
SOL MEYER
EDDIE MAXWELL.

Republic Pictures Page 176
"The Yellow Rose of Texas" Script Revision: #2

CUT TO INTERIOR OF NIGHTCLUB FROM POINT-OF-VIEW OF PATRONS. PAN ACROSS ROOM STOPPING AT STAGE. LATE EVENING.

On their way to find the gun responsible for the slug that hit Weston, Roy and Buster visit the villain's nightclub to speak with Ferguson. They think Ferguson's gun may be the one they're looking for. While they look around, the entertainment begins with Janet's number.

TAKE IT EASY

(As sung by Dale Evans in a showboat production)

words & music by
ALBERT DE BRU
IRVING TAYLOR
VIC MIZZY

(Dale begins instructions to the dancers)

When doing the Rhumba, the movement is slow.
You got to move slow to last. . .
That's better. . . much better. . .
You're getting it now, but. . . Bobby!
You move too fast! . . .

Rhumba

D7 G D7

1. Take it ea - sy. Take it ea - sy. Don't you know it's more ro-man-tic when a
2. (Instrumental ______________________) Why, you're much too far a -way to whis-per

G D7 G

dance is slow.___ Take it ea - sy. Take it ea - sy. What's the
in her ear, ___ (Instrumental __________________________________) Don't you

D7 G7 D7

good of feel - ing high when all the lights are low?__ Take it ea - sy, ____________
know you on - ly get three pairs of shoes a year?__ (Instrumental ______________

G D7 G

ea - sy. We've got lots of time a - head of us, the night is young.__ Take it

D7 G D7

ea - sy. Take it ea - sy. Don't you know this mu-sic should be swayed in -

G D7 G

stead of swung?___ Take your time. Take your time. Dance it with ease.___

G 1. D7 G 2. D7 G

Take your time. Take your time. Slow if you please.__ Take it
_________________________ _____________)

Republic Pictures Page 225
"The Yellow Rose of Texas" Script Revision: #8

CROSS DISSOLVE TO LONG SHOT OF STAGE.

At the evening performance on the showboat, it has been advertised that Roy will open the strong box that was thought ro have been stolen by Weston years ago. The evening's entertainment begins with Betty explaining to a group of dancers how to do the Rhumba, then leads into the song "Take It Easy."

SHOWBOAT

(As sung by Dale Evans in the showboat finale production)

Republic Pictures Page 265
"The Yellow Rose of Texas" Script Revision: #2

FADE UP LONG SHOT STAGE WITH BOAT ARRIVING.

Roy has captured the villain in a spectacular water fight. Later that evening, in the film's finale presentation, Betty and a chorus sing "Showboat."

Produced By
Harry Grey

Directed by
Joseph Kane

Screenplay by
Gordon Kahn, Olive Cooper

Starring
Roy Rogers, Dale Evans,
Mary Lee, Bob Nolan,
The Sons of the Pioneers,
Trigger

with
Lloyd Corrigan, Thrust Hall,
John Eldredge, Forrest Taylor,
George Meeker, Emmet Vogan,
LeRoy Mason, William Davidson,
Kenne Duncan, Si Jenks,
Frank McCarroll, Henry Wills,
Jack O'Shea, Tom Steel,
Helen Talbot

Prod: #1323 Released: 8 May 1944
Black/White - 75min.

Joan (Dale) hears that her father, John Barrabee (Hall), died in a plane crash and she goes outwest to sell the family ranch. Her fiance, Rollo (Eldredge), whom her father hated, conspires with the foreman, Ferguson (Mason), to steal ranch assets. Meanwhile, Barrabee is not really dead and he hires Roy to win his daughter back and oust the villains.

RB

1. Joan is ashamed of her father when he causes a scene at a nightclub.

2. Roy and Barrabee read that his plane has crashed and he's dead.

3. Barrabee hides out and conspires with Roy to win his daughter back.

4. Joan's father's letter that says that Roy will drive her stagecoach in the race.

5. During the race, several stagecoaches meet with mysterious accidents.

6. Roy and Joan enjoy a picnic at the shack where her father is hiding out.

7. When the villains learn that Barrabbe is not dead, Ferguson is sent to kill him.

8. Con-man Hanley tells Joan and Rollo that he bought the ranch.

9. The villains are arrested and Joan is happily reunited with her father.

THERE'S A NEW MOON OVER NEVADA

(As sung by the Sons of the Pioneers around the campfire)

Republic Pictures
"Song of Nevada"

Page 24
Script Revision: #2

CUT TO LONG SHOT OF PIONEERS AND ROY AROUND CAMPFIRE. NIGHT.

Barrabee, who has wandered off after his plane has made an emergency landing, discovers Roy and the Pioneers sitting around a campfire singing "There's A New Moon Over Nevada."

WIGWAM SONG

(As sung by Mary Lee and the Sons of the Pioneers in a Medicine Show)

Republic Pictures
"Song of Nevada"

Page 148
Script Revision: #3

FADE UP TO STREET BANNER ADVERTISING CELEBRATION. CROSS DISSOLVE TO LONG SHOT OF DECORATED STREET. CUT TO LONG SHOT OF LEE ON MEDICINE SHOW WAGON STAGE. ROY ENTERS. DAY

On the day of the "Mesa County Frontier Day Celebration," Roy wonders over to a show wagon and sees Kitty (Mary Lee) dressed as an Indian. She's dancing around a drum trying to attract attention. She tells Roy that she needs a little help. He sees the Sons of the Pioneers across the street and "volunteers" their musical services. Kitty quickly shows them a song sheet and they all sing "The Wigwam Song."

SWEET BETSY FROM PIKE

(As sung by Roy Rogers and the Sons of the Pioneers at the Costume Ball)

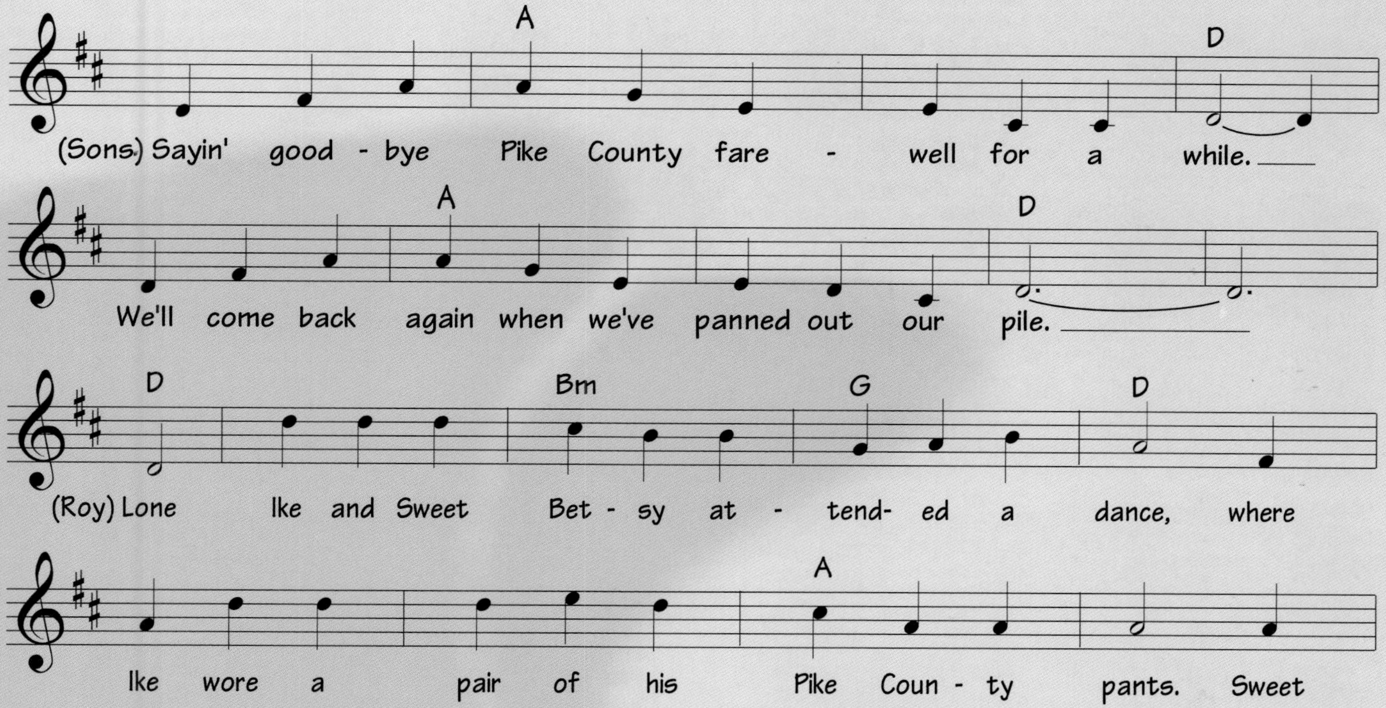

A D

(Sons) Sayin' good - bye Pike County fare - well for a while.

A D

We'll come back again when we've panned out our pile.

D Bm G D

(Roy) Lone Ike and Sweet Bet - sy at - tend- ed a dance, where

A

Ike wore a pair of his Pike Coun - ty pants. Sweet

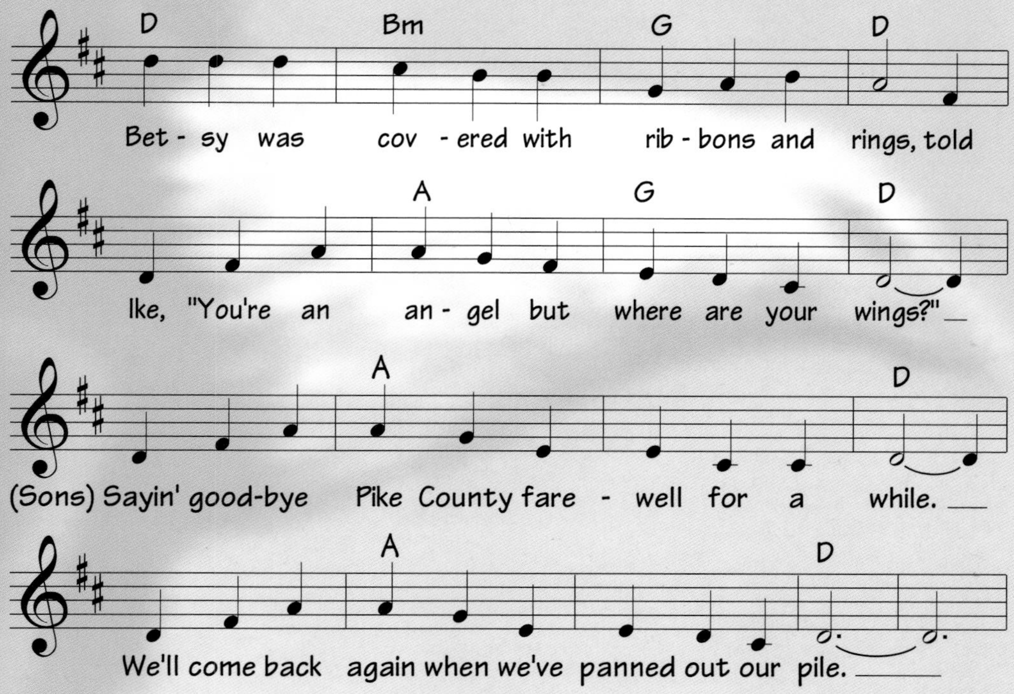

D Bm G D

Bet - sy was cov - ered with rib - bons and rings, told

A G D

Ike, "You're an an - gel but where are your wings?"

A D

(Sons) Sayin' good-bye Pike County fare - well for a while.

A D

We'll come back again when we've panned out our pile.

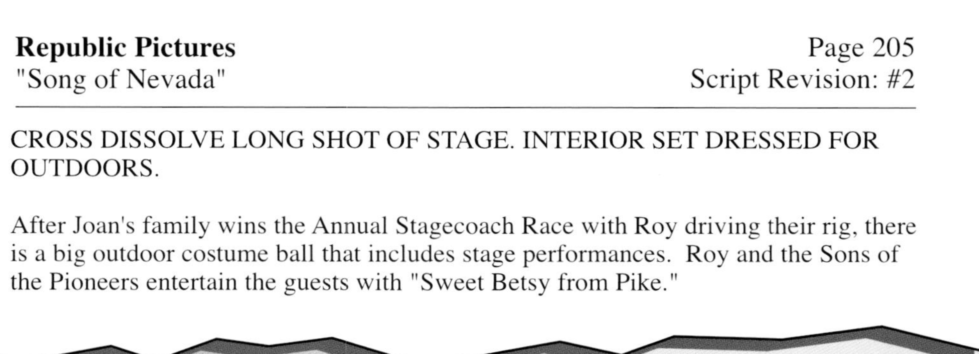

Republic Pictures Page 205
"Song of Nevada" Script Revision: #2

CROSS DISSOLVE LONG SHOT OF STAGE. INTERIOR SET DRESSED FOR OUTDOORS.

After Joan's family wins the Annual Stagecoach Race with Roy driving their rig, there is a big outdoor costume ball that includes stage performances. Roy and the Sons of the Pioneers entertain the guests with "Sweet Betsy from Pike."

AND HER GOLDEN HAIR WAS HANGING DOWN HER BACK

(As sung by Dale Evans and the Sons of the Pioneers at the Costume Ball)

And Her Golden Hair Was Hanging Down Her Back-2

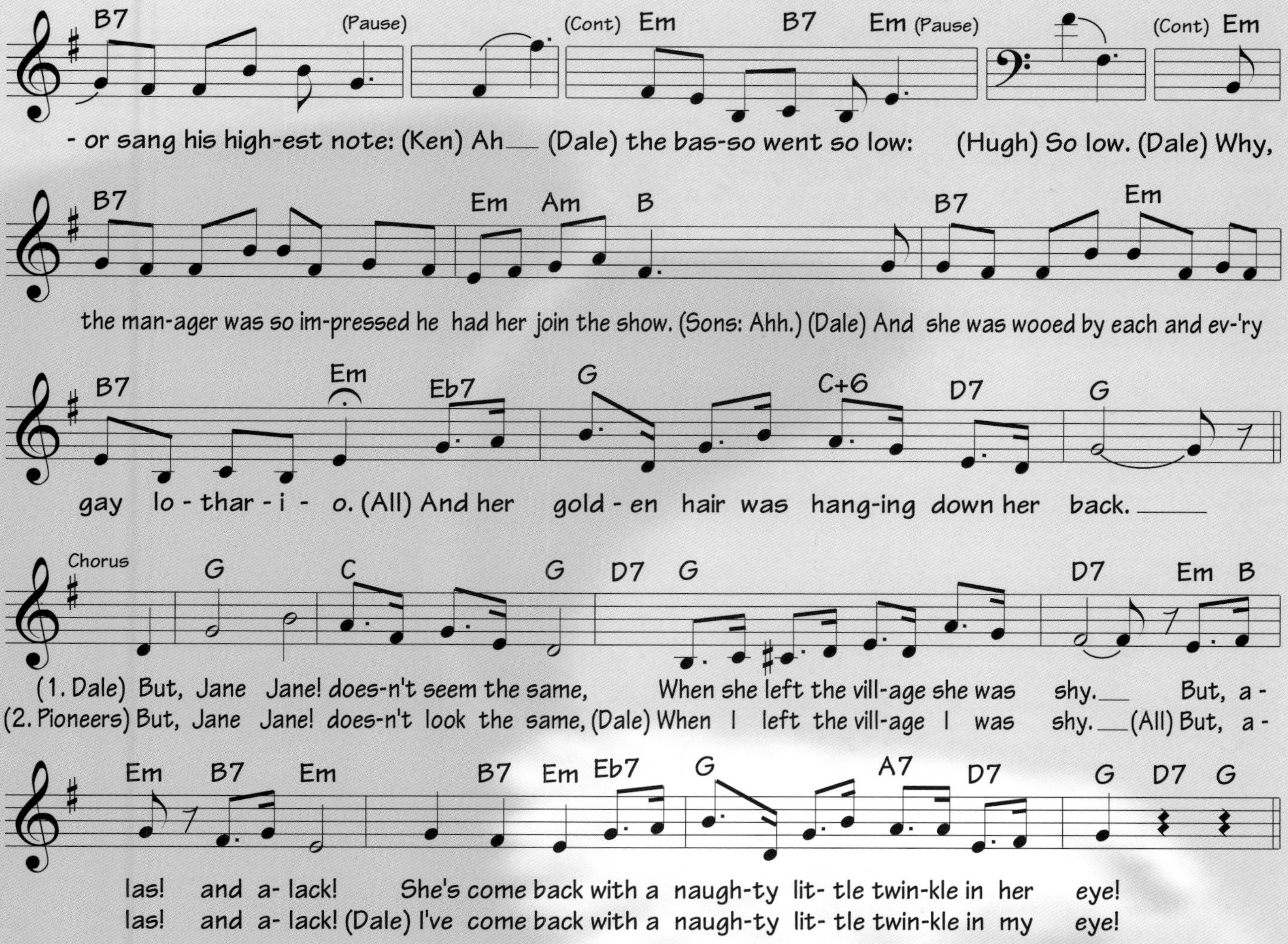
B7 (Pause) (Cont) Em B7 Em (Pause) (Cont) Em
- or sang his high-est note: (Ken) Ah___ (Dale) the bas-so went so low: (Hugh) So low. (Dale) Why,
B7 Em Am B B7 Em
the man-ager was so im-pressed he had her join the show. (Sons: Ahh.) (Dale) And she was wooed by each and ev-'ry
B7 Em Eb7 G C+6 D7 G
gay lo - thar - i - o. (All) And her gold - en hair was hang-ing down her back.___
Chorus
G C G D7 G D7 Em B
(1. Dale) But, Jane Jane! does-n't seem the same, When she left the vill-age she was shy.___ But, a -
(2. Pioneers) But, Jane Jane! does-n't look the same, (Dale) When I left the vill-age I was shy.___(All) But, a -
Em B7 Em B7 Em Eb7 G A7 D7 G D7 G
las! and a- lack! She's come back with a naugh-ty lit- tle twin-kle in her eye!
las! and a- lack! (Dale) I've come back with a naugh-ty lit- tle twin-kle in my eye!

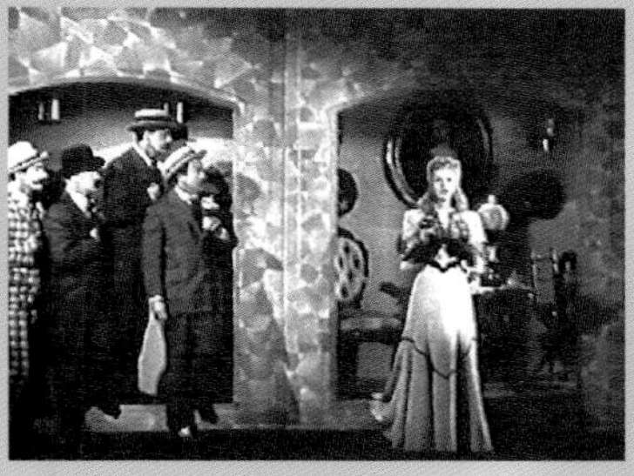

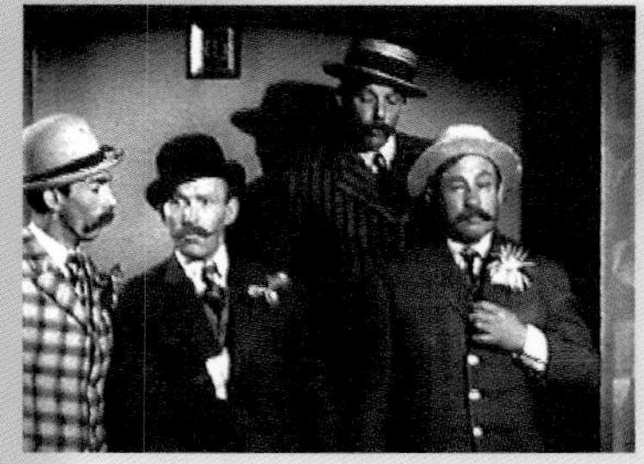

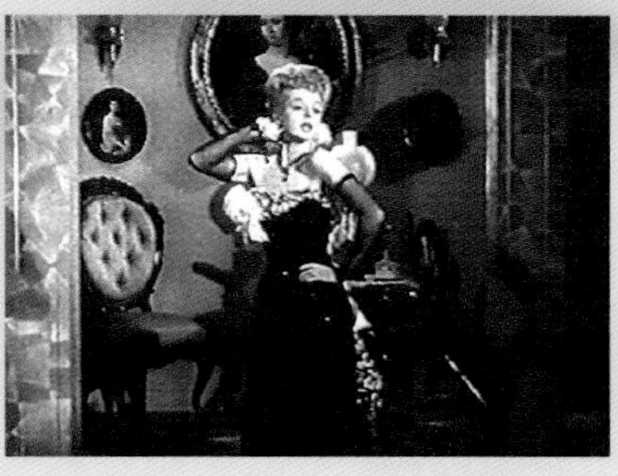

Republic Pictures Page 209
"Song of Nevada" Script Revision: #3

AFTER DANCE SEQUENCE. DALE TAKES THE STAGE. LONG SHOT AND ON CUE, SLOW TRUCK INTO ALBUM BOOK ON TABLE. CROSS DISSOLVE TO LIFE-SIZE BOOK OPENING WITH DALE AND PIONEERS INSIDE. EVENING. OUTDOORS INTERIOR SET.

After Roy sings and a dance number is performed, Joan is asked to sing. She uses a family photo album and the song "And Her Golden Hair Was Hanging Down Her Back" to explain about "Jane," a blacksheep of the family. The Pioneers accompany her and all are dressed in turn-of-the-century city costumes.

NEVADA

(As sung by the cast in the film's finale stage show)

transcribed by
SCOTT HOMAN
ERIC VAN HAMERSVELD

words & music by
CHARLES HENDERSON

Republic Pictures Page 244
"Song of Nevada" Script Revision: #5

FADE UP TO AN OPTICAL MATTE GRAPHIC OF THE NEVADA STATE MAP THAT FRAMES VARIOUS RUNNING FOOTAGE SCENES.

Barrabee and Roy have captured the villains that tried to steal the ranch. At the "Frontier Days Celebration" stage show, which is the film's finale, the cast and chorus opens the show with a special salute to the state of Nevada by singing "Nevada." This production begins with a cutout of the state that frames various scenes depicting life in Nevada, then goes to cast member cameos, and ends with a high-kicking chorus line.

Produced By
Eddy White

Directed by
John English

Screenplay by
Dorrell and Stuart McGowan

Starring
Roy Rogers, Dale Evans, Jean Porter, Bob Nolan, The Sons of the Pioneers, Trigger

with
Andrew Tombes, Edward Gargan, Dot Farley, LeRoy Mason, Charles Smith, Pierce Lyden, Maxine Doyle, Helen Talbot, Pat Starling, kay Forrester, Marguerite Blout, Mary Keyon, Hank Bell, Vernon and Draper, Morell Trio.

Prod: #1325 Released: 15 Sep 1944
Black/White - 74min.

Dale's younger sister, Betty Lou (Porter), has discovered men and is monopolizing the ranch hands' time. Dale fires the men and hires cowgirls. Betty Lou has the horses stolen to be recovered by the men but the villains play for keeps. Roy and Keno (Gargan) are hired as cooks by the ranch owner, Cyclone (Tombes). Roy falls for Dale and winds up capturing the horse thieves.

1. Dale fires the ranch hands for paying too much attention to Betty Lou.

2. Dale hits Roy with her car and he pretends he's really hurt to get her attention.

3. Roy takes Dale on a wild wagon ride to get her to give him her address.

4. Cyclone discovers that Dale has replaced the ranch hands with cowgirls.

5. Cyclone's surrey breaks loose and he's rescued by Roy.

6. Betty Lou's horse stealing plan is being carried out by REAL HORSE THIEVES!

7. Roy catches up with the thieves and has it out with them.

8. Trigger helps Roy bring in the horse thieves.

9. In the end, the Pioneers marry the cowgirls and Roy and Dale get married too.

MY HOBBY IS LOVE

(As sung by Jean Porter in the opening stage show dream sequence)

words & music by
CHARLES HENDERSON

(Opening Verse)

I was quite a gay little gad about.
Never had a romance in view.
Just had a lot of hobbies I was mad about,
and they gave me plenty to do.
Then I met you...

C Cm

I've stopped jit - ter bugg - ing, in

G Gdim Am7

fav - or of moon- light hugg - ing. With you, ba - by, my

D9 G6 F#7 G6

hob - by is love. _____ To prove my af-

fec - tion, I'm sell - ing my stamp col - lec - tion. With

D7 G9 Gdim

you, ba - by, my hob - by is love. _____

G9 Em7 C

__ I used to spend my time _____ up - on a

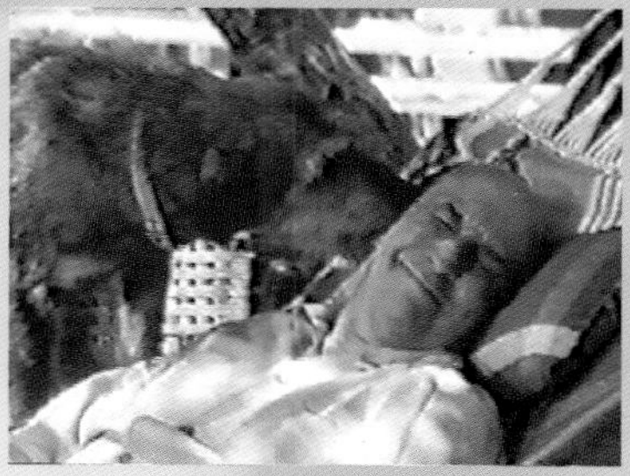

Ebmaj7 Eb6 G

ten - nis court ______ But now I like my

Republic Pictures Page 4
"The San Fernando Valley" Script Revision: #2

CROSS DISSOLVE FROM MAIN TITLE TO MEDIUM CLOSE UP OF CHORUS GIRLS LOOKING INTO REFLECTING POOL ON STAGE SET. DURING SONG DISSOLVE TO MEDIUM LONG SHOT OF HAMMOCK. DAY

While taking a nap in a hammock, "Cyclone," Dale's grandfather and owner of the ranch, is dreaming. His dream includes Dale's younger sister, Betty Lou, and several dancers singing "My Hobby Is Love" just for him in a spectacular nightclub setting. He is suddenly awakened when he falls out of the hammock reaching for his pipe in his dream. He discovers that it was just his young granddaughter, Betty Lou, singing to the ranch hands. He stomps over to the group to break up the goings-on.

ONE THOUSAND EIGHT HUNDRED AND FORTY NINE YEARS

(As sung by the Sons of the Pioneers in the "Days of '49 Celebration parade)

transcribed by
SCOTT HOMAN
ERIC VAN HAMERSVELD

words & music by
TIM SPENCER

Republic Pictures Page 26
"The San Fernanco Valley" Script Revision: #2

FADE UP LONG SHOT OF STREET FROM HOTEL SECOND STORY PORCH.

As the "Days of '49 Celebration" parade rolls along, the Sons of the Pioneers sing "One Thousand Eight Hundred and Forty Nine Years" from atop a stagecoach.

SAN FERNANDO VALLEY

(As sung by Roy Rogers and Dale Evans with the Sons of the Pioneers in the jail-wagon)

words & music by
GORDON JENKINS

Republic Pictures Page 113
"San Fernando Valley" Script Revision: #8

CUT TO MEDIUM LONG SHOT OF ROY, DALE, AND SHERIFF, ENTERING STAGE LEFT WALKING TO BACK OF JAIL WAGON. DAY.

Roy, who's happy, and Dale, who's mad, have been "arrested" and taken to the jail wagon for arguing in the street which is against the "Days of '49 Celebration" rules. They must sing to be released. Accompanied by the Sons of the Pioneers, they sing their own rendition of "The San Fernando Valley."

I DROTTLED A DRIT DRIT

(As sung by Jean Porter and the Sons of the Pioneers on the outdoor street stage at the "Days of '49 Celebration)

transcribed by
SCOTT HOMAN
ERIC VAN HAMERSVELD

words & music by
WILLIAM LAVA

Fm7 Bb7 Fm7 Bb7
It's simp - ly new slang - uage mean - ing,
Eb7 Fdim Bbm7 Eb7
I got a guy and he's right on the beam. I
Ab
drot - tled a drit drit. (Shug: Oh, she's dropping her...mmmm?) (Jean) I
Fm7 Bb7 Fm7 Bb7
drat - tled a grat grat. (Shug: That's confusing, ain't it?) (Jean) He
Bbm7 Eb7 Bbm7 Eb7
wig - gled a fran, dig - gled a tran, bid - dy dad - dy,
Ab Eb7 Ab
just wait - 'll it hap - pens to you. Now
Ebm7 Ab7 Ebm7 Ab7
what is a "drit drit?" I had a hunch you'd be ask - in'. And
Db
may- be you've not-tled and drot-tled a lot -tle and don't ev - en know what it means.
Fm7 Bb7 Fm7 Bb7
Must be a new lang - uage. It
Eb7 Fdim Bbm7 Eb7
means, I got a guy and he's strict - ly on the beam. I

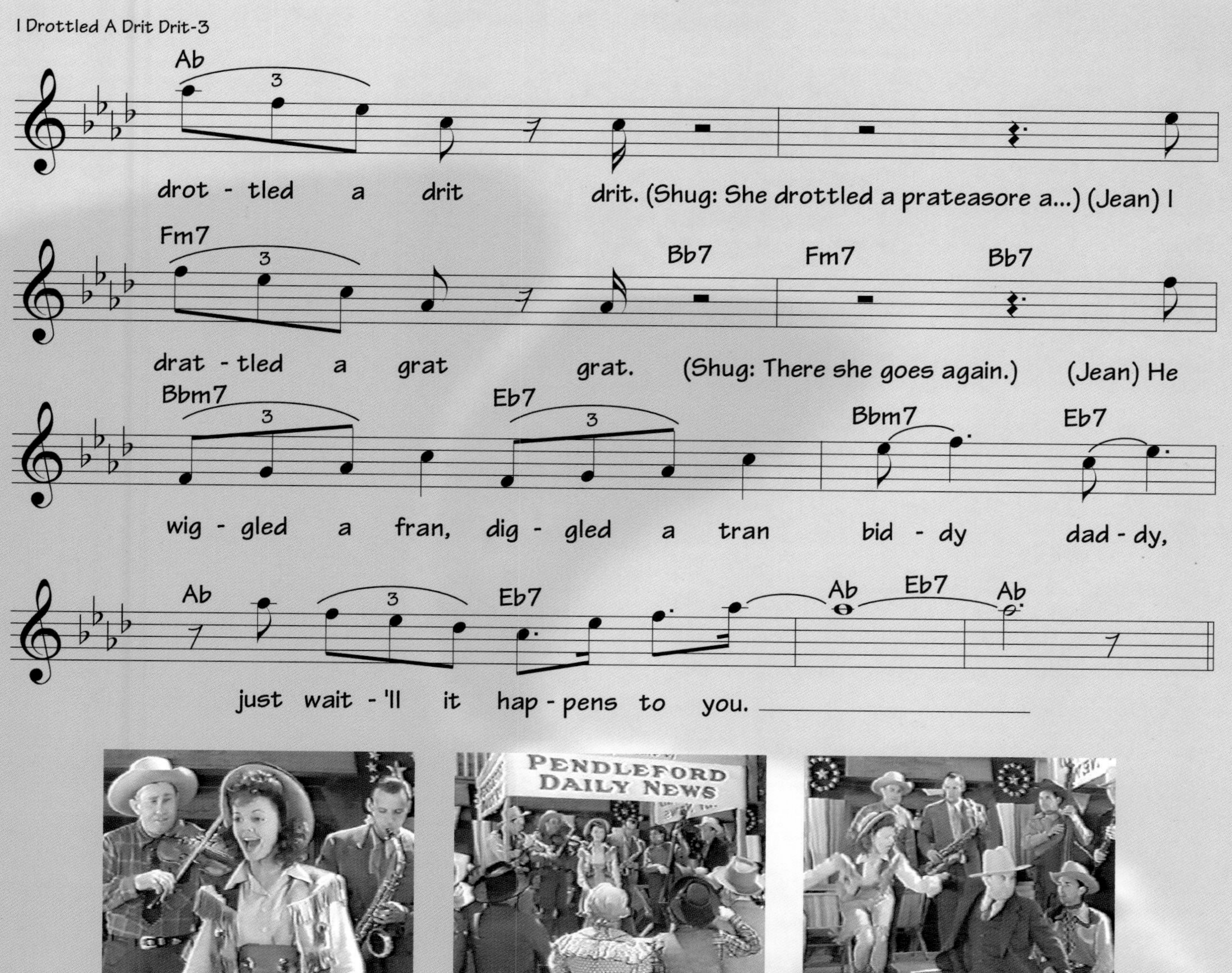

Republic Pictures Page 133
"The San Fernando Valley" Script Revision: #3

CUT TO LONG SHOT OF WESTERN STREET WITH PORTER WALKING IN STAGE RIGHT. PAN LEFT WITH HER STOPPING AT THE OUTDOOR STAGE AND THE PIONEERS. DAY

Dale has hired cowgirl ranch hands to keep Betty Lou away from boys. The Sons of the Pioneers are still out of their jobs at the ranch. Betty Lou sees them performing on a "'49 Celebration" street stage. She has an idea about how to get all the boys back on the ranch and tells them her plan. She explains that if the boys steal some of Cyclone's horses then "find" them before the cowgirl ranch hands do, Cyclone would so pleased he'd fire the gals and hire the guys back!

The boys hesitate and while she is trying to convince them, she sees Cyclone coming down the street. He would be angry seeing her talking with them, so she quickly tells the Sons to play something and she'll pretend that she just came to sing. The Pioneers and Betty Lou sing the novelty song "I Drottled A Drit Drit." At the end of the song, a very upset Cyclone grabs Betty Lou off the stage to take her back to the ranch.

THEY WENT THAT-A-WAY

(As sung by Roy Rogers and Ed Gargon in the kitchen)

transcribed by
SCOTT HOMAN
ERIC VAN HAMERSVELD

words & music by
TIM SPENCER

Republic Pictures Page 152
"San Fernando Valley" Script Revision: #5

CROSS DISSOLVE FROM CLOSE UP OF POT TO MED. SHOT KITCHEN WITH KENO COOKING AND ROY SITTING WITH GUITAR. INDOORS. EVENING.

Roy and Keno have taken jobs as cooks at Dale's ranch to keep an eye on Betty Lou. Using the "Brides Bible" cookbook, they begin to make popovers. The ranch dog steals the book, so they improvise the recipe while singing "They Went That A-Way."

HOW COULD ANYONE BE SWEETER THAN YOU

(As sung by Roy Rogers while sitting with Dale Evans on the porch swing)

transcribed by
SCOTT HOMAN
ERIC VAN HAMERSVELD

words & music by
CHARLES HENDERSON

Republic Pictures Page 213
"The San Fernando Valley" Script Revision: #4

CUT TO MEDIUM LONG SHOT OF ROY AND DALE SITTING ON A PORCH SWING. NIGHT.

To help put a stop to Betty Lou's outrageous flirting and especially her demonstrative crush on Roy, Dale wants to show her the difference between men and boys, and especially that Roy is too old for her. She chats with Roy about the situation and suggests that, if Roy outwardly pays attention to one of the older girl ranch hands in front of Betty Lou, she might get the idea. Dale suggests several of the girls to try this out on but Roy declines in favor of having Dale be the best candidate. She reluctantly agrees and they set up an innocent, but "adult", rendezvous. On the porch swing that evening Betty Lou sees Roy serenading her sister, Dale, with the song "How Could Anyone Be Sweeter Than You."

OVER THE RAINBOW TRAIL

(As sung by the Sons of the Pioneers around the ranch swimming pool)

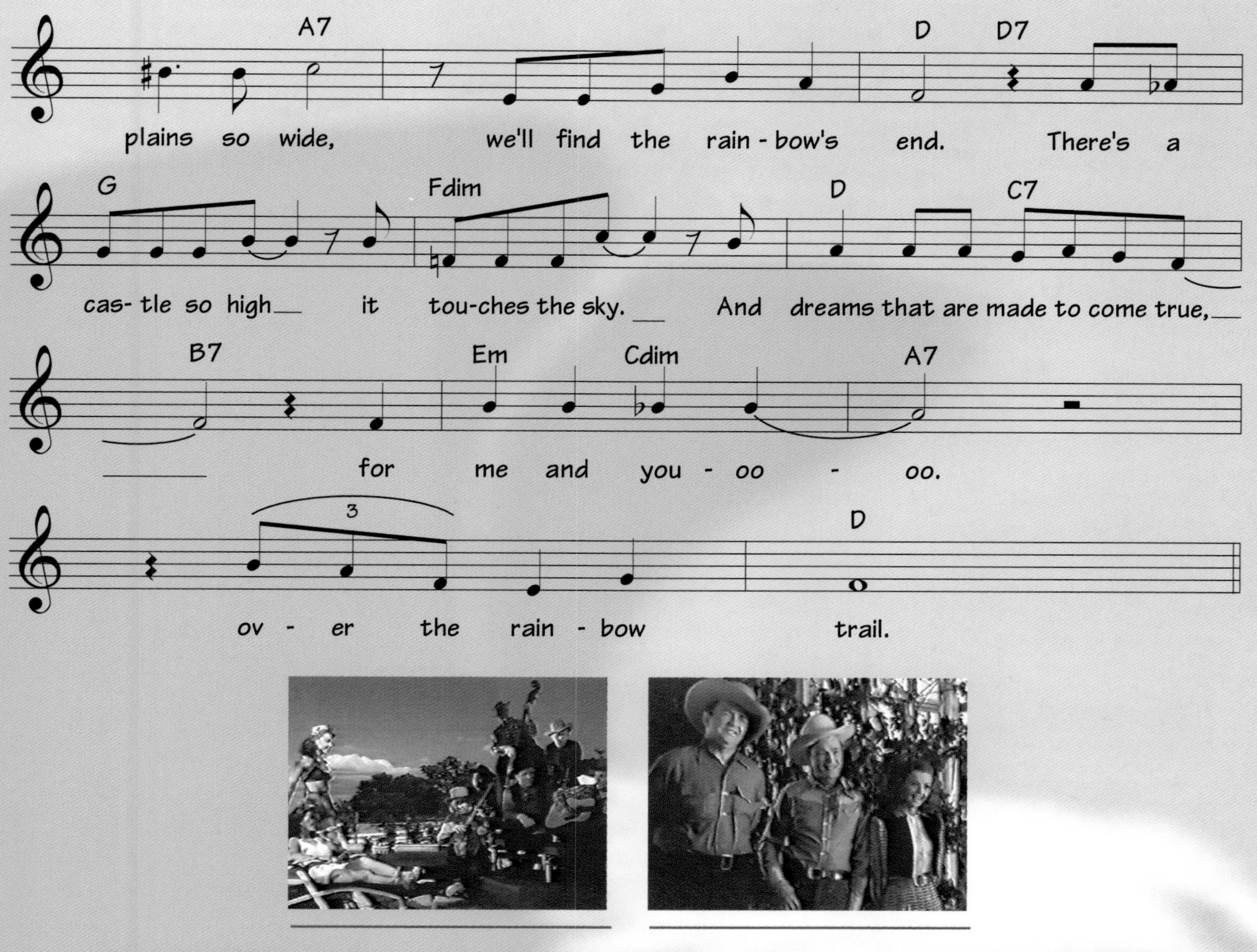

Republic Pictures Page 223
"San Fernando Valley" Script Revision: #3

FADE UP LONG SHOT SWIMMING POOL. FOLLOW PAN PIONEERS RIDING IN STAGE RIGHT. CUT TO GROUP AROUND POOL LOOKING ON. CUT TO PIONEERS WALKING IN STAGE LEFT. CUT TO MEDIUM LONG SHOT OF PIONEERS WITH POOL GROUP. SHOOT DAY FOR NIGHT.

Pioneers arrive for an impromptu evening serenade to the gal ranch hands. Around the ranch's swimming pool they sing "Over the Rainbow Trail." While they're singing Betty Lou sets her plan into action to get Roy interested in her by untying the horses and allowing the villains to steal them.

Produced By
Harry Grey

Directed by
Frank McDonald

Screenplay by
Gordon Kahn, Bob Williams

Starring
Roy Rogers, Dale Evans, Gabby Hayes, Bob Nolan, The Sons of the Pioneers, Trigger

with
Lloyd Corrigan, Clair Dubrey, Richard Powers (Tom Keene), Arthur Loft, Roy Barcroft, Lucien Littlefield, Sam Flint, Jack Kirk

Prod: #1326 Released: 6 Jun 1944
Black/White - 77min.

Marjorie (Dale), the owner of the Brooks Rodeo, has just come home from college to discover that her rodeo, run by Gabby, is in deep financial trouble. A rival rodeo owned by Madden (Powers) is out to finish off the Brooks Rodeo. Roy and the Sons of the Pioneers are hired by Gabby to spruce up his show and they soon learn what Madden is up to.

RB

1. Gabby learns that the rodeo he's managing isn't getting any bookings.

2, Trying to stay in business, Gabby hires Roy, the Pioneers, and Trigger for his show.

3. Marjorie, who owns the rodeo, wants to sell out to competitor Madden.

4. While on a romantic rowboat date with Madden, Roy steals Marjorie away.

5. There's a hair-raising chariot grudge race between Roy and Madden's men.

6. On the way to a performance in Albuquerque, Gabby's rodeo is sabotaged.

7. Roy saves Gabby's life after a runaway wagon goes in the river.

8. Just before his marriage to Marjorie, Roy arrests Madden for the dirty work.

9. They make it to the State Fair and Gabby and Margorie's rodeo is saved.

AMOR
(As sung in English and Spanish by Dale Evans at the Benefit Show)
words & music by
SUNNY SKYLAR
GABRIEL RUIZ
RICARDO LOPEZ MENDEZ
Beguine tempo
C
1. A - mor. A - mor. A -
mor. This word so sweet that I re -
G7
peat means I a - dore you. A -
Dm G7
mor. A - mor. My love, would you de -
Fm6 C
ny that heart that I have placed be - fore you?
Em B7
I can't find an-oth-er word with mean-ing so clear. My
Em G
lips try to whis-per sweet-er things in your ear. But some-how or oth-er noth-ing
D7 G7
sounds quite so dear as this soft ca-ress-ing word I know. A -
C
mor. A - mor. A - mor. No - cio de

Amor-2

Republic Pictures
"Lights of Old Santa Fe"

Page 14
Script Revision: #3

CUT TO LONG SHOT OF STAGE.

Roy, Gabby, and the Pioneers arrive at a benefit show produced by Marjorie, just in time to hear her sing "Amor." Two-part song sequence includes costume change to Spanish.

COWPOKE POLKA
(As sung by Roy Rogers and the Sons of the Pioneers at the Charity Benefit)
transcribed by
SCOTT HOMAN
ERIC VAN HAMERSVELD
words & music by
TIM SPENCER
(Fiddling
) (Sons/Roy) Swing your part - ner
to the right, swing her back and hold her tight.
Swing her far in - to the night, that's the cow - poke
pol - ka. Do - si - do and pro - me - nade,
to some oth - er lit - tle maid. Swing her once and
then you trade. That's the cow - poke pol - ka.
One lit - tle bird in a three ra - il pen, the
bird hops out and the crow hops in.
Chick - en in the bread pan pick - in' out dough, the
crow hops out and a - way you go. Cir - cle late and

C7 F
swing your pard', swing her ea - sy, not too hard.
F C7
Rat - tle your spurs til' you get tired. That's the cow - poke
F 3 3
pol - ka. (Fiddling) (Shug dances around his base fiddle)
C7 3 3 3 3 3 3
F Fast C
(Gabby) One lit - tle bird in a three ra - il pen, the
G7 C
bird hops out and the crow hops in.
Chick - en in the bread pan pick - in' out dough, the
G7 C7 F
crow hops out and a - way you go. (Sons/Roy) Cir - cle late and
C7 F
swing your pard', swing her ea - sy, not too hard.
F C7
Rat - tle your spurs til' you get tired.
F
That's the cow - poke pol - ka.
Republic Pictures
"Lights of Old Santa Fe"
Page 22
Script Revision: #2
CROSS DISSOLVE BALLERINA TO MEDIUM SHOT OF ROY AND GABBY.
Tired of the classy dancing wood nymph dancers, Gabby wants Roy and the Sons of the the Pioneers to play a western tune. They sing "Cowpoke Polka" and attract a crowd that includes Majorie and Madden.

I'M HAPPY IN MY LEVI BRITCHES

(As sung by Roy Rogers and the Sons of the Pioneers traveling in the car)

transcribed by
SCOTT HOMAN
ERIC VAN HAMERSVELD

words & music by
TIM SPENCER

Republic Pictures Page 65
"Lights of Old Santa Fe" Script Revision: #4

CROSS DISSOLVE TO LONG SHOT OF ROY AND THE PIONEERS DRIVING TOWARDS CAMERA. DAY.

Roy and the Pioneers, with Trigger in a trailer, have just turned down a job at Madden's ranch. Along the way they sing "I'm Happy In My Levi Britches."

COWBOY JUBILEE

(As sung by Roy Rogers and the Sons of the Pioneers at the radio station)

transcribed by
SCOTT HOMAN
ERIC VAN HAMERSVELD

words & music by
KEN CARSON

D A
soon we'll be long gone to the Cow - boy
E7 A D
Ju - bi - lee. Just hear that cow - boy
A B7
band a play - in'. (instrumental guitar
E7
) (All) You know your
A
blues won't mean a thing when you get
D A
in the swing. Say, a cow - boy's life
A E7
is for me. Soon all your
A
cares you'll be shed - din' an' like
D A
me, you'll be head - in' to the Cow - boy
E7 A
Ju - bi - lee. (Roy yodels
E7

A
E7
A
D
A
E7
A
D
) (All) Just hear that cow - boy
A
band a play- in'. (Instrumental fiddle
B7
E7
) (All) You know your
A
blues won't mean a thing when you get
D
A
in the swing. Say, a cow - boy's life

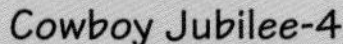

Republic Pictures Page 78
"Lights of Old Santa Fe" Script Revision: #3

CUT TO ROY AND THE PIONEERS BEHIND MICROPHONE IN RADIO ROOM. DURING SONG, CROSS DISSOLVE TO OUTDOOR STAGE. DAY.

Gabby wants to hire Roy and the Sons of the Pioneers but doesn't have the money. So, he takes them to WAKT radio. He has an idea of how to promote his rodeo and have the boys under his control by persuading Martin Masley (Corrigan), the station announcer, to hire them to sing. While he is talking with Masley, Roy and the Pioneers slip into the room and start singing "Cowboy Jubilee." During the song, the scene cross dissolves to an outdoor stage where the boys have been been hired and are singing for Medley's Market Anniversary Celebration. At the end of the song, Marjorie arrives.

THE NERVE OF SOME PEOPLE

(As sung by Roy Rogers and Dale Evans on the outdoor radio stage)

transcribed by
SCOTT HOMAN
ERIC VAN HAMERSVELD

words & music by
JACK ELLIOTT

Freely

Bbm7 Eb7
(Dale) Did you ever break a shoe - lace, when

Bbm7 Eb7 Bbm7 Eb7
you were in a hur - ry? Did you ev - er fail to mail an

Ab Eb7 Cm G7
ur - gent note? And were you ag - gri - vat - ed. Well, you

Cm F7 Eb Cm
know just how I feel, 'cause some - one here has

F7 Bb7 Eb7
real - ly got __ my goat. ____ (Roy says: I wonder who that could be?) (Dale) The

Ab Adim Bbm Eb7 Bbm Eb7
nerve of some peo - ple. ______ The nerve of some peo - ple. __

Ab F7
__ Act - ing just like they know it all, ____

Bb7 Eb7 Ab Adim
of all the nerve. ____ The nerve of some peo - ple. __

Bbm Eb7 Bbm Eb7 Ab
___ (Dale says: The nerve of some peo - ple.)

Ab F7
You're real - ly rid - in' for a fall. ____ (Roy says: Oh, I don't think so.)

Bb7 Eb7 Ab Db
(Dale says: Of all the nerve.) (Dale) You may think that you're

Dbm Ab Eb7 Ab
clev - er. (Dale says: But brain work is not your long suit.) (Dale) And
Bb7 Eb7
if I nev- er see you a - gain, I... (Roy says: You know,
Ab Adim
you're kinda cute.) (Dale says: Well.) (Dale) The nerve of some peo - ple.
Bbm Eb7 Bbm Eb7 Ab
(Dale says: The nerve of some peo- ple.) (Roy says: Say, by the way, when will
F7 Bb7 Eb7 Ab Eb7
I see you again?) (Dale says: Are you kidding?) (Dale) All the nerve. (Roy) The
Ab Adim Bbm Eb7 Bbm Eb7
nerve of some peo - ple. (Roy says: The nerve of some peo - ple.)
Ab 3 F7
(Roy) Can't take a joke when the joke's on you.
Bb7 Eb7 Ab Adim
(Dale says: Well) (Dale) of all the nerve. (Roy) The nerve of some peo - ple.
Bbm Eb7 Bbm Eb7 Ab
The nerve of some peo-ple. (Dale says: That's what I say.) (Roy says: You'll
Ab F7
nev - er make friends act - ing like you do.)
Bb7 Eb7 Ab Db
(Dale) Of all the nerve. I guess I know my own

Republic Pictures Page 82
"Lights of Old Santa Fe" Script Revision: #2

CUT TO MEDIUM LONG SHOT OF DALE WALKING THROUGH CROWD. DAY.

Roy and the Pioneers, who are broadcasting a radio program on an outdoor stage for Medley's Market, have just finished singing a song. Marjorie arrives and is going into Medley's when Roy sees her and asks her to come up and join him. She declines, so he Roy grabs the microphone and comes down to her. He wants to ask her a few simple questions. With a smartalecky attitude she condescends. He then wants her to come up on the stage with him and sing a song. She declines and he says she's lost her nerve. With that she climbs up the stage and joins him. They sing "The Nerve of Some People" with the Pioneers' accompanying.

TRIGGER HASN'T GOT A PURTY FIGURE

(As sung by Roy Rogers to Dale Evans on the way back to the ranch)

transcribed by
SCOTT HOMAN
ERIC VAN HAMERSVELD

words & music by
TIM SPENCER

Eb
Oh, Trig- ger has - n't got a pur - ty fig - ure, but he

Eb Edim Fm7 Bb7
is - n't half as ug - ly as a girl can be. And for

Eb Gdim Ab Bb7
your in - for - ma - tion, he's real trans - por - ta - tion.

Eb Gm Fm7 Bb7
How's a - bout a ride with me?

Eb
Trig - ger has - n't got a pur - ty fig - ure, but his

Eb Edim Fm7 Bb7
ea - sy rid - ing sad - dle's like a rock - ing chair. And if

Eb Gdim Ab Bb7
you're tired of walk - ing, you'd bet - ter do some talk - ing.

Eb Ab Eb
He won't charge you an - y fare.

Fm7 Bb7 Eb
Tramp, tramp down the dus - ty trail,

Fm7 Bb7 Eb Fm7 Bb7
till you get the gout. Tramp, tramp, tramp o - ver

Republic Pictures Page 79
"Lights of Old Santa Fe" Script Revision: #2

CUT TO MEDIUM SHOT OF ROY, DALE, AND TRIGGER. OUTDOORS. DAY.

Roy has just broken up a romantic rowboat date between Marjorie and the villain, Madden, by lassoing the boat, pulling it so hard that Madden has fallen in, and dragging the boat to the shore. Roy's upset because he is a little sweet on Marjorie and she rode Trigger to get there. Marjorie is furious and won't ride back to the ranch on Trigger with Roy. She will walk and that's that! As they head back, Roy sings "Trigger Hasn't Got A Purty Figure." Pretty soon Marjorie gives up and the two ride off together.

RIDE 'EM, COWBOY

(As sung by the Pioneers for the simulated rodeo radio broadcast)

words & music by
TIM SPENCER
ROY ROGERS

Republic Pictures Page 98
"Lights of Old Santa Fe" Script Revision: #4

CUT TO LONG SHOT OF ROY RUNNING TOWARDS CAMERA. MID-DAY.

The villains have ransacked Gabby's rodeo. To keep Marjorie from finding out, the group pretends to be in Albuquerque by broadcasting a simulated rodeo from a borrowed radio transmission truck. To begin the broadcast, Gabby introduces the Pioneers who sing "Ride 'Em Cowboy" while Roy handles the radio engineer duties.

LIGHTS OF OLD SANTA FE

(As sung by Roy Rogers, Dale Evans, and Gabby in the kitchen)

words & music by
JACK ELLIOTT

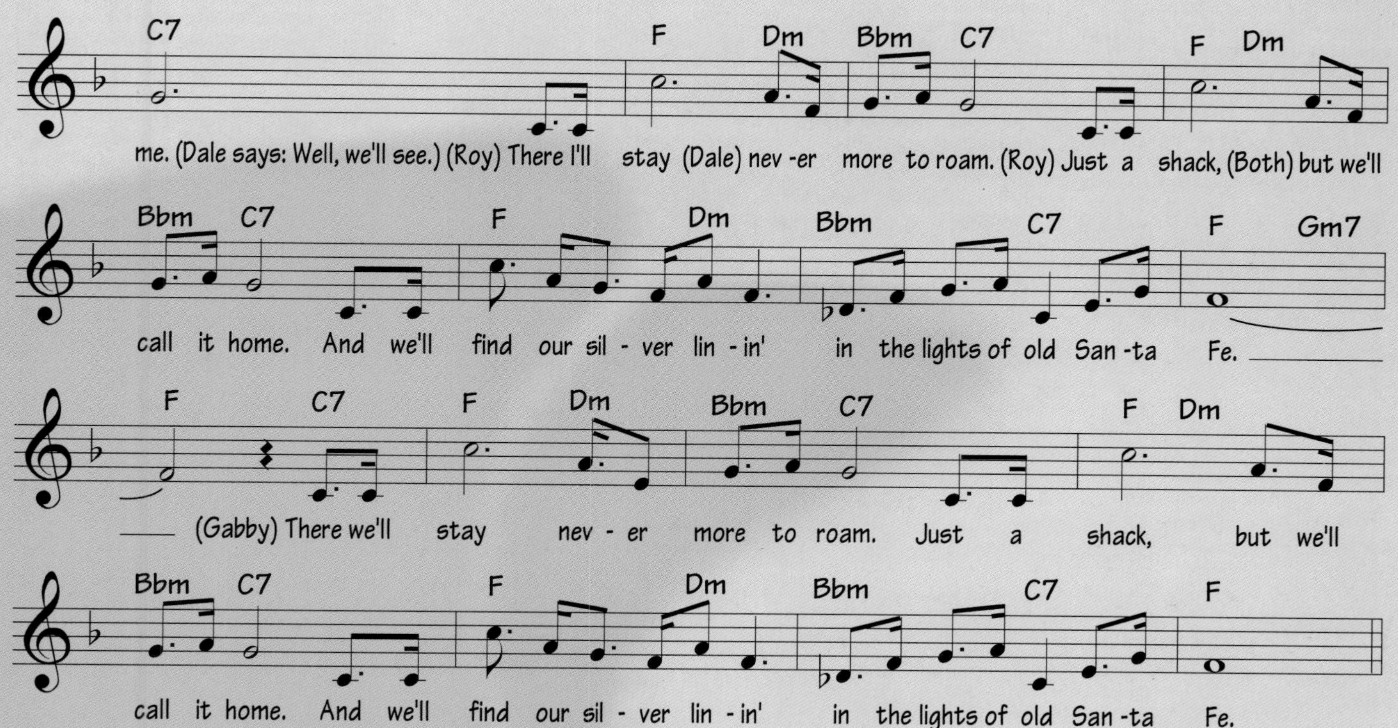

Republic Pictures Page 146

"Lights of Old Santa Fe" Script Revision: #4

CUT TO MEDIUM LONG SHOT OF ROY AND DALE IN THE KITCHEN COOKING OVER AN OPEN BARBECUE. EVENING.

The group is celebrating their "Albuquerque" rodeo show. Marjorie doesn't know about Gabby's rodeo not making it to Albuquerque because of sabotage. She thinks that she heard the "successful" rodeo broadcast over the radio and is chattering about taking the rodeo to Madison Square Garden.

While Marjorie and Roy are tending the steaks over the barbecue, they sing "Lights of Old Santa Fe." Gabby sings the last verse himself.

Produced By
Donald H. Brown

Directed by
John English

Screenplay by
Jack Townley, John K. Butler

Starring
Roy Rogers, Dale Evans, Gabby Hayes, Bob Nolan, The Sons of the Pioneers, Trigger

with
Peggy Stewart, Beverly Loyd, Grant Withers, Jill Browning, Vivian Oakland, Hal Taliaferro, Jack Rutherford, Emmett Vogan, Edward Cassidy, Ralph Colby

Prod: #1329 Released: 23 Mar 1945
Black/White - 78min.

The musical show Dorothy (Dale) is in is broke. She has an idea to raise money by selling a Utah ranch that she recently inherited. She heads west with the all-girl cast. Roy and the Pioneers, who run the ranch, don't want the sale. Bowman (Withers) does and creates trouble. Gabby, Roy's friend, pitches in to stop Bowman, and convince Dorothy not to sell.

RR

1. Dorothy learns the show she is in is closing, so the cast is out of a job.

2. Roy reads a telegram that Dorothy is coming to sell the Bar X ranch.

3. Roy catches up with Bowman who "accidentally" takes a shot at him.

4. Dorothy and the gals arrive. Roy convinces them that Gabby's shack is the Bar X.

5. Bowman makes his pitch to buy Dorothy's Bar X ranch.

6. Roy shows Dorothy that Utah is wonderful and she shouldn't sell the ranch.

7. Roy and Gabby are arrested for stopping the Bar X sale, but they escape.

8. Roy and Gabby bring in Bowman and the cattle thieves.

9. In the musical finale, the gang (without the villains) reenact their story.

THANK DIXIE FOR ME

(As sung by Dale Evans on stage at the rehearsal)

transcribed by
SCOTT HOMAN
ERIC VAN HAMERSVELD

words & music by
JACK ELLIOTT

Republic Pictures Page 4
"Utah" Script Revision: #2

FADE UP AFTER OPENING TITLES TO SLOW TRUCK IN TO SIGN. DISSOLVE TO LONG SHOT OF STAGE.

Dorothy, the chorus line dancers, and an all-girl band, dressed in casual shorts and blouses, are rehearsing the song "Thank Dixie For Me" for an upcoming production.

THE UTAH TRAIL

(As sung by Roy Rogers and the Sons of the Pioneers
while herding cattle)

words & music by
BOB PALMER

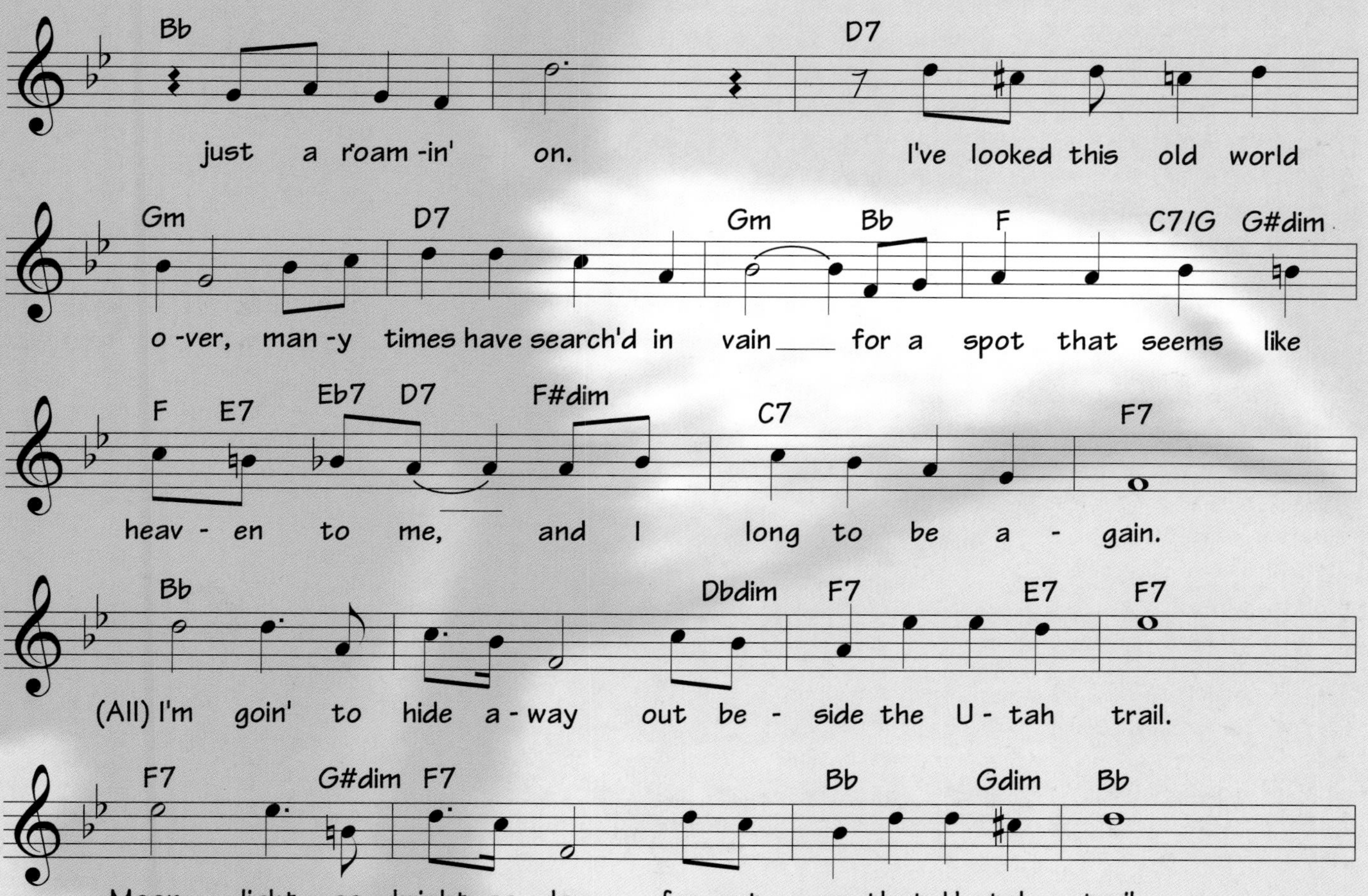

Bb Bb/D Dbdim F7
(Roy) You ask me where I'm go - in' so ear - ly in the

F7 F+7
dawn. I'm just a trav' - ler rov - ing,

Bb D7
just a roam -in' on. I've looked this old world

Gm D7 Gm Bb F C7/G G#dim
o -ver, man -y times have search'd in vain___ for a spot that seems like

F E7 Eb7 D7 F#dim C7 F7
heav - en to me, and I long to be a - gain.

Bb Dbdim F7 E7 F7
(All) I'm goin' to hide a - way out be - side the U - tah trail.

F7 G#dim F7 Bb Gdim Bb
Moon - light as bright as day far out on that U - tah trail

Republic Pictures Page 10
"Utah Trail" Script Revision: #3

CROSS DISSOLVE FROM DALE ON PHONE TO LONG SHOT OF RANCH GATE. THEN DISSOLVE TO MEDIUM LONG SHOT OF ROY RIDING ON TRIGGER TRUCKING FROM STAGE RIGHT TO LEFT. DAY.

Roy and the Pioneers are working cattle on their ranch, the Bar X. While they move their cattle from the pens to the open prairie, they sing "The Utah Trail."

WELCOME HOME MISS BRYANT

(As sung by the Sons of the Pioneers at the train station)

transcribed by
SCOTT HOMAN
ERIC VAN HAMERSVELD

words & music by
KEN CARSON
BOB NOLAN

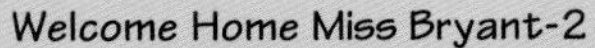

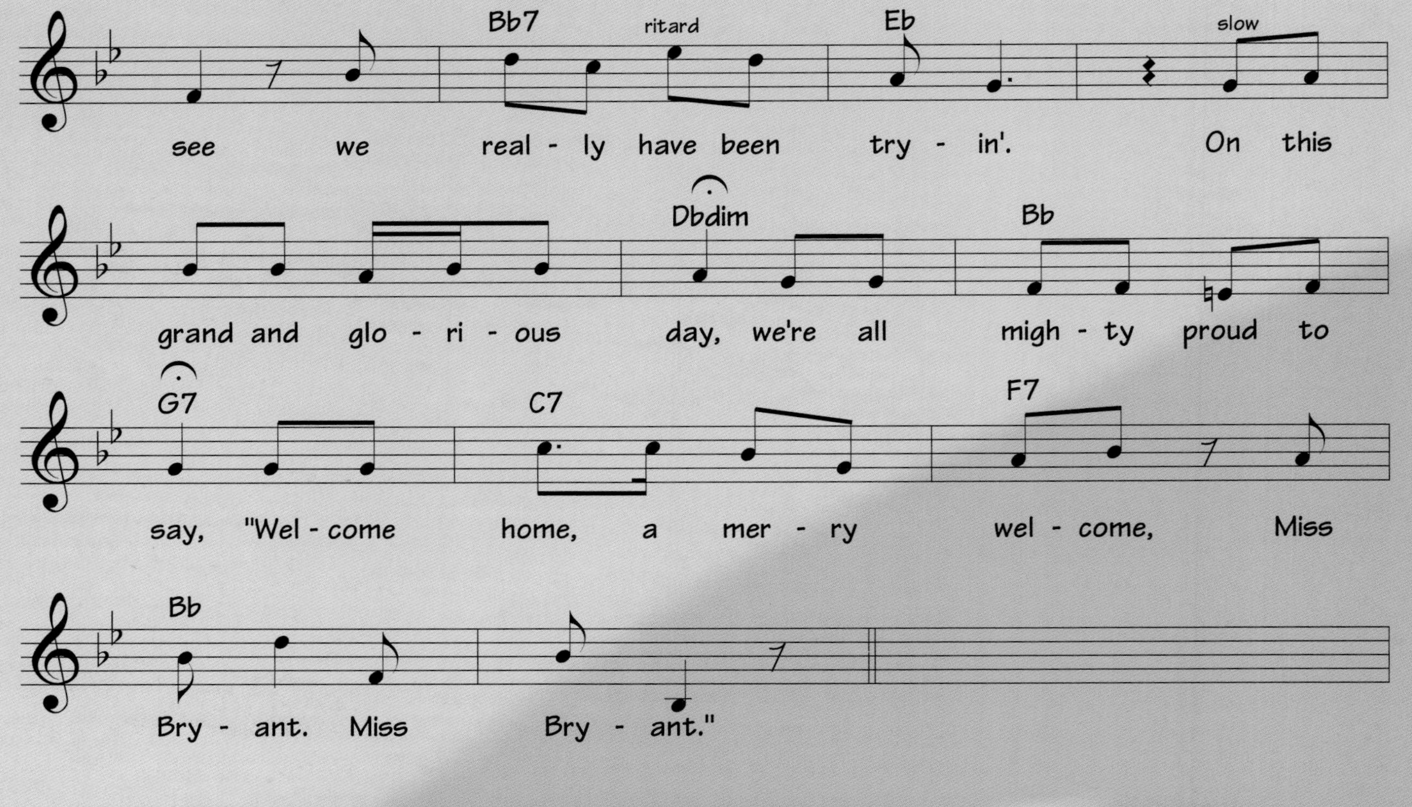

Republic Pictures Page 41
"Utah" Script Revision: #3

CROSS DISSOLVE TO LONG SHOT OF TRAIN. DISSOLVE TO TRAIN STATIONSIGN. TITT DOWN TO ROY AND GABBY. FOLLOW ROY OVER TO PIONEERS. OUTDOORS. DAY

Dorothy and her female band friends arrive by train at Coldbrook where Dorothy's ranch is. Roy and the Sons of the Pioneers welcome them by singing "Welcome Home Miss Bryant."

FIVE LITTLE MILES

(As sung by the Sons of the Pioneers beside the brokendown car)

transcribed by
SCOTT HOMAN
ERIC VAN HAMERSVELD

words & music by
BOB NOLAN

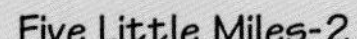

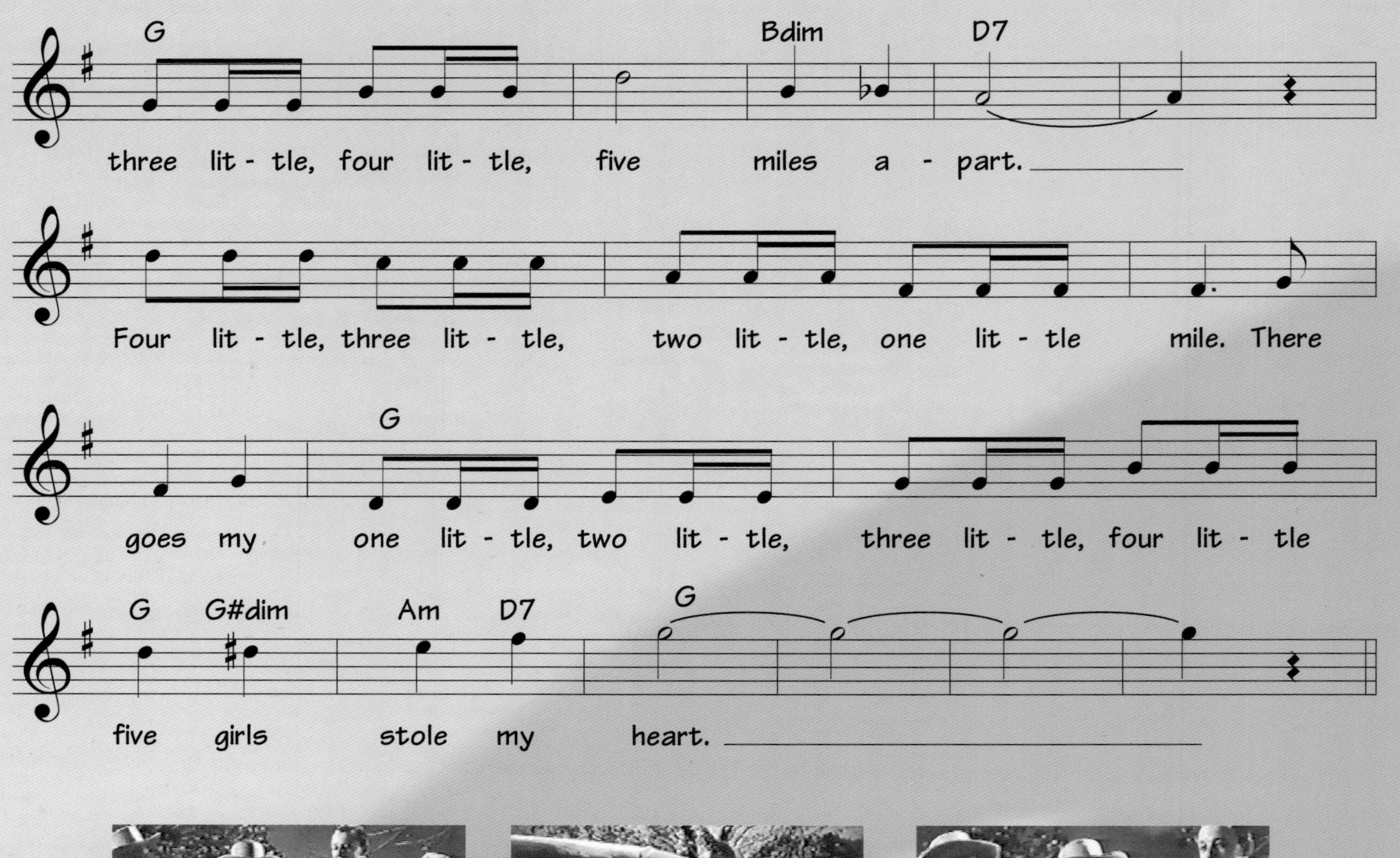

Republic Pictures Page 53
"Utah" Script Revision: #4

CROSS DISSOLVE FROM CLOSE UP OF RANCH SIGN TO LONG SHOT OF PIONEERS. OUTDOORS. DAY.

Roy and the girls in a car, followed by Gabby and the Pioneers on horse back, are headed for the ranch that Dorothy has inherited and wants to sell. The cowboys don't want the ranch sold and become a sheep ranch, so Roy secretly disables their car by pulling wires loose from under the dashboard. Then he tells the Pioneers to keep the girls busy while he and Gabby ride off to switch ranch signs so Dorothy will think that she owns Gabby's worthless shack on the prairie. The Pioneers serenade the gals with "Five Little Miles" over and over and over again until Roy and Gabby return.

BENEATH A UTAH SKY

(As sung by Roy Rogers outside Gabby's cabin)

Republic Pictures Page 197
"Utah" Script Revision: #3

LONGSHOT INTERIOR OF GIRLS IN CABIN. LIGHTS DIM. PAN AND TRUCK STAGE RIGHT TO DALE AS SONG BEGINS. NIGHT.

Outside the cabin Roy and Gabby have been trying to scare Dorothy and the girls to convince them that Roy should stay nearby for the night. They make animal sounds and such. To really scare them, Gabby growls like a bear while holding a bear skin up at the window. This does the trick. The gals take a shot at the "bear" and are scared enough to decide that having Roy outside to protect them might not be such a bad idea. As the gals settle in for the night, Roy serenades them with "Beneath A Utah Sky."

THE WILD AND WOOLLY GALS FROM OUT CHICAGO WAY

(As sung by Roy Rogers on the way back to the ranch)

transcribed by
SCOTT HOMAN
ERIC VAN HAMERSVELD

words & music by
TIM SPENCER

Republic Pictures Page 92
"Utah" Script Revision: #2

CROSS DISSOLVE TO MEDIUM TRUCK SHOT OF ROY RIDING TRIGGER LEFT TO RIGHT. DAY.

Roy has just saved the gals who had a wild ride on a runaway wagon. With the gals in the wagon, Trigger tied behind, and Roy and Dorothy on the wagon's horses, Roy takes them back to Dorothy's ranch (which is actually Gabby's shack). To pass the time, Roy sings "The Wild and Woolly Gals From Out Chicago Way."

UTAH

(As sung by Roy Rogers and the Sons of the Pioneers around the campfire)

transcribed by
SCOTT HOMAN
ERIC VAN HAMERSVELD

words & music by
CHARLES HENDERSON

Utah-2
E C#m F#7 F#m B7
gin - ning where your rain - bow ends.
E E7
Your heart will know, no oth - er place will
A Am E
do. You'll fall in love wi U -
G#m F#m B7 E C#m
tah, and U - tah will love you.
F#m B7 E C#m F#m B7
(Dale says: You know if you close your eyes you can just see Utah. With all its beauty and its grandeur.)
E E7
(Sons) If there's a place more beau - ti - ful to
A Am E
view, more won - der - ful than U -
G#m F#m B7 E C#m
tah, I can't be - lieve it's true.
F#m B7 E
Where paint - ed moun - tains
E7 A Am
climb in - to the blue, and when it's night in
E G#m F#m B7 E
U - tah, the stars come spark - ling through.
A E E7 A
(Bob) Where ev - 'ry man's your

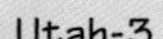

E E7 A
neigh - bor, and friends are real - ly

E E7 A E
friends. You'll find your life be - gin - ning

C#m F#7 B7 E
where your rain - bow ends. (Sons) Your

E7 A
heart will know, no oth - er place will do.

Am E G#m F#m
You'll fall in love with U - tah, and

B7 E
U - tah will love you.

Republic Pictures Page 62
"Utah" Script Revision: #2

TRUCK BACK FROM CLOSE UP OF CAMPFIRE TO MEDIUM LONG SHOT OF DALE AND ROY. STAGE SET FOR OUTDOORS. NIGHT.

To help persuade Dorothy not to sell the ranch, Roy and the Sons of the Pioneers hatch a plan that has Roy take Dale on an evening ride so that she can begin to appreciate the beautiful ranch land. At a campfire, Roy sings, with the help of the Sons of the Pioneers hiding behind the rocks, and teaches Dorothy the song "Utah." During the Pioneers part, a roll over background effect of scenes of Utah appears.

THE LONESOME COWBOY BLUES

(As sung by Roy Rogers and the Sons of the Pioneers from a jail cell)

transcribed by
SCOTT HOMAN
ERIC VAN HAMERSVELD

words & music by
TIM SPENCER

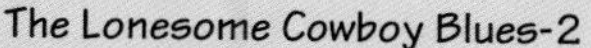

G E7
wish - in' all day ___ I could take wings ___ and

A7 D
fly a - way. ___ (Shug) Far a - way, to where my true love's

D
wait - in', ___ tru - est gal I ev - er knew. (Pioneers) Nev - er

D D7 G Gm
thought we'd ev - er break up. Let me sleep and nev - er wake up,

D D7 G D
then I'll lose the cow - boy blues. Lose the lone-some cow-boy blues.

Republic Pictures
"Utah"

Page 124
Script Revision: #3

FADE UP TO MEDIUM CLOSE UP OF SHERIFF AT DESK. PAN LEFT TO ROY BEHIND BARS IN THE JAIL. NIGHT.

Dorothy thinks she has sold the Bar X ranch, but she has really sold Gabby's place. When Roy tries to stop the villains from taking the Bar X's cattle, he is arrested. Gabby tries to help Roy escape by sawing the jail house window bars with a hacksaw while Roy and the Sons of the Pioneers sing "The Lonesome Cowboy Blues." The sheriff catches on to the situation and goes outside to confront Gabby.

Produced By
Eddy White

Directed by
Frank McDonald

Screenplay by
Jack Townley

Starring
Roy Rogers, Dale Evans, Gabby Hayes, Bob Nolan, The Sons of the Pioneers, Trigger

with
Adele Mara, Grant Withers, Janet Martin, Syd Saylor, Addison Richards, Edward Cassidy, Roy Barcroft, Kenne Duncan, Rex Lease, Bob Wilke, Ted Adams, The Robert Mitchell Boy Choir

Special Guest Stars
Bob Livingston, Wild Bill Elliott, Allan Lane, Don "Red" Barry, Sunset Carson

Prod: #1324 Released: 19 Jun 1945
Black/White - 68min.

Sue Farnum (Dale), who has inherited a circus/ranch that doubles as a refuge for boys, must find a receipt for money that her father borrowed from Ripley (Withers). She gets help from Phillips (Richards), her father's former partner, and Gabby, the ranch foreman. She also gets help from Roy and the Sons of the Pioneers who are making a movie in the area.

1. Sue and Gabby meet with Phillips to see if he knows about the Ripley receipt.

2. Gabby, Sue, Phillips, and his niece arrive in the middle of a western movie shoot.

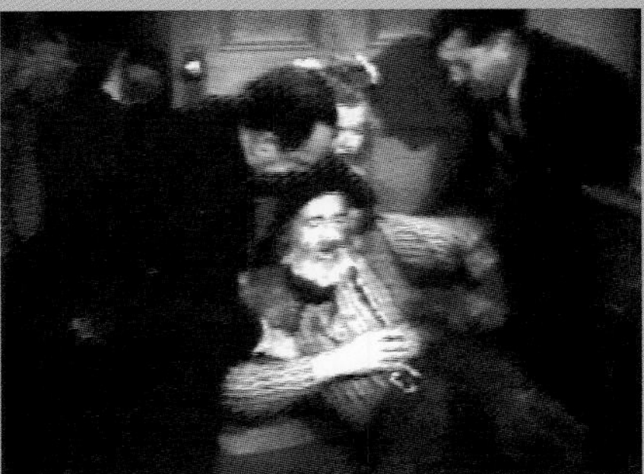
3. Gabby is hog tied and Phillips is kidnapped by Ripley.

4. The boys from Sue's circus ranch want Roy and Bob to save the circus.

5. Roy, Bob, and Gabby find the hideout where Ripley is holding Phillips.

6. Roy captures Ripley and finds the receipt that saves Sue's circus ranch.

7. Roy gets help from his Republic Studio co-stars Bob Livingston, Wild Bill Elliott, Allan Lane, Don "Red" Barry, and Sunset Carson to roundup the rest of the villains and save the show.

8. During the finale, Roy, Sue, Gabby, and the Pioneers sing the title song.

BUGLER'S LULLABY

(As sung by the Mitchell Boys' Choir inside the circus tent)

transcribed by
SCOTT HOMAN
ERIC VAN HAMERSVELD

words & music by
ROBERT MITCHELL
BETTY BEST

Republic Pictures Page 23
"Bells of Rosarita" Script Revision: #4

CUT TO LONG SHOT OF BOYS INSIDE THE CIRCUS TENT. DAY.

Sue, Patty (Sue's friend), Gabby, and Mr. Phillips (friend of Sue's deceased father) have arrived at the ranch just in time to hear the boys practicing the song "Bugler's Lullaby" inside the circus tent. Ken Carson plays the solo trumpet while the Pioneers listen.

BELLS OF ROSARITA

(As sung by Roy Rogers, the Mitchell Boys Choir, and the "leading lady")

transcribed by
SCOTT HOMAN
ERIC VAN HAMERSVELD

words & music by
JACK ELLIOTT

Republic Pictures Page 44
"Bells of Rosarita" Script Revision: #5

CUT TO MEDIUM LONG SHOT OF CAMERA CREW. ON DIRECTOR'S COMMAND OF "ACTION", CUT TO BELLS RINGING THEN CUT TO BOYS SINGING. DAY.

The last scene of the "picture" is being filmed. The camera crew is set, boys' choir is atop the mission and the street below is filled with people. As the wedding party begins to depart, Roy rides in next to a wedding carriage and the boys, Roy, and his co-star sing "The Bells of Rosarita."

UNDER A BLANKET OF BLUE

(As sung by Dale Evans at the barbecue)

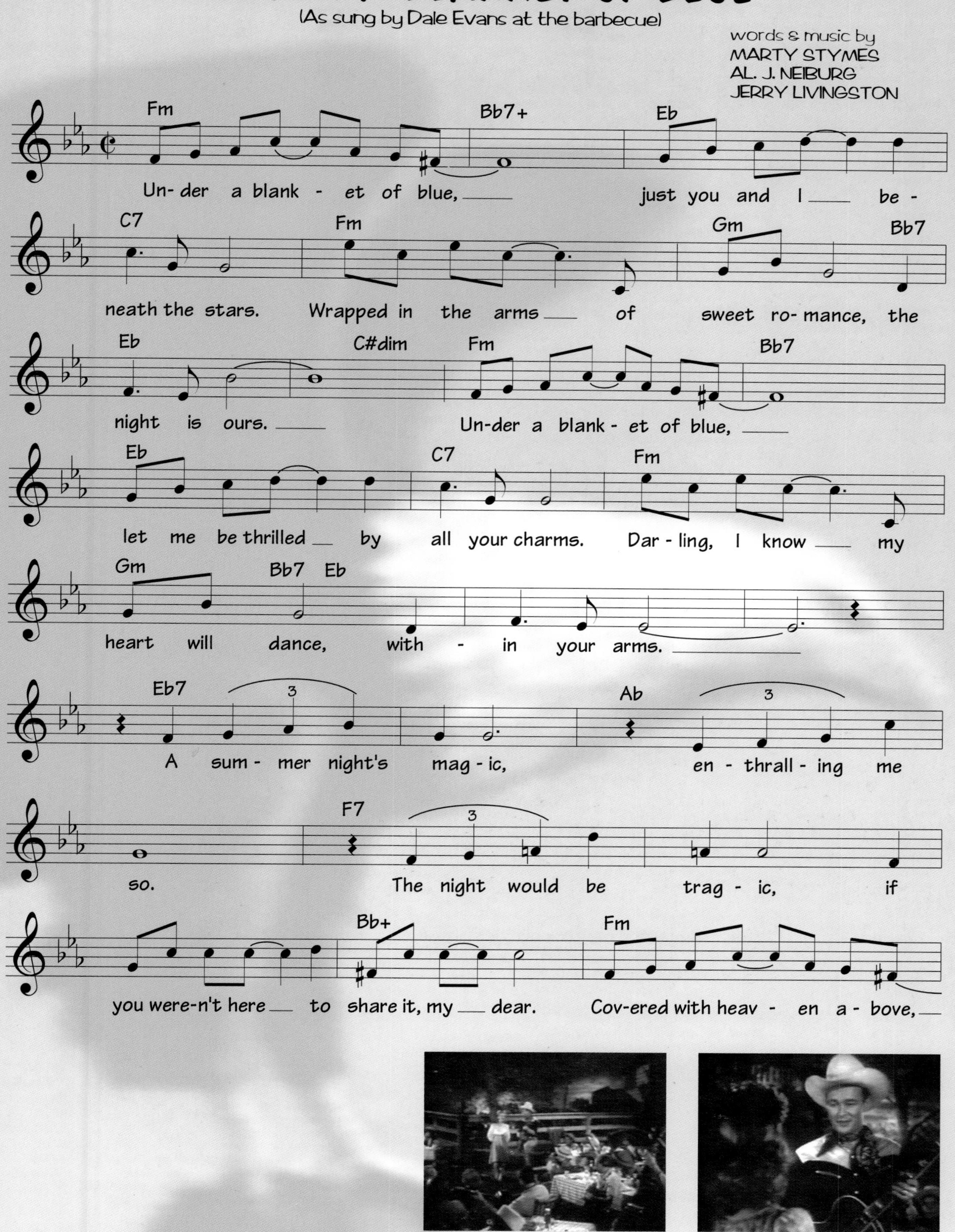

Republic Pictures Page 60
"Bells of Rosarita" Script Revision: #4

CROSS DISSOLVE AND TILT DOWN FROM MOON STILL TO OUTDOOR BARBECUE SCENE. SLOW TRUCK INTO FROM EXTREME LONG SHOT AND PAN RIGHT TO LONG SHOT OF ROY AND DALE. EVENING.

Roy's latest picture, "Bells of Rosarita," has finished filming and the cast and crew have gathered for a barbecue celebration. Sue and her friend, who met the group by driving their car accidentally into a shooting scene, have been invited to the party. As the beef roasts on the pit, Sue sings "Under a Blanket of Stars" with Roy and the Sons of the Pioneers accompanying her.

SINGIN' DOWN THE ROAD

(As sung by Roy Rogers at ranch barbecue)

words & music by
CHARLIE TOBIAS
RAYMOND SCOTT

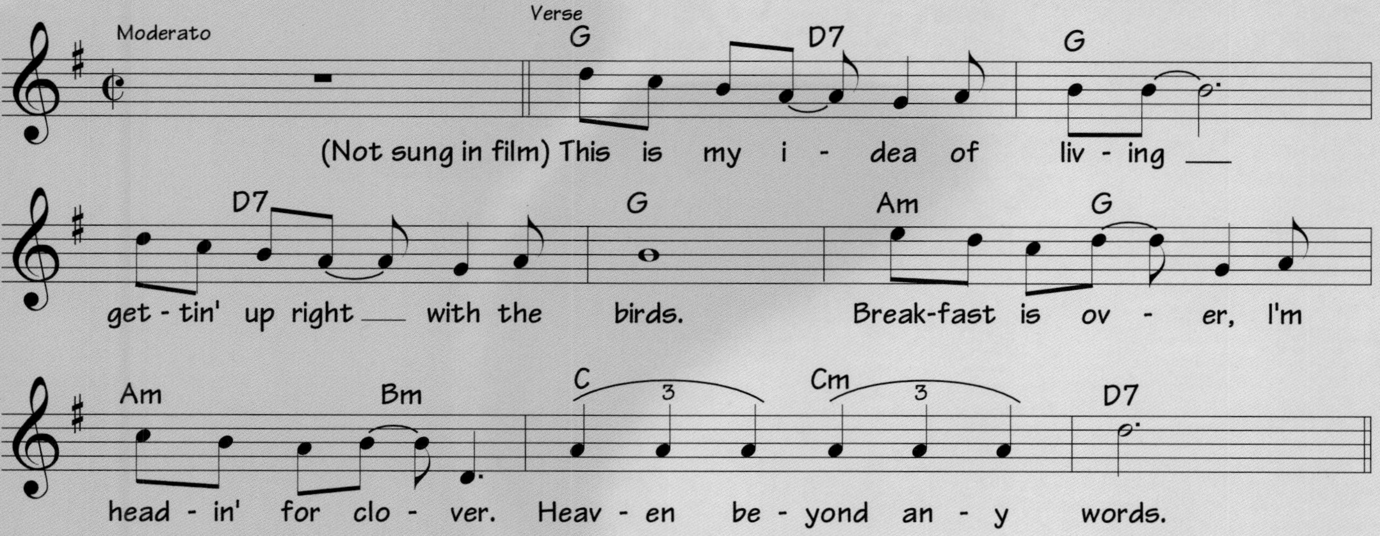
Moderato
Verse
G D7 G
(Not sung in film) This is my i - dea of liv - ing
D7 G Am G
get - tin' up right with the birds. Break-fast is ov - er, I'm
Am Bm C Cm D7
head - in' for clo - ver. Heav - en be - yond an - y words.

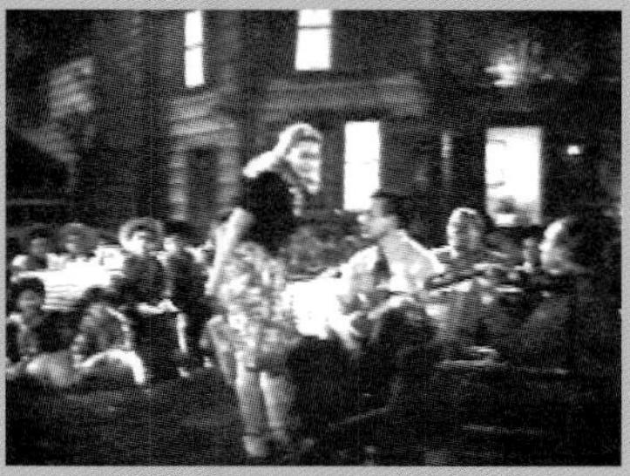

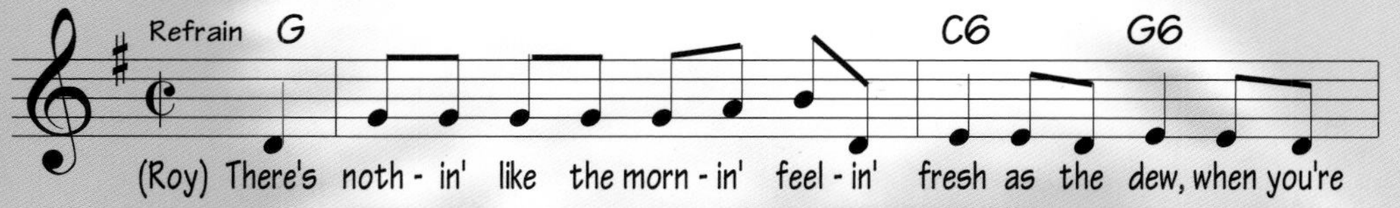
Refrain G C6 G6
(Roy) There's noth - in' like the morn - in' feel - in' fresh as the dew, when you're

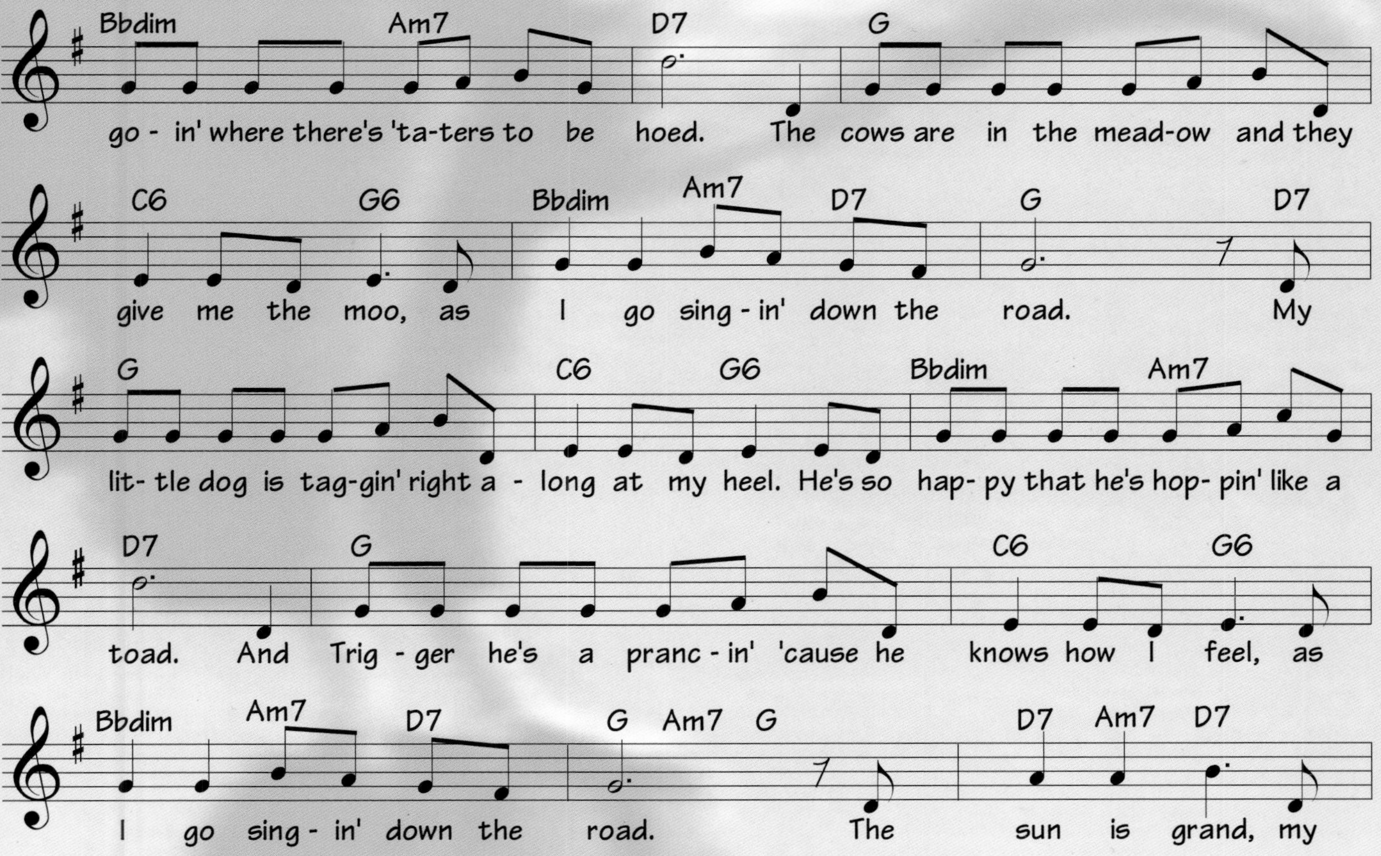
Bbdim Am7 D7 G
go - in' where there's 'ta-ters to be hoed. The cows are in the mead-ow and they
C6 G6 Bbdim Am7 D7 G D7
give me the moo, as I go sing - in' down the road. My
G C6 G6 Bbdim Am7
lit- tle dog is tag-gin' right a - long at my heel. He's so hap- py that he's hop- pin' like a
D7 G C6 G6
toad. And Trig - ger he's a pranc - in' 'cause he knows how I feel, as
Bbdim Am7 D7 G Am7 G D7 Am7 D7
I go sing - in' down the road. The sun is grand, my

Republic Pictures
"Bells of Rosarita"

Page 62
Script Revision: #3

CUT TO MED LONG SHOT OF GROUP OF YOUNG LADIES SITTING ON THE GROUND. EXTERIOR SET OF BACKYARD ON SOUND STAGE. EVENING.

One of the young ladies, Patty, asks Bob Nolan to dance the jitter-bug with her. Roy sings and plays the guitar to "Singin' Down the Road." The Sons of the Pioneers, play backup musical accompaniment. Sue is standing next to Roy holding Trigger's reins. Trigger does a little dance when he's mentioned in the song lyrics. Bob and Patty perform an athletic jitter-bug to the delight of the guests.

GONNA BUILD A BIG FENCE AROUND TEXAS

(As sung by Roy Rogers and the Mitchell Boys' Choir at the hotel)

words & music by
CLIFF FRIEND, GEORGE OLSEU
KATHERINE PHILLIPS

Eb Ab Eb Ebm F7 Bb7 Eb Bb7
build a big fence a-round Tex-as, so they can't steal my ba-by a-way. She's the

Eb Ab Eb Bb7 Eb Bb7
"Lov-en-est" ba-by 'round Tex-as, a-round Tex-as, way 'round Tex-as. And the

Eb Ab Eb Ebm F7 Bb7 Eb
fel-lows all know it in Tex-as that's the rea-son I wor-ry each day. (Roy) She's got that

Ab Eb Bb7
Tex-as sun-shine in her smile. Thrills the cow-boys. Kills the

Eb Ab Eb
cow-boys. She's got those "Lone Star" moon-beams in her eyes.

F7 Bb7 Ebdim Bb7
See what I'm up a-gainst, my trou-bles have just com-menced (Roy/Boys) Got-ta

Eb Ab Eb Bb7 Eb Bb7
build a big fence a-round Tex-as, a-round Tex-as, way 'round Tex-as. Gon-na

Eb
build a big fence a-round Tex-as, so they can't steal my ba-by a-way.

Republic Pictures Page 80
"Bells of Rosarita" Script Revision: #2

CUT TO MEDIUM LONG SHOT OF ROY AND BOB IN HOTEL ROOM. BOYS ENTER STAGE LEFT THROUGH DOOR . EVENING.

Roy and Bob are packing up because the film they've been making is finished. Three boys from the ranch have come to say goodbye. They seem to have something else on their minds but are reluctant to mention it. So, they begin by asking Roy to sing "Gonna Build A Big Fence Around Texas." After the first verse, from outside the window the rest of the boys sing along with him.

MICHAEL FINNEGAN

(As sung by the Mitchell Boys' Choir while doing ranch chores)

words & music by
(TRADITIONAL)

1. There was an old man named Mi-chael Fin-ne-gan. He has whisk-ers on his chin-ne-gan.
2. There was an old man named Mi-chael Fin-ne-gan. He went fish-ing with a pin-ne-gan.
3. There was an old man named Mi-chael Fin-ne-gan, climbed a tree and barked his shin-ne-gan.
4. There was an old man named Mi-chael Fin-ne-gan. He grew fat and then grew thin a-gain.

A - long came the wind and blew them in a- gain. Poor old Mi- chael Fin- ne- gan. Be- gin a-gain.
Caught a fish ___ and drop - ped it in a- gain. Poor old Mi- chael Fin- ne- gan. Be- gin a-gain.
He took off sev- er - al yards of skin a- gain. Poor old Mi- chael Fin- ne- gan. Be- gin a-gain.
Then he died and had to be - gin a- gain. Poor old Mi- chael Fin- ne- gan. Be- gin a-gain.

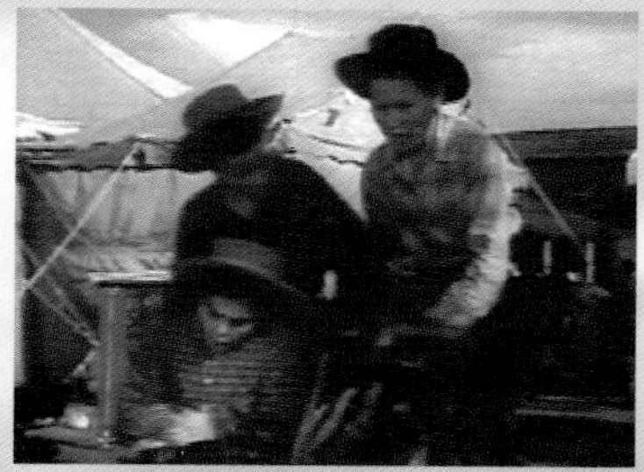

Republic Pictures Page 109
"Bells of Rosarita" Script Revision: #4

CROSS DISSOLVE FROM ROY AND BOB'S HOTEL ROOM TO OUTDOOR CORRAL LONG SHOT.

The boys are seen doing ranch chores: brushing the horses, chopping and sawing wood, oiling leather goods. To pass the time they sing the traditional round, "Michael Finnegan."

WHEN THE CIRCUS CAME TO TOWN

(As sung by the Sons of the Pioneers in the circus parade)

transcribed by
SCOTT HOMAN
ERIC VAN HAMERSVELD

words & music by
JIMMY EATON
JULIAN KAY
TERRY SHAND

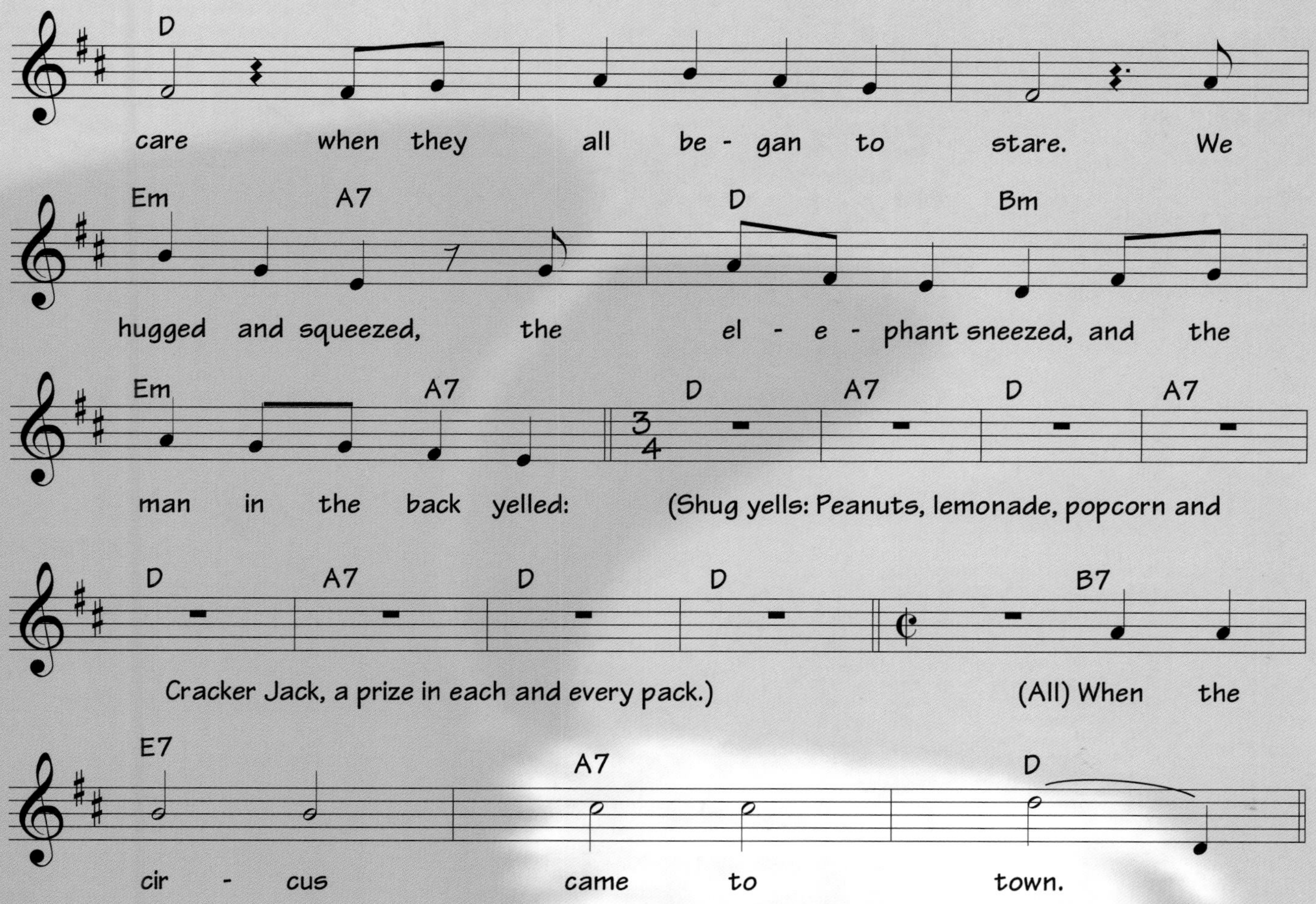

D

care when they all be - gan to stare. We

Em A7 D Bm

hugged and squeezed, the el - e - phant sneezed, and the

Em A7 D A7 D A7

man in the back yelled: (Shug yells: Peanuts, lemonade, popcorn and

D A7 D D B7

Cracker Jack, a prize in each and every pack.) (All) When the

E7 A7 D

cir - cus came to town.

Republic Pictures Page 130
"The Bells of Rosarita" Script Revision: #2

CROSS DISSOLVE TO LONG SHOT OF STREET FROM PARADE WATCHERS POINT OF VIEW. DAY.

Roy has called in all his Republic Pictures' cowboy pals to help Gabby get a big crowd for his circus. To promote the event they planned a street parade but were told by the sheriff that they wouldn't be granted a permit. To get around this problem, they have a "funeral" parade in honor of Shug's recently deceased duck. As the parade passes by, the Sons of the Pioneers sing "When the Circus Came to Town."

TRAIL HERDIN' COWBOY

(As sung by Roy Rogers and the Sons of the Pioneers at the Benefit Circus)

words & music by
BOB NOLAN

Republic Pictures
"Bells of Rosarita"

Page 185
Script Revision: #5

CROSS DISSOLVE TO BANNER ADVERTISING THE "GIGANTIC SHOW".
DISSOLVE TO LONG SHOT OF SMALL STAGE WITH AUDIENCE. EVENING.

For the circus benefit, Roy and the Sons of the Pioneers perform outside the main tent to raise money to save the ranch from being sold to the villain.

Produced By
Louis Gray

Directed by
Frank McDonald

Screenplay by
John K. Butler

Starring
Roy Rogers, Dale Evans, Gabby Hayes, Bob Nolan, The Sons of the Pioneers, Trigger

with
Roger Pryor, Arthur Loft, Maude Eburne, Sam Flint, Si Jenks, June Bryde, Elaine Lange, Charles Soldani, Edmund Cobb, George Sherwood, Eddie Kane, George Chandler, Wally West, Tex Terry, Bob Wilke, Bobbie Priest

Prod: #1328 Released: 1 Aug 1945
Black/White - 68min.

Roy and the Pioneers are broke but must get to the ailing Gabby Whittaker. They solicit financial help from a reluctant Peggy Lane (Dale). The Lanes and Whittakers have had a long standing feud. Gardner (Pryor), who wants both ranches in order to drill for oil. Influences cause them to think that each other is causing the trouble.

RB

1. Shug has lost all the Pioneers' money to a con man promoter.

2. Gabby, a Whittaker, is ailing. Roy goes to Peggy, a Lane, to borrow travel money.

3. Roy discovers that Gabby tricked them to helping him with the feud.

4. Peggy arrives to help her family fight the Whittakers but becomes fond of Roy.

5. Gabby and Mrs. Lane will give away part of their ranches to the wagon race winner.

6. Roy accuses Gardner of causing the feud so he can buy the properties to drill for oil.

7. Gardner sabotages the wagon race so he'll win the race and the ranches.

8. News film of the race shows Gardner's man fixing the race. Gardner is arrested.

9. Everyone makes up. The Lane/Whittaker feud is over.

WE'RE GONNA HAVE A COWBOY WEDDIN'

(As sung by Roy Rogers and the Sons of the Pioneers at the audition)

Republic Pictures Page 4
"Man From Oklahoma" Script Revision: #2

FADE IN FROM OPENING TITLES TO GRAPHIC OF TALL OFFICE BUILDING. TILT UP AND CROSS DISSOLVE TO LONG SHOT OF ROY AND THE PIONEERS IN AN OFFICE.

Roy and the Sons of the Pioneers are auditioning for a job by singing "We're Gonna have a Cowboy Weddin'."

I'M BEGINNING TO SEE THE LIGHT

(As sung by Dale Evans at the Flamingo Club)

words & music by
DON GEORGE
JOHNNY HODGES
DUKE ELLINGTON
HARRY JAMES

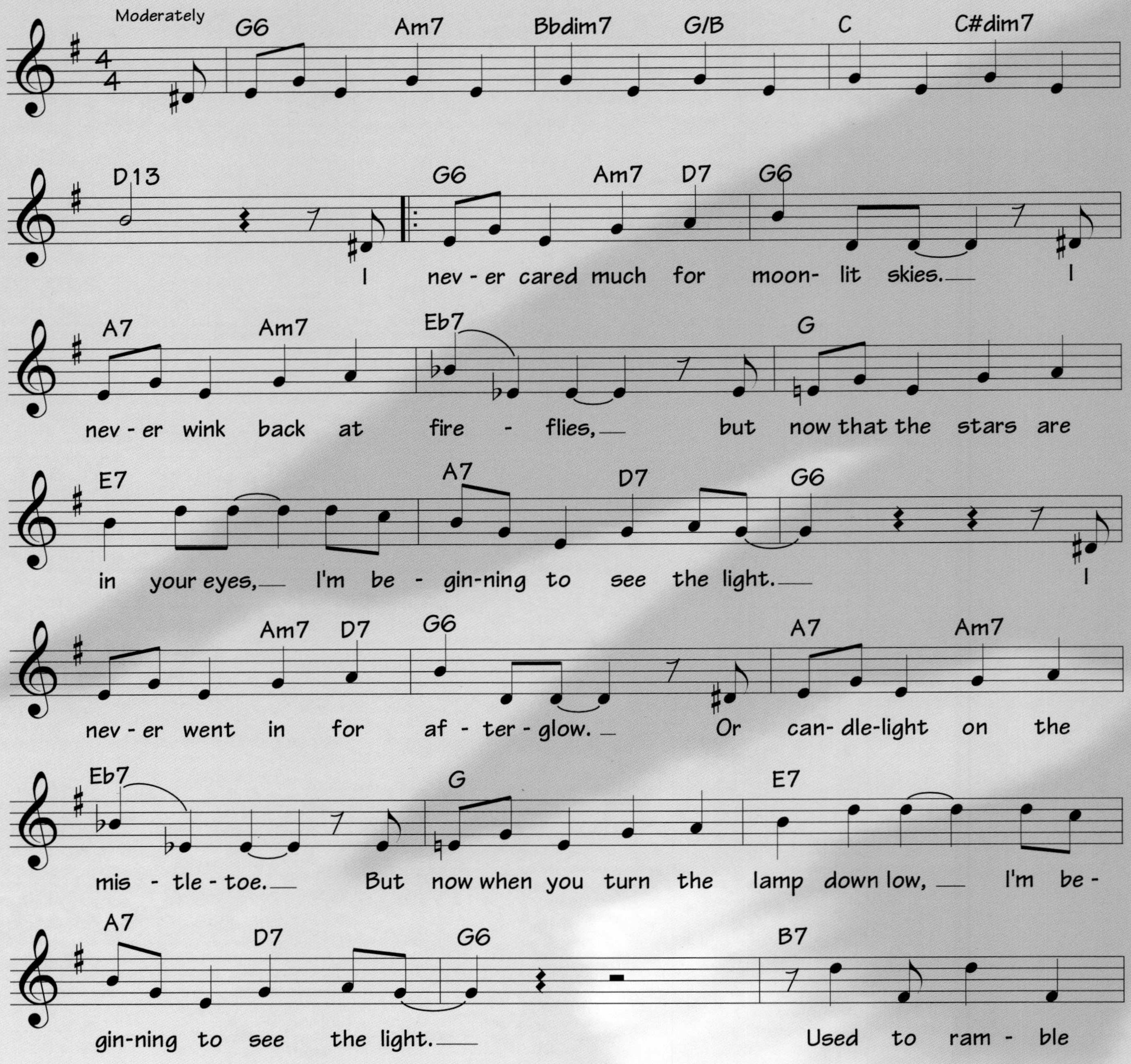
Moderately
G6 Am7 Bbdim7 G/B C C#dim7
D13 G6 Am7 D7 G6
I never cared much for moon-lit skies. I
A7 Am7 Eb7 G
never wink back at fire - flies, but now that the stars are
E7 A7 D7 G6
in your eyes, I'm be - gin-ning to see the light. I
Am7 D7 G6 A7 Am7
never went in for af - ter - glow. Or can- dle-light on the
Eb7 G E7
mis - tle - toe. But now when you turn the lamp down low, I'm be -
A7 D7 G6 B7
gin-ning to see the light. Used to ram - ble

THE FLAMINGO CLUB
MISS PEGGY LANE
Music by Donald Scott
EXCELLENT CUISINE

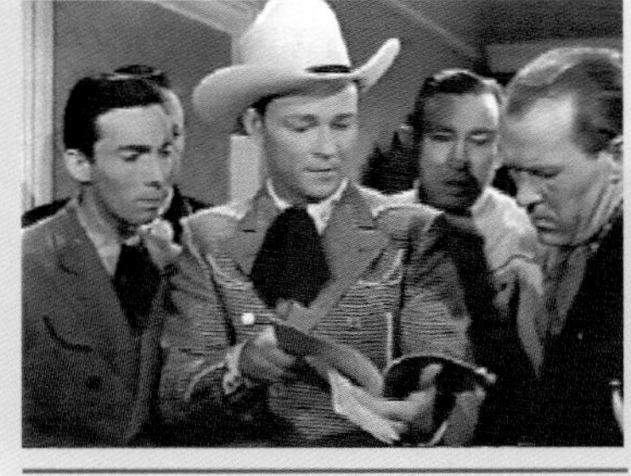

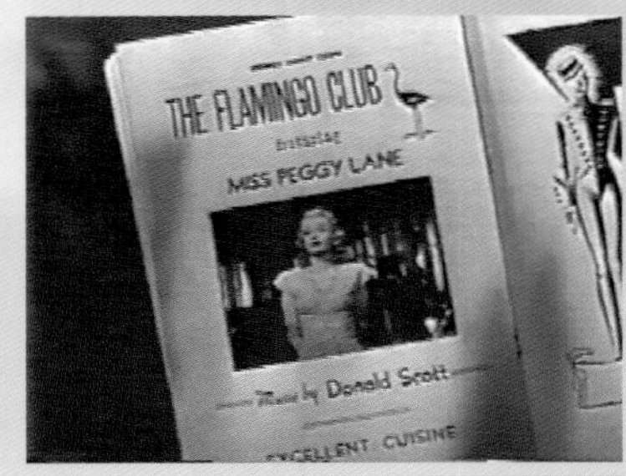

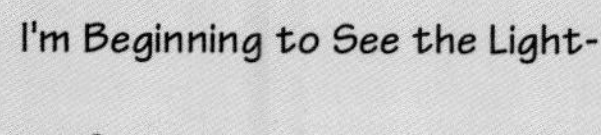

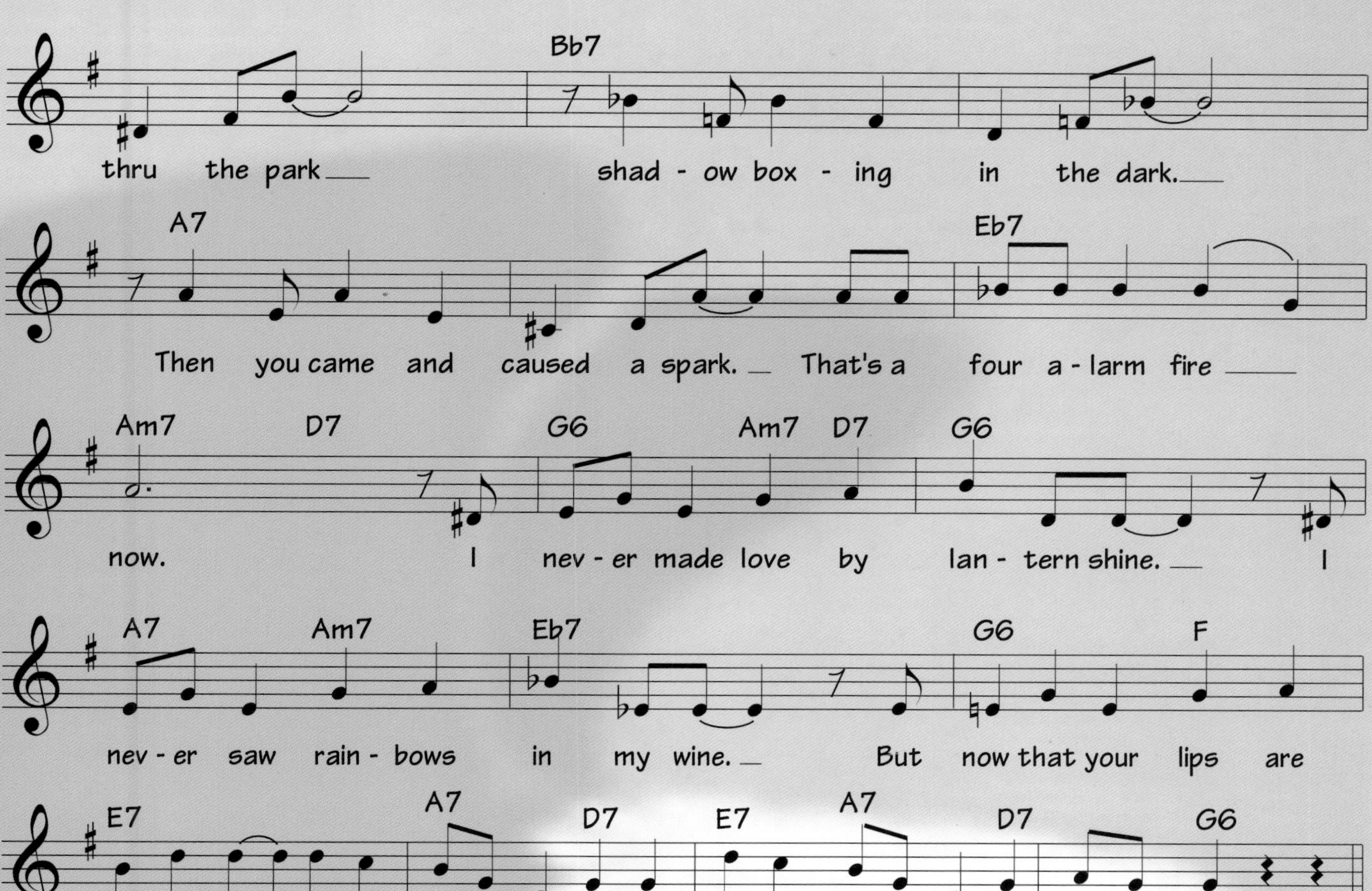

Republic Pictures Page 32
"Man From Oklahoma" Script Revision: #7

HOLD GRAPHIC OF ADVERTISEMENT FOR FLAMINGO CLUB THAT HAS FREEZE FRAME OF DALE. ZOOM INTO FREEZE FRAME THEN CONTINUE RUNNING FOOTAGE OF DALE SINGING.

Roy and the Sons of the Pioneers need money. Roy suggests visiting with Peggy Lane and ask for funds to get them home. The "Lane's" are enemies of the the "Whittaker's," and Roy and the Sons are on the Whittaker side of the feud. Roy knows where Peggy is working and has an advertisement to show the boys. The ad shows Peggy singing "I'm Beginning to See the Light" at the Flamingo Club.

FOR YOU AND ME

(As sung by Dale Evans on the Flamingo Club stage)

transcribed by
SCOTT HOMAN
ERIC VAN HAMERSVELD

words & music by
KIM GANNON
WALTER KENT

Republic Pictures Page 34
"Man From Oklahoma" Script Revision: #2

PAN FROM LONG SHOT OF DALE ON STAGE TO ROY AND PIONEERS.

Roy and the Sons of the Pioneers have arrived at the Flamingo Club where Peggy works to show her the telegram about Gabby dying and, get a loan from her to get home. The host doesn't want to seat them, so they threaten to start singing. With that, they are immediately taken to a table but on the way they make enough noise to drown out Peggy while she's trying to sing "For You and Me."

SKIES ARE BLUER

(As sung by the cast and chorus during the celebration street parade)

transcribed by
SCOTT HOMAN
ERIC VAN HAMERSVELD

words & music by
SANFORD GREEN
JUNE CARROLL

Dm G7 C Cm F7
Ok - la - ho - ma, U. S. A.
Bb C7 F7
Men don't roam - a from Ok - la - home, sweet ho - ma.
G7 Cm C7 F7
Ok - la - ho - ma where my heart lies.
Bb C7 F7
(Dale) Gals are slim - mer and an - kles trim - mer, in
G7 Cm F7 Bb
Ok - la - ho - ma life is king - size.
Gb F7 Gbmaj7
(All) There's where a fra - grance fills the air, keeps the
F7 Gbmaj7 Db
folks with a smile on their face.
Gb F7 Bb
(Sons) There's where the oi - l tastes like rum. So, come
Gm C7 F9
take some, it's flood - in' the place.
Bb C7 F7
(All) Bells are ring - in' and voi - ces sing - in'.
G7 Cm A7 Dm
Oil is gush - in' and the folks are rush - in' out to

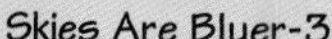

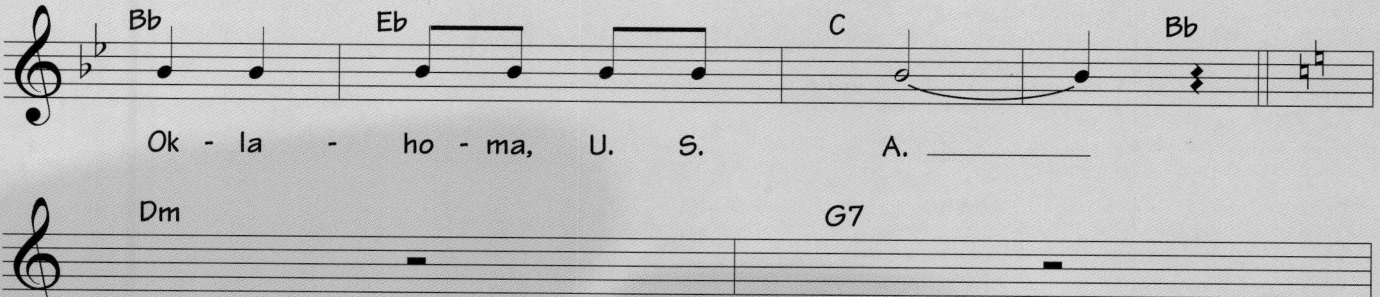

(Gabby says from inside of teepee: Can't a man have a little privacy around here?)

Republic Pictures Page 104
"Man From Oklahoma" Script Revision: #3

CUT TO LONG SHOT OF STREET FROM ELEVATED END-OF-STREET CAMERA POSITION. DAY.

The Oklahoma Gold Rush Celebration is kicking off with a street parade complete with dignitaries in coaches, decorated floats, costumed horsemen, dancing girls, Indians, and covered wagons. Everyone, including Roy, Peggy, Gabby, and the Sons of the Pioneers, is singing "Skies Are Bluer."

CHERO CHERO CHEROKEE

(As sung by the Sons of the Pioneers at the celebration show)

Republic Pictures Page 171
"Man From Oklahoma" Script Revision: #5

FADE UP ON SIGN ADVERTISING THE AWARDS CELEBRATION. SIGN INCLUDES A "PICTURE" OF THE PIONEERS DRESSED AS INDIANS. PICTURE IS ACTUALLY THE LIVE STAGE SET. ZOOM INTO PIONEERS.

The annual Gold Rush Wagon Race is finished with Roy losing because the villains sabotaged his wagon. That evening is the awards presentation which includes a lavish stage show. It opens with the Sons of the Pioneers singing "Chero, Chero, Cherokee." This production number includes Indian maidens and braves dancing on a stage set that includes a log fort, trampoline drums, and fire rings.

Produced By
Louis Gray

Directed by
Frank McDonald

Screenplay by
John K. Butler

Starring
Roy Rogers, Dale Evans, Gabby Hayes, Bob Nolan, The Sons of the Pioneers, Trigger

with
Hardie Albright, Margaret Dumont, Roy Barcroft, Tom London, Stanley Price, Bob Wilke, Ed Cassidy, Dorothy Granger, Hank Bell, Bud Osborne

Prod: #1421 Released: 24 Sep 1945
Black/White - 66min.

Lucille (Dale) is an engaged, dissatisfied travel agent who goes west to find out more about her grandmother, Kansas Kate. On the way she meets Roy who takes her to the the ghost town saloon where Kate had worked. In a dream sequence, Lucille becomes Kansas Kate and helps keep Gabby from losing his gold mine.

RB

1. Lucille gives a travel lecture at the World Wide Travel Agency in New York.

2. Lucille's car broke down. Roy discovers her wondering the desert looking for help.

3. Lucille finds the saloon, where her grand-mother worked, and Gabby, her mother's friend.

4. Lucille is dreaming she's her grandmother and Gabby tells her about his gold mine.

5. The villainous owner of the saloon, Mr. Earl (Albright), learns about Gabby's mine.

6. Mr. Earl's bouncer decides to help Roy instead of going to jail for shooting at him.

7. To get Gabby's gold mine map, Mr. Earl has Gabby drink until he passes out.

8. Roy captures Mr. Earl as he tries to escape.

9. The dream is over and Lucille begins her new life touring the west with Roy.

GO WEST YOUNG MAN

(As sung by the Sons of the Pioneers on the Western Tour bus)

words & music by
TIM SPENCER

Republic Pictures Page 35
"Sunset In El Dorado" Script Revision: #2

FADE UP EXTERIOR OF TRAVELING BUS. FOLLOW TRUCK. CUT TO INTERIOR. DAY.

Singing "Go West Young Man" on the Western Tour bus, the Sons of the Pioneers entertain the travelers, including the "runaway" Lucille. Solos by Shug Fisher, Bob Nolan, and Ken Carson.

BELLE OF THE EL DORADO

(As sung by Roy Rogers and Dale Evans in the Golden Nugget Saloon)

Cm G7 Cm Bb7
all men on the run. (Roy says: You mean all ex-cep-tin' one.) (Roy) So, she's the
Eb Fm Bb7
Belle of the El Do - ra - do. (Dale) She could
Fm C7 3 Fm
win you if she tried. (Roy says: Not e - ven if I was roped and
C7 F7 Bb7
tied.) (Roy) Not the Belle of the El Dor - ra - do.
Bbm Eb Ab
No, the girls that I pre - fer are not an - y-thing like
Fm Cm F7 Bb7
her. They're the type who are con - tent to set - tle down.
G7 Cm G7 Cm
(Dale) She's the dar - ling of the west. (Roy says: Well, a man's just got the
Bb7 Eb Bb7
best of her. (Roy) The Belle of the El Do - ra -

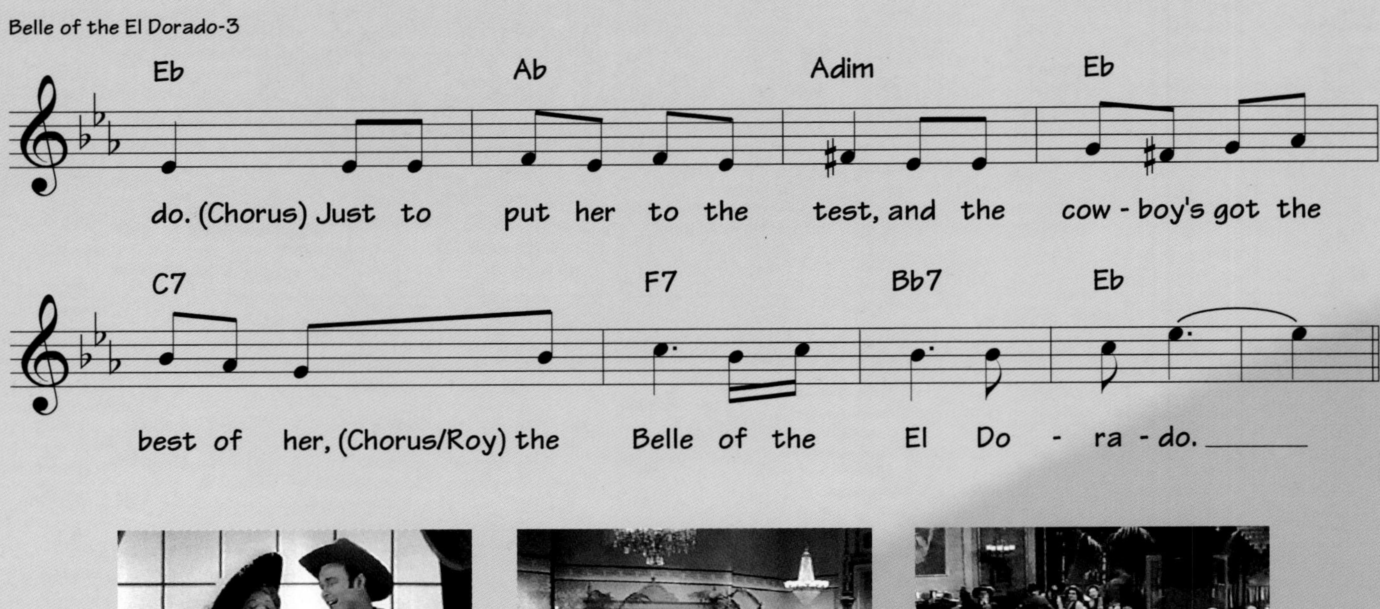

Republic Pictures Page 78
"Sunset In El Dorado" Script Revision: #5

DURING MUSIC OPENING CUT FROM DALE AND DANCERS TO ROY ENTERING THE SALOON SHOOTING HIS GUNS.

Lucille is deep in her dream sequence playing the part of her grandmother, Kansas Kate, a singer in the Golden Nugget saloon in the boomtown of El Dorado. As one of her production numbers begins, Roy enters and joins in singing "Belle of the El Dorado."

I'M AWFULLY GLAD I MET YOU

(As sung by Dale Evans in Mr. Earl's saloon)

words & music by
JACK DRISLANE
GEORGE W. MEYER

F F7
(Dale) I used to won-der why all

Bb+ G7
lov - ers love to sigh, and hold each oth-er's hand at night. With

C7 F D7 G7
them I've of- ten chaffed, at times I've ev- en laughed, and thought it such a fun- ny

C7 F F7 Bb+
sight. But since I met you, dear, it does - n't seem so queer. It

G7 Bb Fdim
seems the pro- per thing to do. For when you are a- way, I'm

F D7 G7 C7
lone - ly all the day, and think of noth - ing else but you.

Republic Pictures
"Sunset In El Dorado"

Page 132
Script Revision: #4

CROSS DISSOLVE FROM MR. EARL'S OFFICE TO MEDIUM LONG SHOT OF DALE WALKING DOWN FROM SALOON STAGE TO CHAT WITH BUSTER.

Mr. Earl, the villain owner of the saloon that Lucille sings in, has just helped Gabby drink himself into unconsciousness. Mr. Earl then steals Gabby's map to the gold mine and locks it in the office desk.

Roy and Buster, who was Mr. Earl's bouncer but is now Roy's friend, want to search Mr. Earl's office to find the map. Their plan is to have Lucille sing a song to keep Mr. Earl occupied while they search. Lucille sings "I'm Awfully Glad I Met You" but he gets suspicious, and, along with his men, rushes into the office. He discovers Roy and Buster prying open the desk, grabs Roy, and shoots Buster with his gun. Roy is arrested for murder.

THE LADY WHO WOULDN'T SAY YES

(As sung by Roy Rogers, Dale Evans and a chorus in the Golden Nugget Saloon)

Republic Pictures
"Sunset In El Dorado"

Page 156
Script Revision: #3

CUT TO LONG SHOT OF SALOON STAGE.

After a brief fist fight, Roy and the sheriff take Earl, the villainous saloon owner, to jail. Roy joins Lucille on stage for her production of "The Lady Who Wouldn't Say Yes." At the end of the production, Lucille's dream is over and the scene transitions back to present time.

CALL OF THE PRAIRIE

(As sung by Roy Rogers and Dale Evans on the trail)

transcribed by
SCOTT HOMAN
ERIC VAN HAMERSVELD

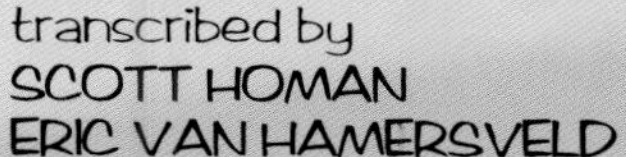

words & music by
KEN CARSON

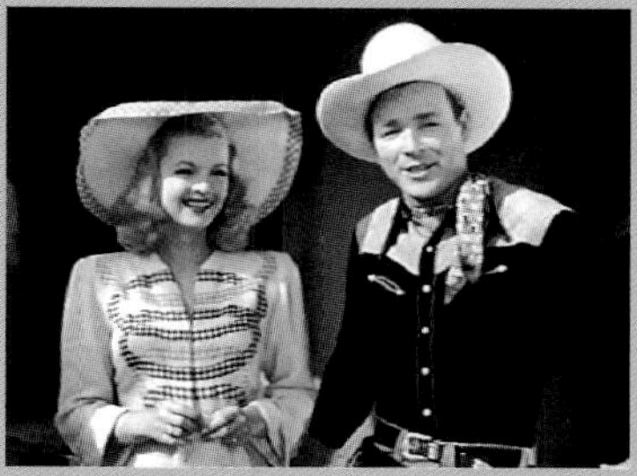

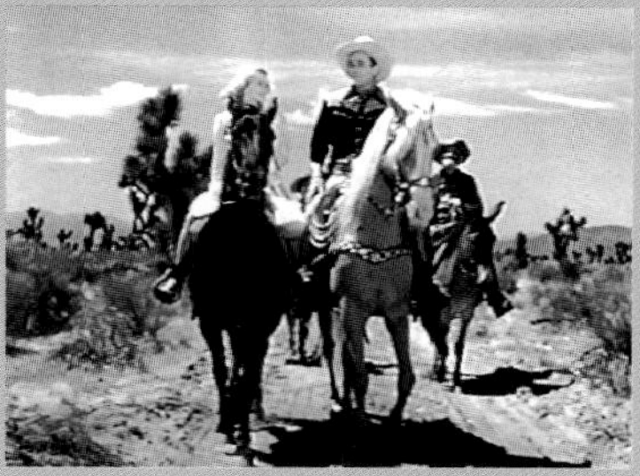

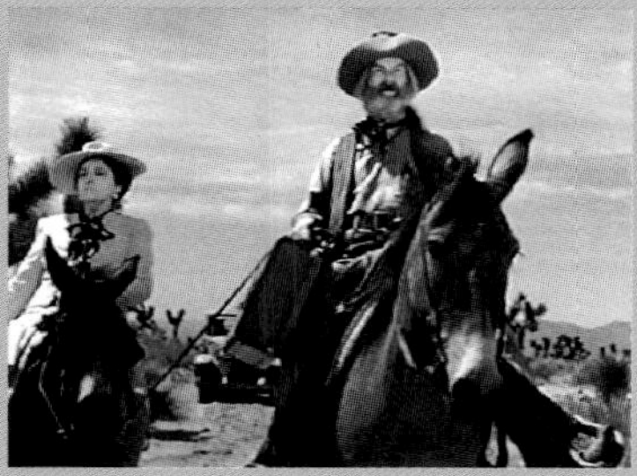

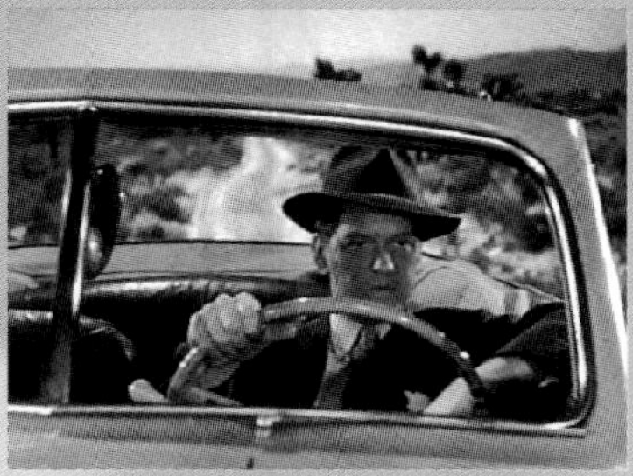

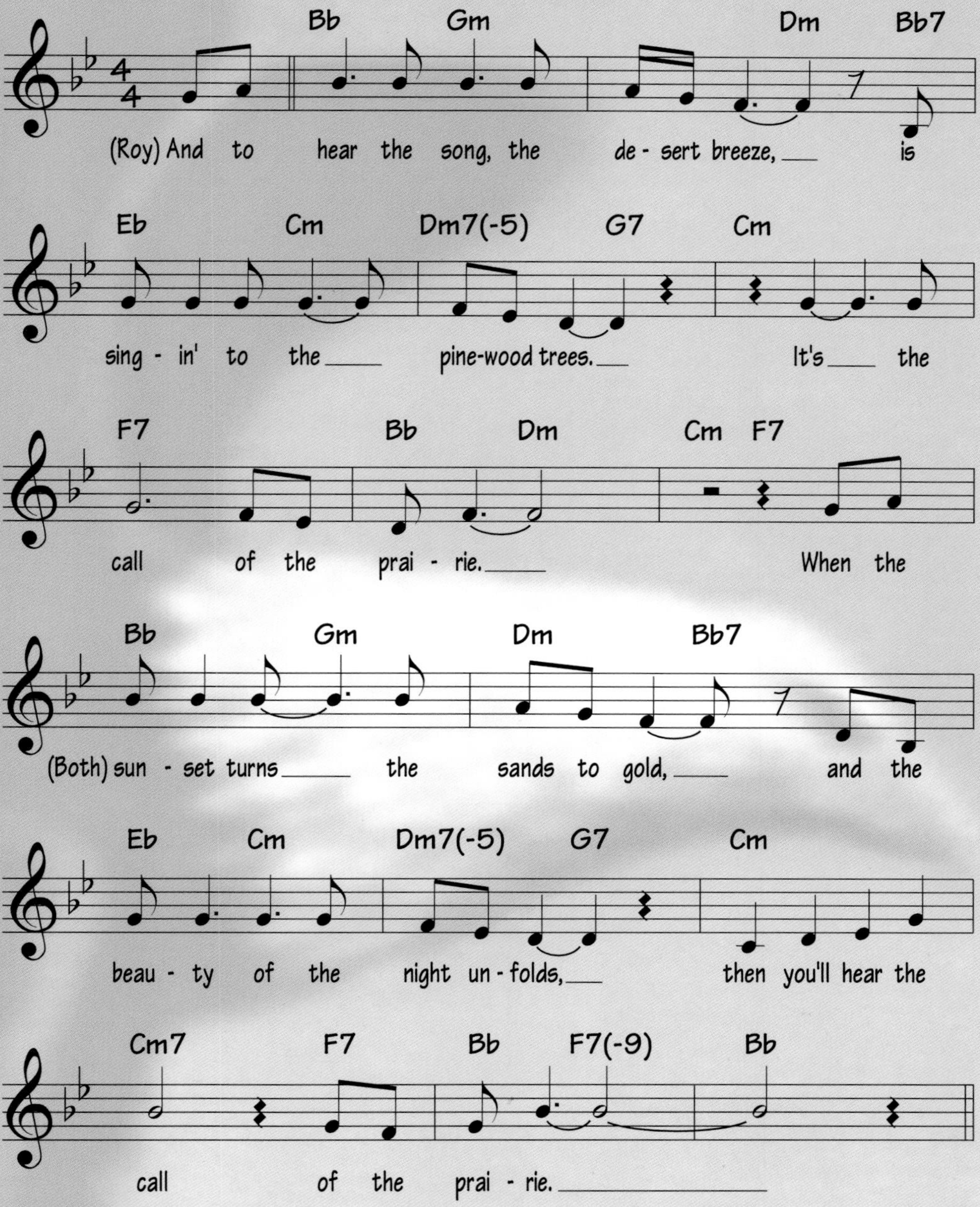
Bb Gm Dm Bb7
(Roy) And to hear the song, the de - sert breeze, is
Eb Cm Dm7(-5) G7 Cm
sing - in' to the pine-wood trees. It's the
F7 Bb Dm Cm F7
call of the prai - rie. When the
Bb Gm Dm Bb7
(Both) sun - set turns the sands to gold, and the
Eb Cm Dm7(-5) G7 Cm
beau - ty of the night un - folds, then you'll hear the
Cm7 F7 Bb F7(-9) Bb
call of the prai - rie.

Republic Pictures Page 173
"Sunset In El Dorado" Script Revision: #2

CROSS DISSOLVE FROM TWO-SHOT OF DALE AND ROY TO LONG SHOT OF RIDERS AND CAR BEHIND CAMERA TRUCK. DAY.

Lucille's aunt and fiancé want her to return to the city, but she decides to continue her visit to the west on a horseback camping tour with Roy and Gabby. So, while Roy and Lucille sing "Call of the Prairie" they all hit the trail: Roy, Lucille, Lucille's aunt, and Gabby, with the pack mule, and Lucille's fiancé following in the car.

Produced By
Donald H. Brown

Directed by
John English

Screenplay by
Dorrell and Stuart McGowan

Starring
Roy Rogers, Dale Evans, Gabby Hayes, Bob Nolan, The Sons of the Pioneers, Trigger

with
Robert Livingston, Moroni Olsen, Marc lawrence, Lucille Gleason, Andrew Tombes, Paul Harvey, Tom London, Steven Barday, Douglas Fowley

Prod: #1327 Released: 10 Oct 1945
Black/White - 71min.

Toni Ames (Dale) is sent west to investigate a tip that the old outlaw, Wildcat Kelly (Gabby), isn't dead. While staying at Roy's dude ranch, she discovers that Gabby, who is working for Roy, is Wildcat and she publishes an article about him. Bennett, who conspired with Gabby's old partner to illegally receive the reward for Wildcat's capture, wants Gabby dead.

1. Toni gets her assignment to check out a story about Wildcat Kelly.

2. Toni is at Wildcat's grave and meets Gabby who is painting the tombstone.

3. Toni pushes Roy into the pool because of his smart aleck attitude towards her.

4. Toni uncovers proof that Wildcat is really the much alive Gabby!

5. Bennett learns that Wildcat isn't dead.

6. The sheriff wants to know who was buried in Wildcat's grave.

7. Bennett's man tries to kill Gabby.

8. Gabby catches up with Bennett and captures him.

9. Gabby tells the Governor that the money he stole was given to charity.

A KISS GOODNIGHT

(As sung by Dale Evans at Mayor Cartwright's campaign meeting)

words & music by
FREDDIE SLACK
FLOYD VICTOR
R. N. HERMAN

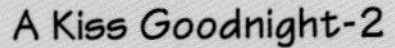

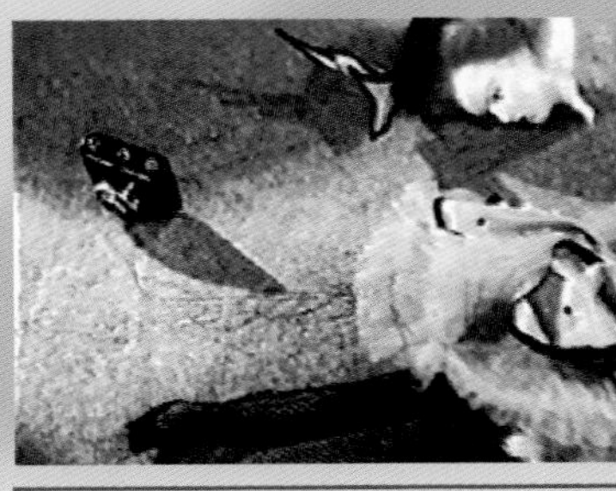

Republic Pictures
"Don't Fence Me In"

Page 5
Script Revision: #3

CROSS DISSOLVE FROM EXTERIOR CITY AERIAL VIEW. SLOW TRUCK INTO SIGN OUTSIDE OF CLOSED BANQUET ROOM DOORS WITH BELLHOP LOOKING ON. CUT TO "THROUGH-THE-KEYHOLE" SHOT INTO THE BANQUET ROOM WITH A SLOW TRUCK INTO SCENE. EVENING.

The mayor is having a campaign meeting behind closed and guarded banquet room doors. Outside the doors, the bellhop is reading the posted sign that includes the statement: "The man that wants to keep our city clean." He looks through the door's keyhole.

Male guests are seated around a large banquet table. Scantily clad girls are going from man to man kissing them, sitting on their laps, etc. A real stag party. Toni, dressed like the girls, is standing on the table singing "A Kiss Goodnight" and holding a doll dressed like her. The doll is actually a prop that hides a camera because Toni is a writer for a sleazy magazine called the "Spread." At the end of her number the mayor hugs her, she drops the doll, the camera falls out, the mayor and all the guests are in an uproar. She grabs the camera and takes a final picture before escaping.

CHOO-CHOO POLKA

(As sung by Roy Rogers the Sons of the Pioneers at the train station)

transcribed by
SCOTT HOMAN
ERIC VAN HAMERSVELD

words & music by
MIKE SHORE
ZEKE MANNERS

C6 C C6 C Gdim G
no one cared when they were com - ing back. (Roy) Ev - 'ry bod - y

G7 C B B7
sang this hap - py song ___ as the choo - choo pol - ka'd right a -

Em B G7 Gdim G7
long. ___ (All) Boys and girls in mo-ments so ___ sub -

G7 C6 C C6
lime. Their hearts beat- ing out in pol - ka time.

C(#7) C7 Am C D7(9) D7 F
Ev - 'ry one was jump- in' on the beam ___ till the en- gin -eer blew his

F F6 C6
whis - tle, then he let off steam.

Republic Pictures Page 21
"Don't Fence Me In" Script Revision: #4

CROSS DISSOLVE TO LONG SHOT OF ROY AND THE PIONEERS OUTSIDE THE TRAIN STATION. DAY.

While Roy and the Sons of the Pioneers await a train load of guests for their R Bar R Dude Ranch, they sing "Choo-Choo Polka." On cue at the end of the song, a big blast of steam from the engine sends them running.

MY LITTLE BUCKAROO

(As sung by Roy Rogers while driving the Dude Ranch stagecoach)

words & music by
JACK SCHOLL
M. K. JEROME

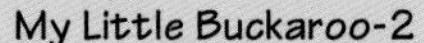

D Em7 A7 D6 D
go to sleep, ___ my lit - tle buck - a - roo. ___

Dmaj7 D6 Dmaj7
___ Soon your gon - na ride the range like grown - up

Gmaj7 G A7 Em A7 D Dmaj7
cow - boys do. ___ Now it's time that you were

D7 D+ G G6 C#7
round - in' up a dream or two. ___ So,

D Em7 A7 D6 D
go to sleep, ___ my lit - tle buck - a - roo. ___

Republic Pictures Page 34
"Don't Fence Me In" Script Revision: #5

CROSS DISSOLVE FROM DALE IN STAGECOACH BOOT TO LONG SHOT OF STAGE ON TRAIL. DAY.

At the train station, Roy sees Toni stowing away in the back of the stagecoach. He puts a package of Limburger cheese in with her. Then he climbs aboard with Gabby and takes her on a wild cross country ride while singing "My Little Buckaroo" at the top of his lungs.

DON'T FENCE ME IN

(As sung by Roy Rogers and the Sons of the Pioneers to the ranch guests)

words & music by
COLE PORTER

Bb F
use. Let me wan-der o - ver yon - der till I see the moun-tains rise.

F Fmaj7 F7
I want to (All) ride to the ridge where the West com - menc - es.

Bb Bbm F Cm/Eb
Gaze at the moon till I lose my sens - es. Can't look at hob - bles, and I

D7 Bbm/Db F/C C7 F
can't stand fenc - es. Don't fence me in."

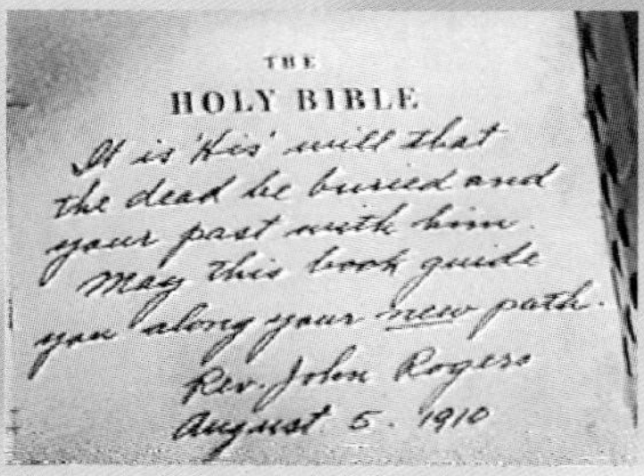

Republic Pictures Page 52
"Don't Fence Me In" Script Revision: #3

CUT TO LONG SHOT OF ROY PICKING UP GUITAR. RANCH LIVING ROOM.

Roy has decided to entertain the ranch guests by singing "Don't Fence Me In" with the Pioneers joining in. While he is singing this song that tells about the deceased Wild Cat Kelly, Toni slips out to snoop in Gabby's room. She suspects that Wild Cat Kelly is not dead, that Gabby is Wild Cat. Roy sees her leave and, while the Pioneers finish the song, he follows her. Toni finds evidence in Gabby's Bible just as Roy breaks in on her.

THE LAST ROUND-UP

(As sung by the Sons of the Pioneers at Gabby's "funeral")

words & music by
BILLY HILL

(Additional verses not in film)

I'm head-in' for the last round-up;
Gon-na sad-dle Old Paint for the
last time and ride.
So long, old pal, it's time
your tears were dried;
I'm head-in' for the last round-up.

I'm head-in' for the last round-up;
There'll be Buf-fa-lo Bill with his
long snow-white hair;
There'll be old Kit Car-son and
Cus-ter wait-in' there;
I'm head-in' for the last round-up.

Republic Pictures Page 112
"Don't Fence Me In" Script Revision: #3

FROM LONG SHOT OF GABBY IN COFFIN WITH PIONEERS AND ROY, PAN-FOLLOW ROY TO DOOR STAGE RIGHT.

Gabby has been shot, but not killed. A plan is devised to catch the shooter, a pretend funeral. As the Sons of the Pioneers sing "The Last Roundup," Roy has Toni taking pictures of mourners in the hope that Gabby can later identify the person who shot him.

ALONG THE NAVAJO TRAIL

(As sung by Roy and the Sons of the Pioneers
at the Westward Ho Club)

words & music by
LARRY MARKES
DICK CHARLES
EDDIE DE LANGE

Republic Pictures Page 136
"Along the Navajo Trail" Script Revision: #2

CROSS DISSOLVE FROM FROM "WESTWARD HO" SIGN TO LONG SHOT OF STAGE. TRUCK RIGHT.

Roy, Toni, and the Sons of the Pioneers find out that the guy who took a shot at Gabby works and lives at Bennet's Westward Ho Club. Roy calls Jack Gorden at Gorden's Theatrical Agency to have him book the Pioneers at the club. Scene opens with Roy and Pioneers on the club's stage singing "Along the Navajo Trail." During the song Roy spies Toni, dressed as a table photographer... she's gotten a job at the club too!

TUMBLING TUMBLEWEEDS

(As sung by the Sons of the Pioneers at Ansen's dinner show cluub)

G7 C
drift - ing a - long with the tum - bling tum - ble-weeds. I

Fm6 G7 C Am6# B7
know when night has gone that a new world's born at

Em B7 G9 G7 F F7
dawn. I'll keep roll- ing a - long,

E E7
Deep in my heart is a song,

F C C#dim
Here on the range I be - long,

G7 C
drift - ing a - long with the tum - bling tum - ble - weeds.

Republic Pictures Page 161
"Don't Fence Me In" Script Revision: #3

CROSS DISSOLVE FROM EXTERIOR TO MED LONG SHOT OF SONS ON STAGE. EVENING.

Roy, Toni, Gabby, and the Sons have a plan to catch Ansen. While waiting for the right opportunity to spring their trap, the Sons, who have been hired as entertainers, sing "Tumbling Tumbleweeds" while Roy looks on.

Produced By
Edward J. White

Directed by
Frank McDonald

Screenplay by
Gerald Geraghty

Starring
Roy Rogers, Dale Evans, Gabby Hayes, Bob Nolan, The Sons of the Pioneers, Trigger

with
Estelita Rodriguez, Douglas Fowley, Nestor Paiva, Sam Flint, Emmett Vogan, Roy Barcroft, David Cota, Ed Cassidy, Hank Bell

Prod: #1425 Released: 15 Dec 1945
Black/White - 66min.

To force them to sell, someone is rustling cattle from the Alastair ranch belonging to Laurie (Dale) and her father, Breck (Flint). Roy, as an undercover agent, is sent from the Cattlemen Assn. to investigate. In order to lay a pipeline. Bentley (Fowley) and his man, Rusty (Barcroft) are being paid by the Santa Fe Drilling Co. to acquire the Alastair ranch at any cost.

1. Roy arrives just in time to rescue Laurie from the lake.

2. Breck gets word that the Cattlemen's Assn. won't be sending an investigator.

3. Rusty is forcing himself on the gypsy girl, Narita (Estelita), and Roy steps in.

4. The Santa Fe Drilling Co. gives Bentley an ultimatum to get Alastair's ranch.

5. There's a bit of jealously brewing between Narita and Laurie over Roy.

6. Roy has it out with Rusty after he tries to shoot him.

7. In Bentley's office, Gabby and Roy find the phoney telegram they had sent .

8. Bentley goes over a cliff while being chased by Roy.

9. Gabby sold a horse to the Gypsies and they paid in ink-wet counterfeit money.

FREE AS THE WIND

(As sung by Estelita Rodriguez and the Gypsies on the trail)

transcribed by
SCOTT HOMAN
ERIC VAN HAMERSVELD

words & music by
JACK ELLIOTT

Republic Pictures
"Along the Navajo Trail"

Page 2
Script Revision: #2

DURING OPENING CREDITS. CUT TO GYPSY WAGON TRAIN. DAY.

A wagon train of gypsies, including Narita, are singing "Free As the Wind" as they seek a place to camp. Laurie comes along and they ask her where they might stop. She warns them to continue on because of the local feud.

IT'S THE GYPSY IN ME

(As sung by Estella Rodriguez outside the Cantina)

transcribed by
SCOTT HOMAN
ERIC VAN HAMERSVELD

words & music by
JACK ELLIOTT

Republic Pictures Page 25
"Along the Navajo Trail" Script Revision: #4

CROSS DISSOLVE TO FOLLOW PAN OF ROY ENTERING TOWN. CUT TO LONG SHOT OF RODRIGUEZ SINGING IN FRONT OF CANTINA. DAY.

As Roy enters town, he sees Narita entertaining patrons of the cantina by singing "It's the Gypsy In Me."

SASKATOON

(As sung by Roy Rogers at his campsite)

transcribed by
SCOTT HOMAN
ERIC VAN HAMERSVELD

words & music by
JACK ELLIOTT

Republic Pictures Page 54
"Along the Navajo Trail" Script Revision: #3

CROSS DISSOLVE TO LONG SHOT OF DALE RIDING IN ON A RIDGE TOP.
CUT TO LONG SHOT OF ROY AT CAMPSITE. DAY.

Roy has set up camp on Laurie's ranch. While he composes a tune called "Saskatoon," Laurie rides up to shoo him off. She takes a pot shot at him which doesn't faze him. She then confront's him.

SAVING FOR A RAINY DAY

(As sung by Roy Rogers and Dale Evans at Roy's campsite)

transcribed by
SCOTT HOMAN
ERIC VAN HAMERSVELD

words & music by
JACK ELLIOTT

Fm Bb7 Eb
There's a shel - ter in you.
Gm C7
Why wor - ry 'bout the wea - ther, as
F Cm
long as we're to - geth - er. We can al - ways see it
F F7 Bb D7
through. Here's a sol - id lit - tle plan al - most
Cm
an - y girl and man can find sil - ver in their
F7 Bb
clouds of gray. Why, they'll nev - er have a care
D7 Cm
if they're just con - tent to share all the
F7 D7 Gm
lit - tle dreams they may have stored a - way,
Cm F7 Bb
sav - in' for a rain - y day. (Dale) So
Fm Bb7 Eb Fm
now let it rain hel - ter skel - ter. There's a
Bb7 Eb Gm
shel - ter in you. (Both) Why wor - ry 'bout the

Republic Pictures
"Along the Navajo Trail"

Page 62
Script Revision: #4

CUT MEDIUM SHOT OF ROY AND DALE SITTING. DAY. RAIN.

As Roy is pretending to be a drifter/musician writing songs along the trail, he is really an investigator for the Cattlemen's Protective Association. Laurie doesn't know this. As he and Laurie begin discussing the trouble on the ranch, it begins to rain. Roy offers her shelter until it's over. While it rains, she looks through the book of songs he's writing and he begins to sing "Saving for a Rainy Day." Laurie joins in and, when they finish the song, the rain has stopped and the sun is out.

COOL WATER

(As sung by the Sons of the Pioneers on the ranch patio)

words & music by
BOB NOLAN

Republic Pictures Page 80
"Along the Navajo Trail" Script Revision: #2

CUT TO LONG SHOT OF PIONEERS ON PATIO. DAY.

The Pioneers, who are hands on Laurie's ranch, pass the time on the patio singing "Cool Water" while Laurie and her father look on.

ALONG THE NAVAJO TRAIL

(As sung by Roy Rogers at the Gypsy Festival)

words & music by
LARRY MARKES
DICK CHARLES
EDDIE DE LANGE

F7 B9 Bb9 Bb7+ Eb Bb7+

al-ways finds me wish-in' on a star. Well, what do you know?___ It's morn-in' al-

Eb Bb7+ Eb Bb7+ Eb Eb7

read- y,___ There's the dawn - in'___ so sil- ver and pale. It's

Ab7 Bb7 Eb Ab

time to climb in - to my sad-dle ___ and ride_______ the Na- va- jo

Eb Ab7 Bb7+ Ab7

trail. I'm go - in' to ride, ___ get a - long there, boy, ___

Ab7 Eb

the Na - va - jo trail. _______________

Republic Pictures Page 155
"Along the Navajo Trail" Script Revision: #4

AT END OF DANCE NUMBER, CUT TO LONG SHOT OF LITTLE GYPSY GIRL WALKING ALONG EDGE OF STAGE TOWARDS ROY. NIGHT.

A little gypsy girl "reads" Roy's palm stating that he is going to sing. He agrees and sings "Along the Navajo Trail" for the crowd. The Sons of the Pioneers, Gabby, Laurie, Narita, and the villain look on.

HOW'RE YA DOIN' IN THE HEART DEPARTMENT

(As sung by Dale Evans at the Gypsy Festival)

Eb7 Bbm Eb7 Ab

in the dark de - part - ment? Why do you act my -

Ab7

ster - i - ous - ly? I'm

Db Db F7 Bbm

gon - na be in the bro - ken heart de - part - ment,

Eb7

for - ev - er, I guess, un - less you fall for

Ab Adim Bbm

me. (Says: And by the way,) How - 're ya do - in'

Eb7 Bbm Eb7 Ab

in the sigh de - part - ment? (Says: Give me

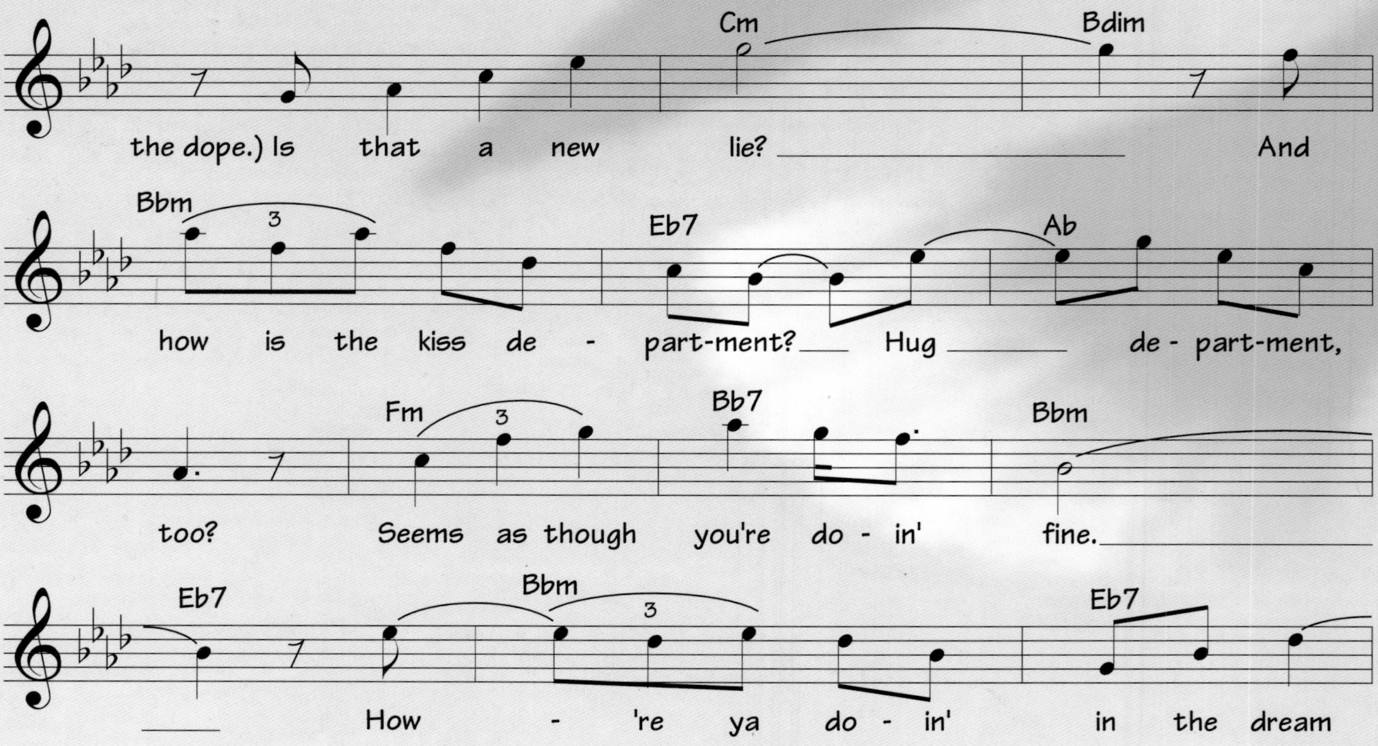

Cm Bdim

the dope.) Is that a new lie? And

Bbm Eb7 Ab

how is the kiss de - part-ment? Hug de - part-ment,

Fm Bb7 Bbm

too? Seems as though you're do - in' fine.

Eb7 Bbm Eb7

How - 're ya do - in' in the dream

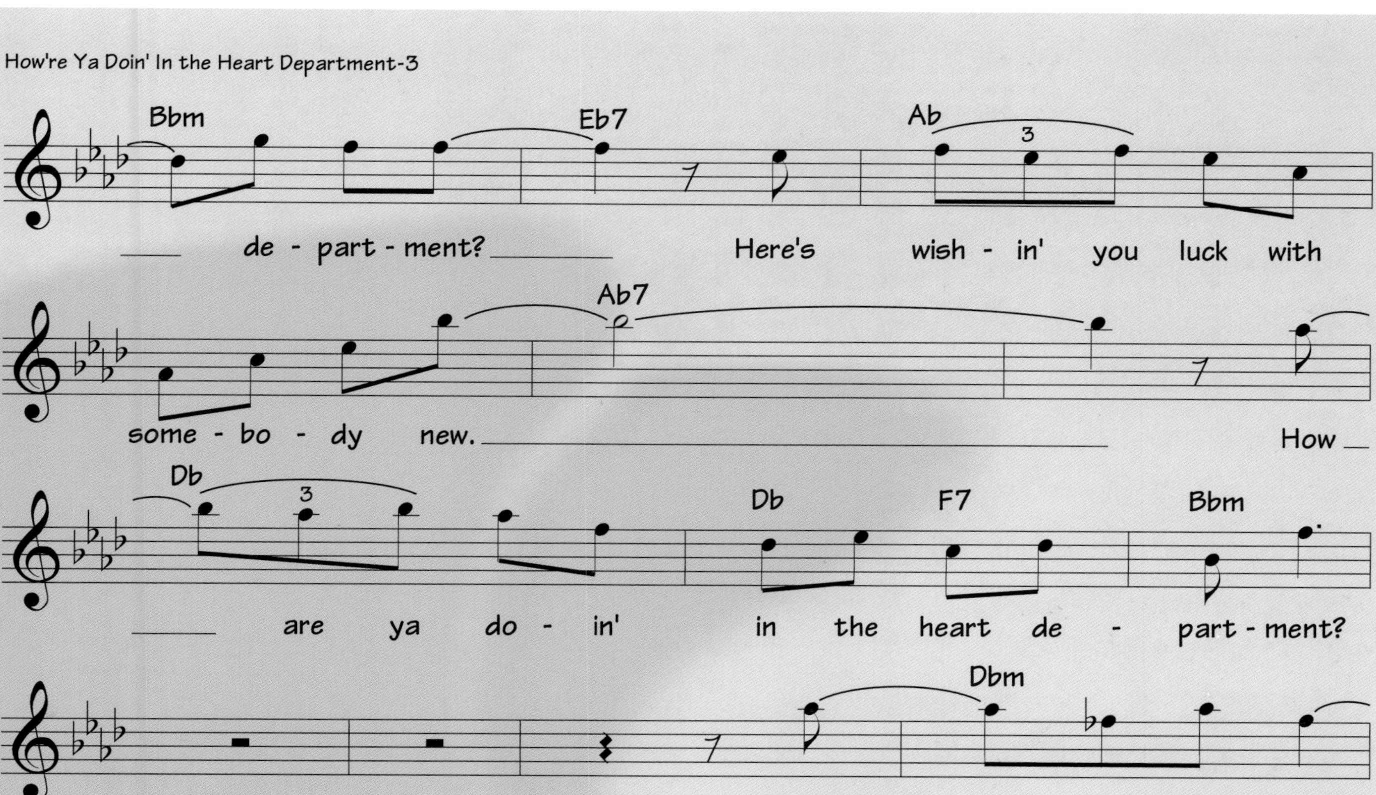

Republic Pictures Page 157
"Along the Navajo Trail" Script Revision: #3

CUT TO MEDIUM SHOT OF DALE WITH GYPSY MUSICIANS. NIGHT.

During the gypsy festival, Roy is having his palm read by Narita. Laurie is jealous and is even mistaken for one of the gypsy singers. She'll show Roy! So, as her father, Gabby, and the gypsies look on she sings "How're Ya Doin' In the Heart Department," while keeping an eye on Roy and Narita.

TWENTY-ONE YEARS IS A MIGHTY LONG TIME

(As sung by Roy Rogers and the Sons of the Pioneers on the trail to Laurie's ranch)

transcribed by
SCOTT HOMAN
ERIC VAN HAMERSVELD

words & music by
TIM SPENCER

Republic Pictures Page 164
"Along the Navajo Trail" Script Revision: #4

CUT TO LONG SHOT OF GROUP ON HORSEBACK RIDING ON A TRAIL. DAY.

Roy has not returned to the ranch after the gypsy festival last night. Laurie thinks that the gypsy, Narita, has something to do with his absence and packs up his stuff to throw him off the ranch when she hears singing. She doesn't know that Roy was shot at after the festival and the shooter, Rusty, was captured by him and the Sons of the Pioneers. As they bring Rusty for questioning, they sing " Twenty-One Years Is a Mighty Long Time."

Produced By
Edward J. White

Directed by
Frank McDonald

Screenplay by
M. Coates Webster

Starring
Roy Rogers, Dale Evans, Gabby Hayes, Bob Nolan, The Sons of the Pioneers, Trigger

with
Lyle Talbot, Tommy Cook, Johnny Calkins, Sara Edwards, Tommy Ivo, Michael Chapin, Dick Curtis, Edmund Cobb, Tom Quinn, Kid Chissell, Robert Mitchell Boy Choir

Prod: #1422 Released: 9 Mar 1946
Black/White - 68min.

Gabby runs a ranch for homeless boys that is in financial trouble. Roy, once a boy on the ranch, offers to help Gabby out. Outlaw, King Blaine (Talbot), is shot but just before he dies he leaves stolen bank money to his son, Chip (Cook), one of Gabby's boys. Roy finds Claire (Dale) and takes her to be with her brother, Chip. Blaine's gang wants the stolen money and goes after Chip.

1. The bank manager, Dolly, tells Gabby to payoff his loan or lose his ranch.

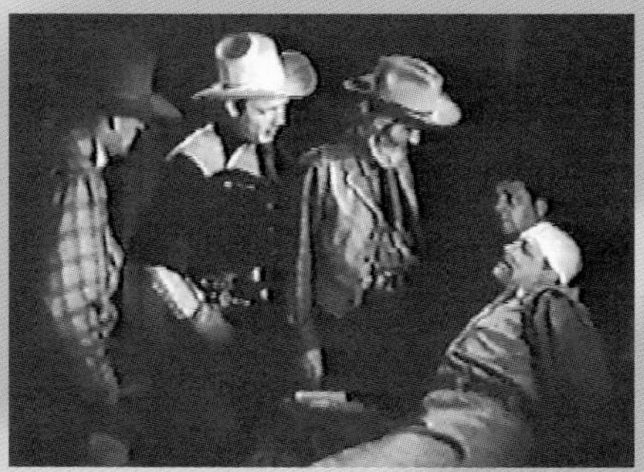

2. Before he dies Blaine wants to give Chip and his sister a little inheritance.

3. Roy tells Claire about the death of her stepfather, Blaine.

4. Blaine's gang wants Chip to hand over the stolen money his father gave him.

5. Gabby, Roy, the Pioneers, and the sheriff shoot it out with Blaine's gang.

6. Chip digs up his inheritance which had been hidden in the barn.

7. Chip secretly delivers $25,000 of the stolen money to Dolly to pay Gabby's loan.

8. Roy and the sheriff ride out to round up the gang.

9. As a reward for the return of the bank's stolen money, Dolly cancels Gabby's debt.

SONG OF ARIZONA

(As sung by Roy Rogers and the Sons of the Pioneers at the radio station)

words & music by
JACK ELLIOTT

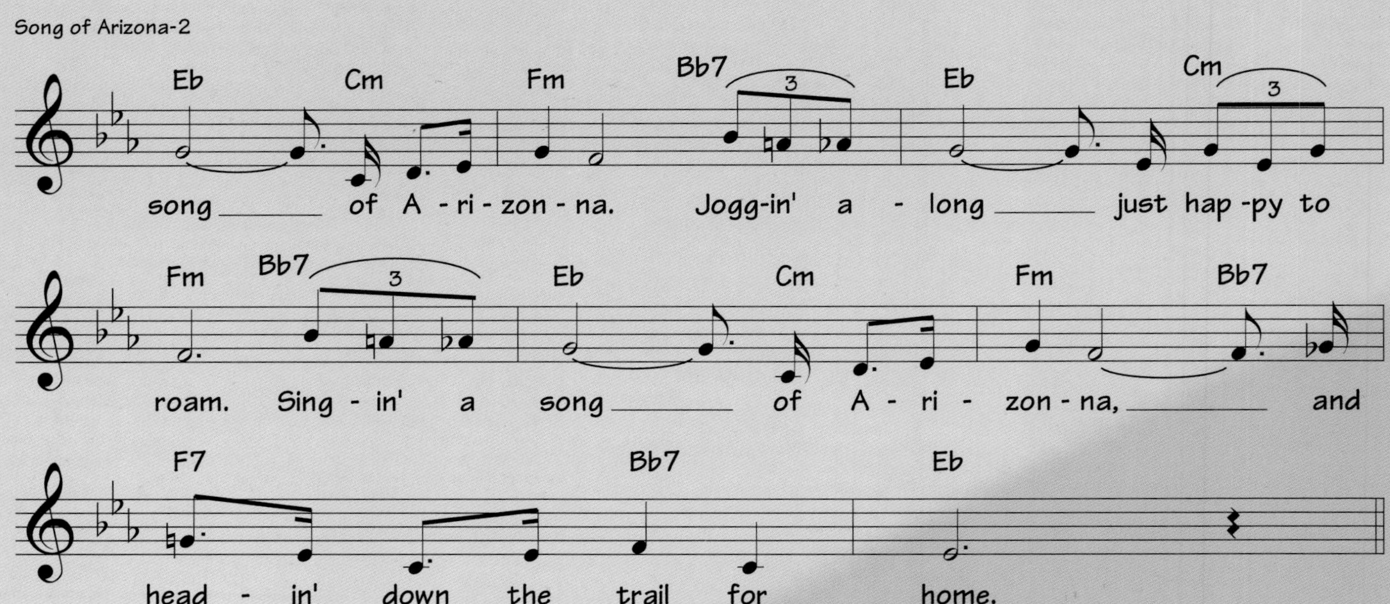

Republic Pictures Page 12
"Song of Arizona" Script Revision: #3

CROSS DISSOLVE FROM GABBY WITH BOYS TO RADIO STATION STATION SIGN. THEN CROSS DISSOLVE TO MEDIUM SHOT OF ROY WITH ANNOUNCER ON THE RADIO STATION'S BROADCAST STAGE.

Roy and the Sons of the Pioneers are singing "Song of Arizona" as the last song in their WYZ radio program. At the end of the song, Roy announces that he and the Pioneers are taking a break from show business and going out to Gabby's ranch. Gabby has set up a ranch that will give troubled boys a better start in life.

WAY OUT THERE

(As sung by the Mitchell Boys Choir in the wagon with Gabby)

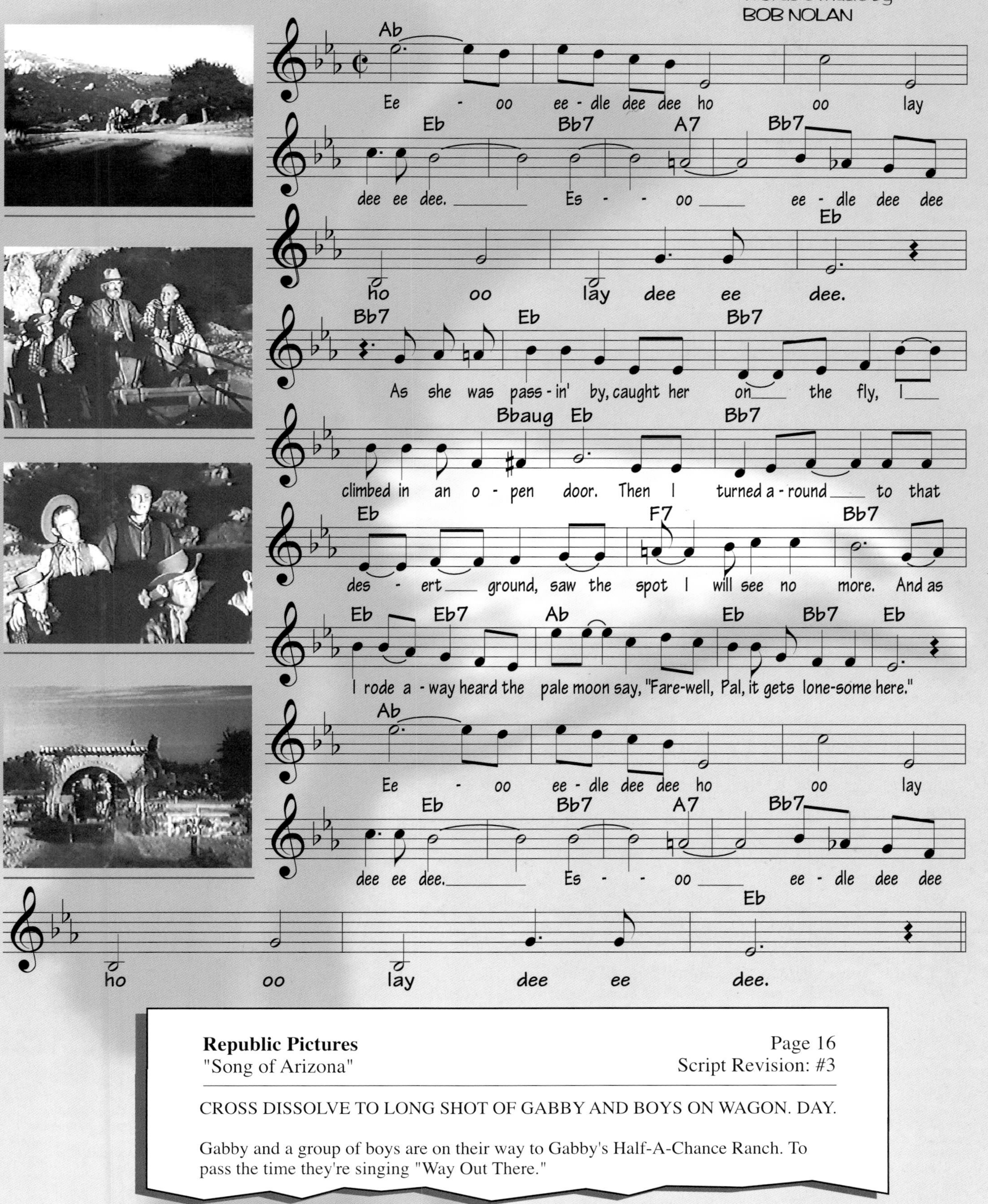

Republic Pictures Page 16
"Song of Arizona" Script Revision: #3

CROSS DISSOLVE TO LONG SHOT OF GABBY AND BOYS ON WAGON. DAY.

Gabby and a group of boys are on their way to Gabby's Half-A-Chance Ranch. To pass the time they're singing "Way Out There."

HALF-A-CHANCE RANCH

(As sung by Roy Rogers and the Mitchell Boys Choir at Gabby's ranch)

transcribed by
SCOTT HOMAN
ERIC VAN HAMERSVELD

words & music by
JACK ELLIOTT

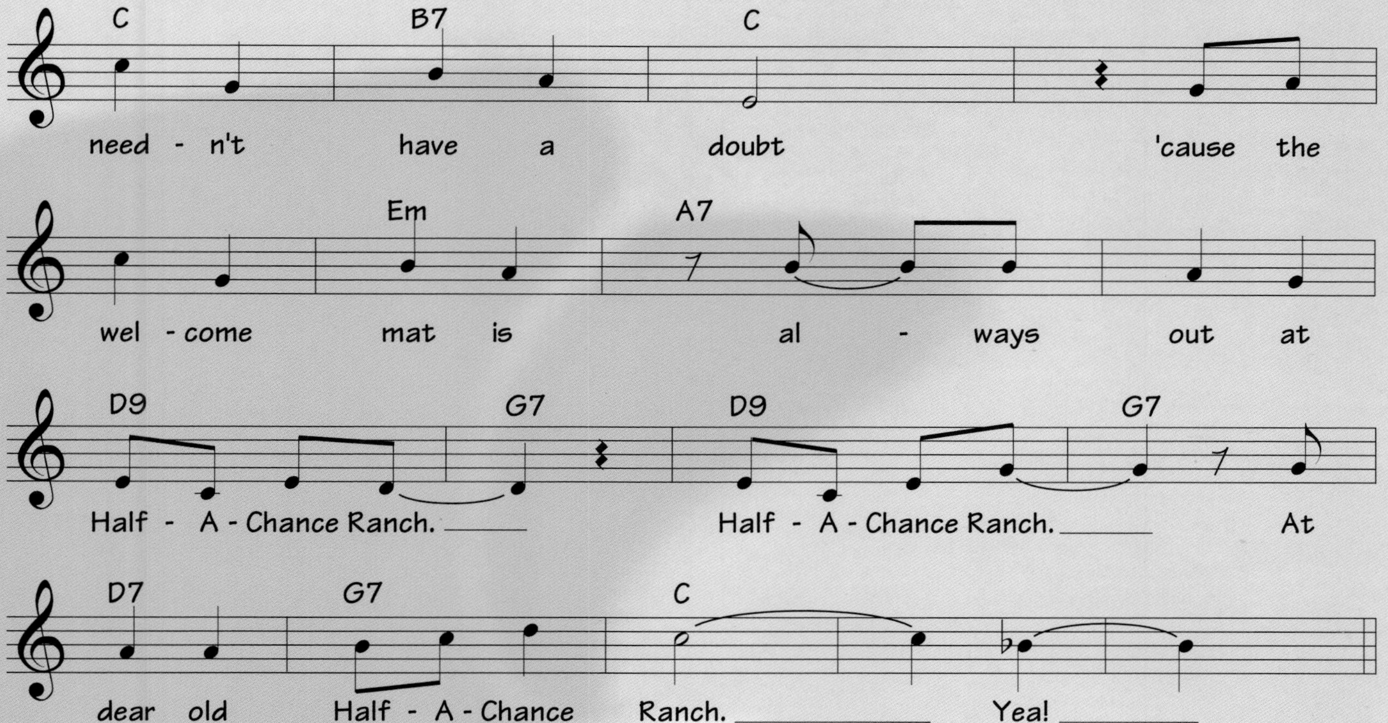

Republic Pictures
"Song of Arizona"

Page 49
Script Revision: #3

CUT TO LONG SHOT OF WITH THE BOYS. CUT TO LONG SHOT OF ROY AND PIONEERS ARRIVING ON HORSEBACK. DAY.

Gabby has just explained what happens during the ranch's graduation exercises when Roy and the Sons of the Pioneers arrive. They all run over to greet them. Gabby turns to boys and has them line up to sing, with Roy pitching in, the ranch's theme song, "Half-A-Chance Ranch."

ROUND AND ROUND, THE LARIAT SONG

(As sung by Dale Evans at the Golden Spur nightclub)

transcribed by
SCOTT HOMAN
ERIC VAN HAMERSVELD

words & music by
JACK ELLIOTT

Republic Pictures Page 82
"Song of Arizona" Script Revision: #5

CUT TO LONG SHOT OF DALE ON STAGE WITH BAND AND DANCERS.

The outlaw father of one of Chip, one of Gabby's boys, has been killed. Before he dies he leaves money to Gabby and a garage in Kansas City to the boy. He also mentions that the boy has a sister, Claire, in Kansas City. Roy has gone to Kansas City to find both Claire and the garage that, when sold, would bring money to the boy. He finds out that the garage burned down years ago, so he is off to find Claire. She is a singer at the Golden Spur nightclub. During her number "Round and Round, the Lariat Song," Claire is to get a guest on stage to join her in a song. She spies Roy and lassos him up onto the stage.

THAT FEELING IN THE MOONLIGHT

(As sung by Roy Rogers and Dale Evans on the Golden Spur stage)

words & music by
JAMES CAVANAUGH
LARRY STOCK
IRA SCHUSTER

Republic Pictures Page 83
"Song of Arizona" Script Revision: #2

CUT TO LONG SHOT OF ROY AND DALE ON STAGE.

Claire has lassoed Roy and pulled him up on to the stage to include him in her show. They sing "That Feeling In the Moonlight."

MICHAEL O'LEARY O'BRIEN O'TOOL

(As sung by the Sons of the Pioneers at Gabby's ranch house)

transcribed by
SCOTT HOMAN
ERIC VAN HAMERSVELD

words & music by
TIM SPENCER

Republic Pictures
"Song of Arizona"

Page 101
Script Revision: #3

CROSS DISSOLVE TO LONG SHOT OF PIONEERS INSIDE RANCH HOUSE.

The Pioneers are entertaining the boys by singing "Michael O'Leary O'Brien O'Tool." During the song, Chip sneaks out to meet with some of his dad's old outlaw gang.

WILL YA BE MY DARLIN'?

(As sung by Roy Rogers and Dale Evans out on the ranch)

transcribed by
SCOTT HOMAN
ERIC VAN HAMERSVELD

words & music by
JACK OWENS
MARY ANN OWENS

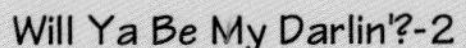

Bb
snoot. (Dale) You're just the sweet - est thing I've

F9
found. ______ (Dale says: Yes, you are.) (Roy) But you'll grow up to

Bb n.c. Bb
be a cow. (Roy bawls like a cow: Moooo) (Dale) Will ya be my dar - lin',

F9
and hold me tight? (Roy) Will ya be my

Bb
dar - lin', and start to - night? (Both) Could you learn to

Eb
love me as I love you? Will you be my

Bb F7 Bb
dar - lin' and make my dreams come true? ______

Republic Pictures Page 128
"Song of Arizona" Script Revision: #3

CUT TO LONG SHOT OF DALE RIDING TOWARDS A RUNNING CALF. DAY.

Roy and Claire chase down a runaway calf during the boys' rodeo competition. Roy says the bawling calf sings like one of Claire's stooges in her Golden Spur act and begins to sing "Will Ya Be My Darlin'" to the calf. Claire joins in. As the song progresses it is apparent that they are really singing to each other.

WHEN MISTER SPOOK STEPS OUT

(As sung by Roy Rogers, the Sons of the Pioneers, Dale Evans, and Gabby at the party)

words & music by
JACK ELLIOTT

Abm Abm7 E7 Eb7
spook - i - est sight you've ev - er seen, and on
Abm Abm7 E7 Eb7
poor lit - tle girls he's ver - y keen,
Abm Eb7
when Mis - ter Spook steps out.
Abm Abm7 E7
When Mis - ter Spook steps out for the big af -
Abm Abm7 E7
fair, he will con-stant - tly look for lad - ies
Eb7 Abm Abm7 E7
there. So don't you re - turn his i - cy
Eb7 Abm Eb7
stare, when Mis - ter Spook steps
Ab Eb Ebm
out. (Roy) He'll hold a ren-dez-vous with a ghost or two un - der
Bb Eb
neath the weep-ing will - ow. (Dale) And per - haps he may try to
Ebm C7 F7
steal you a - way, so you'd bet-ter hide your head be-neath the pil-low. (Roy/Dale) When Mis -ter
Bbm Bbm7 Gb7 F7 Bbm Bbm7
Spook steps out, lock your door up tight. It's a dan - ger - ous thing to

Republic Pictures
"Song of Arizona"

Page 162
Script Revision: #6

CUT TO LONG SHOT OF ROY AND PIONEERS ON STAGE IN GABBY'S RANCH BARN. NIGHT.

At the Halloween party for the boys, Roy, the Pioneers, Claire, and Gabby present a production number complete with a witch and costumed dancers singing "When Mister Spook Steps Out." During the dance line at the end of the song, they are interrupted by the owner of the bank who accuses Gabby of paying off his ranch loan with stolen money.

Produced By
Edward J. White

Directed by
Frank McDonald

Screenplay by
Gerald Geraghty

Starring
Roy Rogers, Dale Evans, Gabby Hayes, Bob Nolan, The Sons of the Pioneers, Trigger

with
Sheldon Leonard, Minerva Urecal, Robert Emmett Keane, Kenne Duncan, Pierce Lydon, Gerald Oliver Smith, Dick Elliott, George J. Lewis, Bud Osborne, Jo Ann Dean, George Chesebro

Prod: #1428 Released: 9 May 1946
Black/White - 65min.

Jackie Dalrymple (Dale) runs away from home. Roy accidentally finds her, disguised as a boy, on his way to Dalrymple, Texas. Gabby, the town sheriff, is looking for the missing Jackie. Meanwhile, Roy enters the annual horse race but casino owner, Haynes (Leonard), wants to win and tries to sabotage Roy's attempt. Roy knows who is behind the sabotage and goes after Haynes and his men.

1. While on his yacht, Jackie has yet another argument with her father about Roy's music.

2. Jackie decides to run away and swims to shore.

3. Roy finds her on the train in Trigger's car under the hay disguised as a boy.

4. Gabby receives a telegram from Dalrymple telling him to look for his missing daughter.

5. Gabby suspects that a senorita is the missing Jackie Dalrymple.

6. In a horse race rigged by Haynes, Roy still takes the lead and wins with Trigger.

7. Mr. Dalrymple is pleased that Roy is going to ride his horses in the race.

8. Haynes tries to shoot Roy but misses. Roy returns the fire and Haynes is hit.

9. There's a big celebration barbecue at the Dalrymple ranch.

LIGHTS OF OLD SANTA FE

(As sung by Roy Rogers, on a record, and Dale Evans in her yacht stateroom)

words & music by
JACK ELLIOTT

Republic Pictures Page 12
"Rainbow Over Texas" Script Revision: #3

FADE UP TO LONG SHOT OF LARGE YACHT. THEN DISSOLVE TO INTERIOR OF YACHT STATE ROOM. PAN TO DALE AT MIRROR. DAY.

Jackie, the daughter of a rich tycoon, is on her father's yacht listening and singing along to a record of Roy singing an abbreviated version of "Lights of Old Santa Fe." At the end of the song, her father and butler rush in. Claiming she's in love with the cowboy, Roy, her father goes into a rage and breaks the record over his knee.

TEXAS, U.S.A.

(As sung by Roy Rogers and the Sons of the Pioneers on the train)

Republic Pictures Page 25
"Rainbow Over Texas" Script Revision: #3

CUT TO LONG SHOT OF ROY AND PIONEERS IN FREIGHT CAR. NIGHT.

On the way to their next performance, Roy and Tim have just written a new song, Texas U.S.A." They try it out for rest of the Sons of the Pioneers.

LITTLE SENORITA

(As sung by Roy Rogers and Dale Evans in the antique store)

transcribed by
SCOTT HOMAN
ERIC VAN HAMERSVELD

words & music by
JACK ELLIOTT

Em7 A7 Dm
chant-ment sure to make each ca - bal - le - ro
G7 C Ddim
fall. Won't you smile for me, lit - tle sen - no -
C Bm7(-5)
ri - ta? You were meant to be
E7 Am C
al - ways bright and gay. You're a
F D#dim
po - em set to mus - ic. You're a
C A7 Dm
pro - mise of ro - mance. Weave your spell for
G7 C Bb7
me, Se - no - ri - ta, dance.
Eb Fdim
(Roy in Spanish) Tu can - tar lin - da se - ño -
Eb Dm7(-5)
ri - ta, la - gua dul - ce, vu
G7 Cm Eb
es mi ins - pi - ra - ción. Tu eres

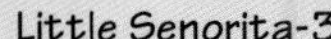

Republic Pictures Page 49
"Rainbow Over Texas" Script Revision: #2

CUT TO CLOSE UP OF SENORITA MUSIC BOX DANCER.

Jackie disguised as a boy steels Trigger in order to get out of town. Roy has raced after her in a buckboard wagon and captured her. In the tussle he discovers that he's a "she." She lies about her background and Roy takes pity on her, taking her back to town and to the Dalrymple Antique Shop to get her some "girl" clothes. While she tries on clothes, he turns on a music box and she sings "Little Senorita." During the song she hands Roy a guitar and he plays and sings along.

OUTLAW

(As sung by the lead singer in the saloon show)

transcribed by
SCOTT HOMAN
ERIC VAN HAMERSVELD

words & music by
JACK ELLIOTT

Republic Pictures
"Rainbow Over Texas"

Page 76
Script Revision: #4

CUT TO LONG SHOT OF SALOON ENTRANCE.

Jackie, closely followed by Gabby the sheriff, who suspects that she is the missing person on a flyer he has just been handed, has slipped into a saloon . As Gabby tries to catch up to her, the saloon's show starts with gunshots as a singer and her "gang" enter in a simulated holdup. They go from table to table demanding wallets, champagne, diamonds, etc. (which they immediately give back) while the singer sings "Outlaw." While roaming the audience, she comes to Roy's table. Instantly recognizing him as the western singing star, she immediately stops the show to introduce him.

RAINBOW OVER TEXAS

(As sung by Roy Rogers and the Sons of the Pioneers on stage in the saloon)

transcribed by
SCOTT HOMAN
ERIC VAN HAMERSVELD

words & music by
JACK ELLIOTT

Dm G7 3 C7
just be - cause there's Spring in the air. There's a
F C7 F C7
rain - bow o - ver Tex - as. See the
F A7 Dm D7
skies are clear - in' and I'm here to say, It's
Gm F Eb7 D7
gon - na be just a real nice da.y, Good
G7 C7 F F7
morn - in' to you. There's a
Bb
blue - bird high in the branch - es ser - e -
Db F
na - din' his la - day fair. And you
C G7 C Am
know for cer - tain all the dog - gies are flirt - in'
Dm G7 3 C7
just be - cause there's Spring in the air. There's a
F C7 F C7
rain - bow o - ver Tex - as, with the

Rainbow Over Texas-3

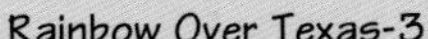

F A7 Dm D7
coun - try - side a - wake and feel - in' great. Ev - 'ry -
Gm F Eb7 D7 G7 C7
thing's first rate in the lone star state. Good morn - in' to
F G7 C7 F
you. Good morn - in' to you.

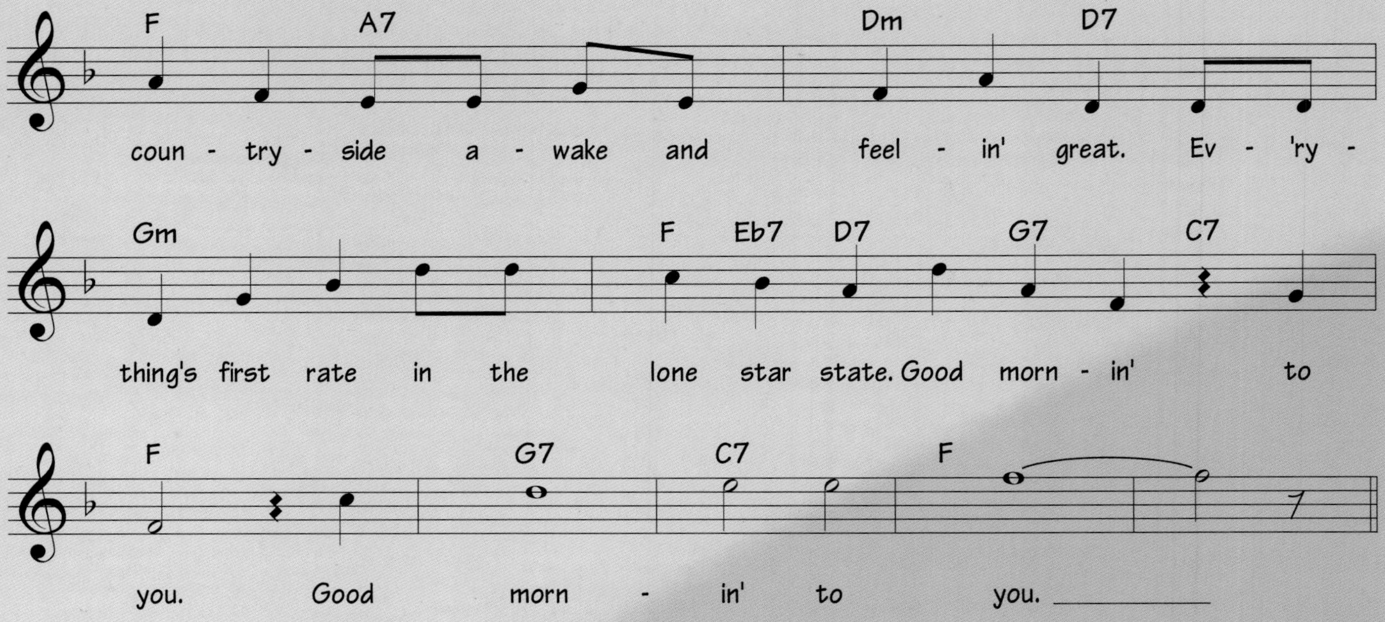

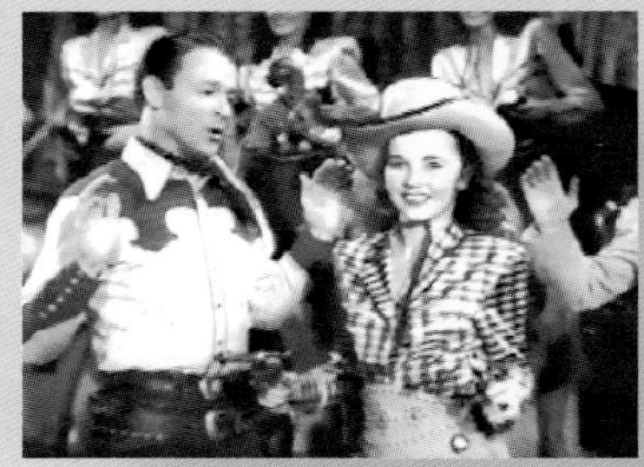

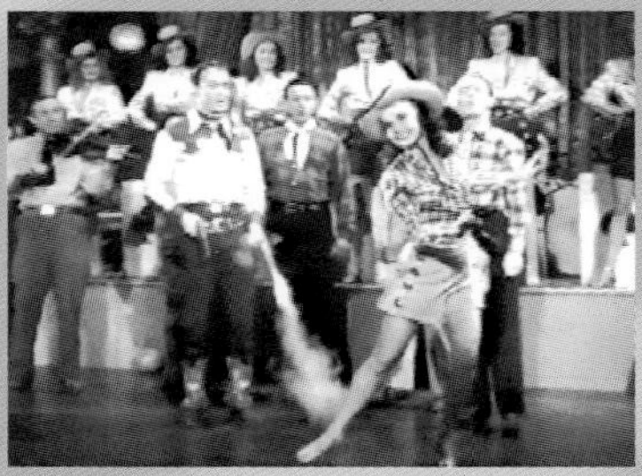

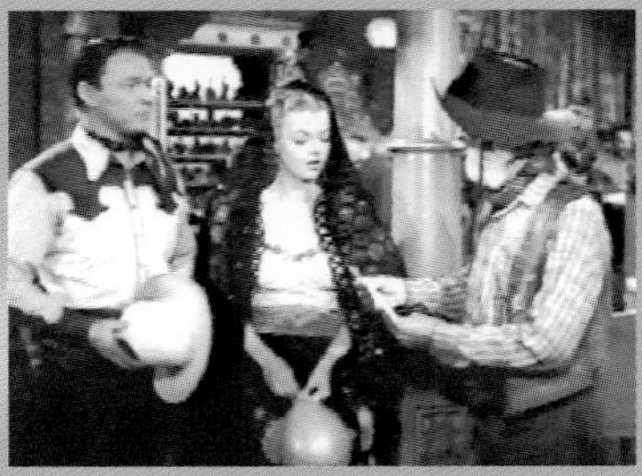

Republic Pictures Page 81
"Rainbow Over Texas" Script Revision: #4

CUT TO MEDIUM LONG SHOT OF ROY AND LEAD SINGER AT TABLE.

During the saloon show the lead singer discovers Roy in the audience. She wants him to sing a song. He says he will if she rounds up the Sons of the Pioneers who are sitting at other tables. They gather on stage and sing "Rainbow Over Texas." Meanwhile, Sheriff Gabby is looking around the room for Jackie and, at the end of the song, challenges her about whether she is the missing person on the flyer.

COWBOY CAMP MEETIN'

(As sung by the Sons of the Pioneers on the saloon stage)

words & music by
TIM SPENCER

G G7 C
sis - ter Lou's gon - na be there, Broth - er, like me an' you. An'
G D7
old Kit Car - son, he will too, 'way up in the
G D7 G
sky. (All) They're gon - na ride at the Cow - boy Camp Meet - in'.
C7 G
Ride at the Cow - boy Camp Meet - in'. Ride on the Cow - boy
D7 G
Camp Meet - in'. Ride on the gold - en range up in the
C G
sky, up in the sky.
G
yes, we'll ride at the Cow - boy Camp Meet - in',
D7 G
'way up in the sky. (Hugh) Lit - tle Da - vid slew the
G7 C
gi - ant so tall, proved right was might for big and small. He'll
G D7
play his harp as I re - call, 'way up in the

Republic Pictures Page 104
"Rainbow Over Texas" Script Revision: #5

FADE UP ON LONG SHOT OF GABBY ENTERING SALOON. FOLLOW PAN TO PIONEERS ON STAGE.

Gabby has come into the saloon looking for Roy to tell him about some fine horses that he has picked for the wagon race. As he ambles through the tables, he pauses to watch the Pioneers sing their production number, "Cowboy Camp Meetin'."

Produced By
Armand Schaffer

Directed by
Frank McDonald

Screenplay by
Jack Townley, John K. Butler

Starring
Roy Rogers, Dale Evans, Mary Lee, Bob Nolan, The Sons of the Pioneers, Trigger

with
Jack Holt, LeRoy Mason, Roy Barcroft, Sam Flint, Kenne Duncan, Ralph Sanford, Francis McDonald, Harlan Briggs, William Haade, Tom London, Fred Graham, Ted Mapes, Alan Bridge

Prod: #1427 Released: 10 Jul 1946
Black/White - 79min.

Roy wants to mate his horse, Lady, with Gabby's Golden Sovereign. He refuses. Scoville (Holt) steals Sovereign so he can get a colt. Sovereign is killed and Susan (Dale), Gabby's daughter, accuses Roy of the killing. Unknown to everyone, Sovereign and Lady did mate before he was killed. Roy names the colt Trigger and rides him in the big horse race.

RB

1. Roy asks Gabby about mating his horse with the prize palomino, Golden Sovereign.

2. Scoville's men steal Sovereign from the ranch.

3. Susan rides up to see Roy standing over the body of Sovereign.

4. Months later, Roy's horse, Lady, gives birth to a colt Roy names Trigger,

4. Gabby is heartbroken over the loss of Sovereign and turns to gambling.

6. Roy is arrested and Trigger is sold at auction to the casino owner, Scoville.

7. Scoville offers Gabby a bet on the horse race: Gabby's ranch against the IOUs.

8. During the race, Roy, riding for Scoville, helps Susan and ends up losing the race.

9. Gabby wins his ranch from the Scoville bet, apologizes to Roy, and gives him Trigger.

LIVIN' WESTERN STYLE

(As sung by Roy Rogers in his wagon traveling down the road)

words & music by
JUNE HERSHEY
DON SWANDER

Republic Pictures
"My Pal Trigger"

Page 12
Script Revision: #3

CROSS DISSOLVE TO LONG SHOT OF WAGON ON ROAD. DAY.

Roy, who buys, sells, and trades horses, is in his covered wagon traveling down the road singing "Livin' Western Style." At the end of the song he pulls up in front of the Golden Horse Ranch, the home of Golden Sovereign.

HARRIET

(As sung by Roy Rogers and Dale Evans at the El Dorado dinner party)

words & music by
ABLE BAER
PAUL CUNNINGHAM

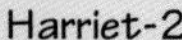

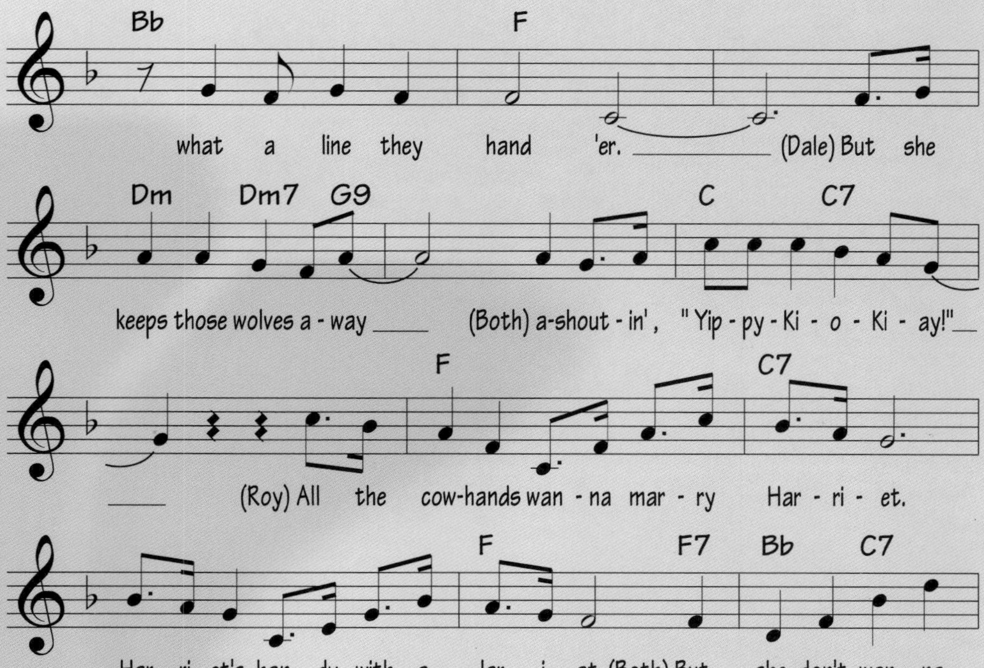

Bb F
what a line they hand 'er. ____ (Dale) But she

Dm Dm7 G9 C C7
keeps those wolves a - way ____ (Both) a-shout - in', "Yip - py - Ki - o - Ki - ay!"__

F C7
____ (Roy) All the cow-hands wan - na mar - ry Har - ri - et.

F F7 Bb C7
Har - ri - et's han - dy with a lar - i - at. (Both) But she don't wan - na

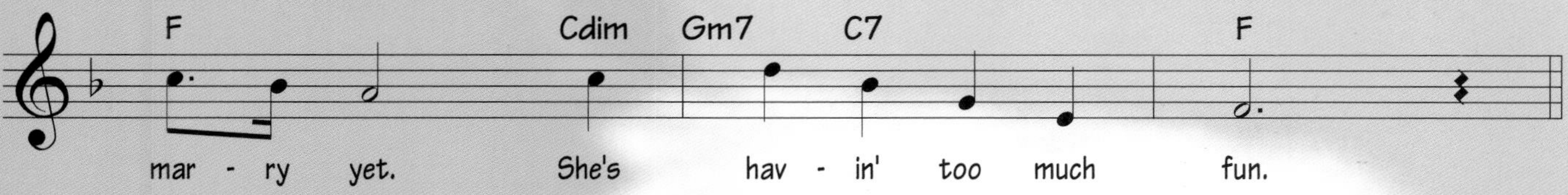

F Cdim Gm7 C7 F
mar - ry yet. She's hav - in' too much fun.

Republic Pictures
"My Pal Trigger"

Page 29
Script Revision: #3

FADE UP TO LONG SHOT OF DINNER PARTY.

Roy has met up with his old friends the Sons of the Pioneers who are working on Gabby and Susan's Golden Horse Ranch. The Pioneers ask Susan if Roy can join them for supper. She agrees and invites him to join all of them at the El Dorado Club for a dinner party. After dinner, to entertain the group, Susan drags Roy up on stage to sing "Harriet." During the song, Bret Scoville, the villain, sends his henchmen out on an errand.

EL RANCHO GRANDE

(As sung by the Pioneers at the El Dorado dinner party)

words & music by
SILVANO RAMOS
BARTLEY COSTELLO
J. del ORAL

Republic Pictures Page 36
"My Pal Trigger" Script Revision: #3

FADE UP TO LONG SHOT OF PIONEERS ON STAGE.

During the El Dorado dinner party, the Sons of the Pioneers sing "El Rancho Grande" with a solo by Lloyd Perryman.

OLE FAITHFUL

(As sung by Roy Rogers riding at night on horseback)

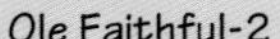

Gm7 C7 F Bb F C7
up, ole fel - ler, 'cause we got - ta get home to - night.

F Bb F Bb
Ole Faith - ful, we rode the range to -

F Bb F
geth - er. Ole Faith - ful, in

C7 F
ev - 'ry kind of weath - er. When your round - up days are

F7 Bb F
ov - er, there'll be pas - tures white with clo - ver, for

Dm7 C7 F Bb F
you, Ole Faith - ful, pal o' mine.

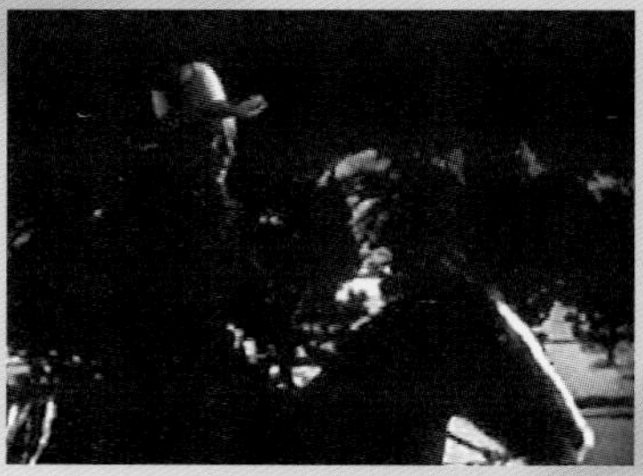

Republic Pictures Page 108
"My Pal Trigger" Script Revision: #4

CROSS DISSOLVE TO LONG SHOT OF ROY ON HORSEBACK. DARK, COLD, SNOWY NIGHT.

Roy is accused of killing Gabby's horse, Golden Sovereign, and has to put up everything he has, including his horse, Lady, as collateral for his bail bond. The crooked bail bondsman wants possession of his horse. Roy decides to get as far away as possible and rides off into the unknown. It's a sad time for Roy. He doesn't have much money and one evening he has to sell his prize silver saddle for horse feed. Later that night, while on a cold, dark trail, it begins to snow and Roy sings "Ole Faithful" softly to Lady, his only friend.

LONG, LONG AGO

(As played on the piano and sung by
Dale Evans in her living room)

words & music by
(TRADITIONAL)

(Dale) 1. Tell me the tales that to me were so dear, long, long a-go, long, long a-go.
(Additional) 2. Do you re-mem-ber the path where we met, long, long a-go, long, long a-go.
(Additional) 3. Tho' by your kind-ness my fond hopes were rais'd, long, long a-go, long, long a-go.

Sing me the songs I de - light - ed to hear, long, long a - go, long a - go.
Ah, yes, you told me you ne'er would for - get, long, long a- go, long a - go.
You by more el - o-quent lips have been prais'd, long, long a- go, long a - go.

Now you are come all my grief is re- moved. Let me for- get that so long you have rov'd.
Then, to all oth- ers, my smile you pre-ferr'd. Love, when you spoke, gave a charm to each word.
But by long ab-sence your truth has been tried. Still to your ac - cents I list - en with pride.

Let me be - lieve that you love as you loved, long, long a - go, long a - go.
Still my heart treas-ures the prais - es I heard, long, long a - go, long a - go.
Blest as I was when I sat by your side, long, long a - go, long a - go.

Republic Pictures Page 112
"My Pal Trigger" Script Revision: #4

CROSS DISSOLVE TO WIDE SHOT OF LIVING ROOM, DALE AT PIANO, GABBY IN EASY CHAIR. NIGHT.

Susan plays the piano and sings "Long, Long Ago" while Gabby, smoking his pipe in his wing-backed easy chair, quietly listens.

Produced By
Edward J. White

Directed by
Frank McDonald

Screenplay by
Paul Gangelin, J. Benton Cheney

Starring
Roy Rogers, Dale Evans, Gabby Hayes, Bob Nolan, The Sons of the Pioneers, Trigger

with
Douglas Dumbrille, Tris Coffin, Leyland Hodgson, Tom Quinn, Rudolph Andres, Steve Darrell, George J. Lewis, LeRoy Mason, Peter George Lynn, Iron Eyes Cody,

Prod: #1429 Released: 26 Aug 1946
Black/White - 69min.

Craig (Hodgson) is shot and his safe is burgled. Helen (Dale), whose father was a friend of Craig's, tells Gabby, the sheriff, and Roy about a crest stolen from her father. Courtney (Dumbrille), a foreign secret agent, arrives and is also looking for the crest. The crest holds a secret that is worth much more than its jewelry value.

1. Craig tells Gabby that someone tried to break into his safe.

2. Helen arrives and asks Craig for a singing job in his club.

3. Dan discovers a man robbing the safe in Craig's office and shoots him.

4. Helen tells Roy and Gabby about the crest that she's looking for.

5. To flush out the villains, Gabby pretends to be drunk and tells of finding the crest.

6. Gabby finds the crest inside an old clock.

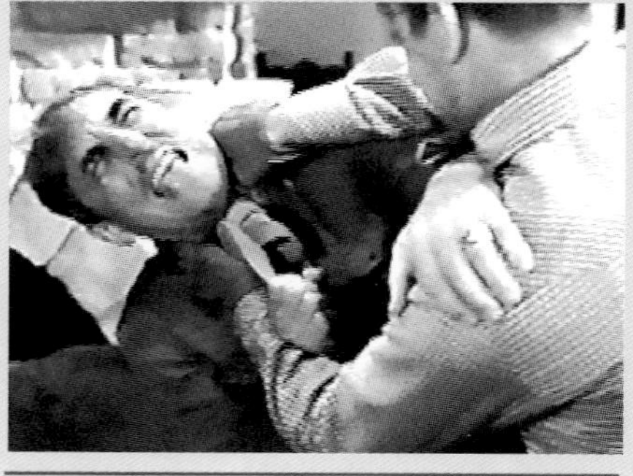

7. Roy fights with one of men who is trying steal the crest.

8. In a blazing shootout, the villains are surrounded by Roy and his Indian friends .

9. Courtney confesses that the crest contains a map to a pitchblende deposit.

NE-HAH-NEÉ
(Clear Water)

(As sung by Roy Rogers and the Sons of the Pioneers
at the annual Indian Pow-Wow)

words & music by
BOB NOLAN

BEAR VALLEY
INDIAN
RESERVATION

Smoothly, with rippling effect

Dm Caug F A7
Long a - go 'twas here I know

Gm6 A7 Dm Gm6 A7
lived the fair- est In - dian maid, daugh - ter of a Chief - tain

Dm Eb7 Dm Caug
brave. Here be - side the lake she stayed. Far and near the

F A7 Gm6 A7 Dm
wa - ters clear blessed her from their deep do - main.

Gm6 Gm7 Caug F
Blessed her with this love - ly name: Ne - Hah

F C7 F
Neé. It must be she is heav - en's daught - er ________

Fdim Gm C7
____ for her eyes and the skies form the lake's clear

F C7 Gm C7
wa - ter. ________ Sun - light plays danc - ing

C7 F
rays when the rip - ples bless her. ________ On the

Republic Pictures Page 5

"Under Nevada Skies" Script Revision: #3

CROSS DISSOLVE FROM OPENING TITLE. PAN RIGHT FOLLOWING HORSEBACK RIDER TO SIGN. HOLD. PAN AND TRUCK LEFT FOLLOWING RIDER TO INDIAN CAMP ENTRANCE. DAY.

Roy and the Pioneers are on vacation. Roy, an honorary member of the tribe, and the Pioneers are giving a performance at the annual Pow-Wow, singing "Ne-Hah-Neé."

I WANT TO GO WEST

(As sung by Dale Evans on the Trading Post Hotel stage)

transcribed by
SCOTT HOMAN
ERIC VAN HAMERSVELD

words & music by
JACK ELLIOTT

Bm Bbdim Am D7
see the smoke when a five gun shoots, to
Bm Bbdim Am D7
meet all the ran - gers in fur pants suits.
G G7/B C C#dim
I want to see them in plat - form boots.
G D7 G C
I want to go west. Oh, let me ride
C G
the lone prai - rie, (yodels) ah - lo - hoo - hee.
G Am D7
With my lit - tle dog - gie bark - in' at my
G G7 C
side. Just let me see,
C G
a cac - tus tree, (yodels) ah - lo - hoo - hee. And I'm
A7 D7
dy - ing to cross the great di - vide.
G Em Am D7
Now, I want to go west, young man. I want to
Bm Bbdim Am D7
rope cor - rals with my old las - sue, to

Republic Pictures
"Under Nevada Skies"

Page 32
Script Revision: #5

CUT TO LONG SHOT OF BOB AND DALE ON STAGE.

Helen goes to see a friend of her father's who owns the Trading Post Hotel. She asks him for a job as a singer in the dinner show. He agrees. Bob overhears the conversation but Roy and the rest of the Pioneers, who are also in the show, don't know she's been hired. On her debut night that evening, Bob introduces her and she sings "I Want To Go West."

UNDER NEVADA SKIES

(As sung by Roy Rogers and Dale Evans at the Indian Pow-Wow)

transcribed by
SCOTT HOMAN
ERIC VAN HAMERSVELD

words & music by
JACK ELLIOTT

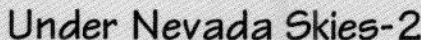

Republic Pictures Page 93
"Under Nevada Skies" Script Revision: #3

FADE UP ON LONG SHOT OF POW-WOW SET AUDIENCE POINT OF VIEW. NIGHT.

Roy and the Sons of the Pioneers have invited Helen to one of the evening get togethers during the Indian Pow-Wow. For entertainment, Roy sings "Under Nevada Skies" accompanied by the Pioneers. During the song, Helen gets up and sings along. Flying Eagle (Lewis) is so impressed with Helen that he says that they may have to make her an honorary member of the tribe.

SEA-GOIN' COWBOY

(As sung by the Sons of the Pioneers on the Trading Post Hotel stage)

transcribed by
SCOTT HOMAN
ERIC VAN HAMERSVELD

words & music by
TIM SPENCER

Dm C Bb A
(Pat) I'm a sea go - in' cow - boy. I ride the waves. I

Dm C Bb A Dm Dm A7
ride the rol - lin' seas. Heave ho, ___ me lads, heave

Dm Dm C
ho. (All) Heave Ho! (Pat) I'm a rough rid - in' pi - rate. I

Bb A Dm C Bb A Dm
have me slaves. They all be - long to me. Heave ho, ___ me

Dm A7 Dm Gm
lads, heave ho. (All) Heave Ho! We sold our sad - dles. We

Bb A7
sold our spurs. We quit herd - in' cat - tle. We hate the curds.

Dm Dm C Bb F C F C7
Ho, ___ me lads, heave ho, heave ho. Heave ho, me ___

F F7
lads, heave ho. (Hugh) Ho, give me a home, on the

Bb Bbm F
bil - low - y foam, where the dear - est of mer - maids

C7 F F7 Bb

play. Where al - ways is heard this en - cour - ag - ing

Bbm Dm Dm A7 Dm

word. Heave, me lads, heave ho. Heave Ho! (Instrumental

Dm A7 Dm A7 Dm

) (Pat) You can

Dm C Bb A Dm C

send all your do - gies to Da - vy Jones, and lock them up be -

Bb A Dm Dm A7 Dm

low. Heave ho, me lads, heave ho. (All) Heave

Dm C Bb A

Ho! (Pat) You can have all your bron - cos and blast their bones, I

Dm C Bb A Dm Dm A7

know where they can go. (All) Heave ho, me lads, heave

Dm Gm

ho. Heave Ho! The sage that's bloom - in', the

Republic Pictures Page 128
"Under Nevada Skies" Script Revision: #4

CUT TO MEDIUM LONG SHOT OF DALE AT TABLE.

Gabby has arrived at the Trading Post Hotel pretending to be drunk. He and Roy have a plan to fool the hotel owner into revealing himself. He makes a bit of a scene and, to calm him down, the hotel owner sits him at Helen's table. On the stage, the Sons of the Pioneers begin their portion of the evening's entertainment, by singing "Sea-Goin' Cowboy."

ANYTIME THAT I'M WITH YOU

(As sung by Roy Rogers and Dale Evans in Gabby's clock shop)

transcribed by
SCOTT HOMAN
ERIC VAN HAMERSVELD

words & music by
JACK ELLIOTT

Bb7 Eb
(Both) Then each mo - ment is like an hour. Each
F7 Bb7
hour just like a day. But
Eb Bb7
let the hands go round with their tick tock sound.
Bb7 Eb
Nev - er mind, we'll find a lot to do.
Eb Bb7
Just for - get the clock and the tick, tick, tock,
Bb7 Eb
an - y - time that I'm with you.
Eb Cm Fm Bb7
(Roy says: You know, they sing this song very nicely south of the border, too.)
Fm Bb7 Eb
(Dale says: Well, here's your guitar, Senior.) (Roy says: Si, si, Senorita.) (Dale says: Bueno.)
Ab Gdim Fm
(Roy in Spanish) Na - da me im - por - ta la vi - da si
Ab7 Db
la - he de vi - vir sin ti.
Bb7 Eb
nun - ca te ol - vi - da - re mi a - mor. Pues

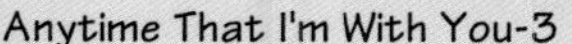

F7 Bb7
morir de - jo tu a - mor si tu

Eb Bb7
me ha - ces que - rer. Yo te ado - ra ___ re

Bb7 Eb
nun - ca nun - ca te ol - vi - da - re ___

Eb Bb7
re - cor - dar que tú e - res ___ pa - ra mi

Bb7 Eb
to - da una fe - li - ci - dad. ___

Bb7 Eb
An - y - time that I'm with you. ___

Republic Pictures Page 137
"Under Nevada Skies" Script Revision: #2

AS SONG BEGINS, FADE UP ON CLOSE UP OF CLOCK SHOP SIGN PAINTED ON WINDOW. THEN CROSS DISSOLVE TO MEDIUM CLOSE UP OF ROY AND DALE INSIDE. DAY.

Helen is taking care of Gabby's clock shop and "Temporary Sheriff Office" while he is fulfilling his sheriff duties. Romance is blossoming and, while Roy is at the shop waiting for Gabby to return, he and Helen, sing "Anytime That I'm With You." Part way into the song, Helen hands Roy a guitar and they sing a verse in Spanish. At the end of song Gabby arrives and is a little miffed that Roy has so much time on his hands when there's so much trouble afoot.

Produced By
Edward J. White

Directed by
William Witney

Screenplay by
Paul Gangelin, Mauri Grashin

Starring
Roy Rogers, Dale Evans, George Hayes, Bob Nolan, The Sons of the Pioneers, Trigger

with
Dennis Hoey, Elizabeth Risdon, Francis McDonald, Edward Keane, Kenne Duncan, Tom London, Harry Strang, Edward Cassidy, Lee Shumway, Steve Darrell, Pierce Lyden

Prod: #1523 Released: 12 September 1946
Black/White - 67min.

Roy, who is working for the "Whirligig" Cattleman's Syndicate, brings peace to a cattlemen-sheepmen range war created by outlaws lead by Gregory (Hoey). Jill (Dale) and Kate (Risdon), are the sheep owners on one side, and Gabby, with the Sons of the Pioneers, are the cattlemen on the other.

1. Gabby, a cattleman, is accused of killing a sheepman.

2. The "Whirligig" Cattleman's Syndicate hires Roy to stop the range war.

3. Gabby takes aim on a lamb that has taken a likin' to him but he doesn't shoot.

4. The Pioneers get a kick out of finding the baby lamb that Gabby hid away.

5. Bad feelings lead to a public fist fight between the cattlemen and sheep owners.

6. Jill is rescued by Roy and Gabby after her sabotaged car goes in the river.

7. Trouble maker, Gregory, tries to persuade Jill to sell her ranch to him.

8. Roy and Trigger are chased by the outlaws.

9. Gabby brings cattlemen and sheep owners to help Roy capture the outlaws.

WHAT'S DOIN' TONIGHT IN DREAMLAND

(As sung by Roy Rogers and the Sons of the Pioneers on Gabby's front porch)

transcribed by
SCOTT HOMAN
ERIC VAN HAMERSVELD

words & music by
JACK ELLIOTT

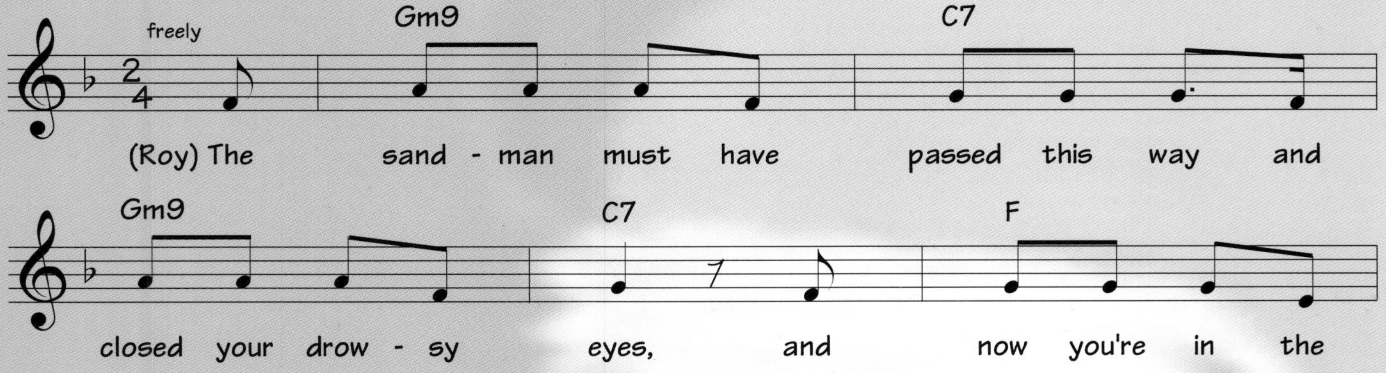

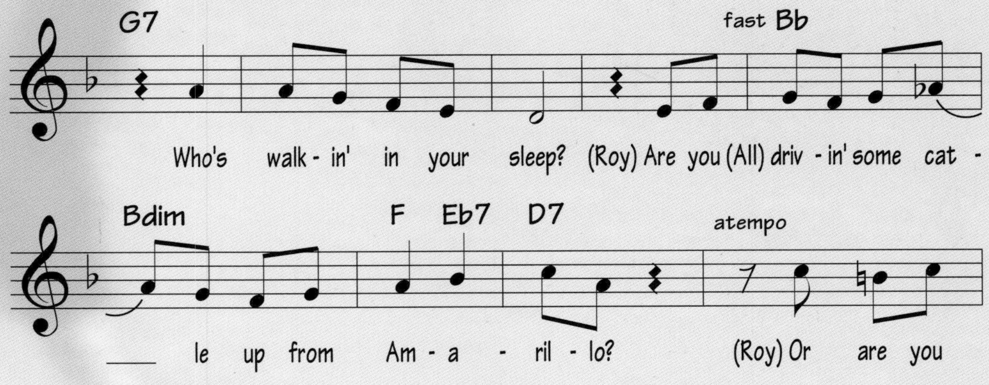

freely
Gm9 C7
(Roy) The sand - man must have passed this way and

Gm9 C7 F
closed your drow - sy eyes, and now you're in the

Dm G9 C7
land of nod so won't you put me wise.
GLISS

tempo
F D7
What's (All) do - in'___ to - night in dream - land?

G7 fast Bb
Who's walk - in' in your sleep? (Roy) Are you (All) driv - in' some cat -

Bdim F Eb7 D7 atempo
___ le up from Am - a - ril - lo? (Roy) Or are you

G7 C7 F
(All) peace-ful - ly count - ing sheep? (Roy) What's (All) do - in'___ to -

What's Doin' Tonight In Dreamland-2
D7 G7
night in dream - land? What's run - nin' through your
G7 fast Bb Bdim
head? (Roy) Are there (All) rust - lers a - fight - in' all a -
F Eb7 D7 atempo G7
cross your pil - low? (Roy) Or is it (All) love on your
C7 F Cm
mind in - stead? (Roy) Are you dream - in' of a
F7 Bb Cm
se - no - ri - ta? Are you keep - in' a
F7 Bb fast G7
ren - dez - vous? Or (All) may - be your chas -
in' a big fat ban - dit. (Pat) More than
C7 Adim C7
like - ly he's chas - in' you. (Bob says: Shhhhh.) (Pat says: QUIET!
slowly atempo F
QUIET!) (All) He's chas - in' you. (Roy) What's (All) do - in' to
F D7 G7
night in dream - land? Your slum - ber - time is

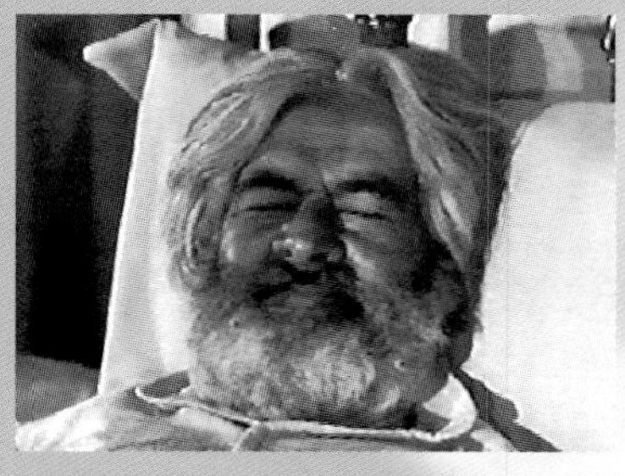

Republic Pictures Page 31
"Roll On, Texas Moon" Script Revision: #2

CUT TO LONG SHOT OF STATION WAGON WITH HORSE TRAILER ENTERING GABBY'S RANCH. NIGHT.

The Pioneers have just found the lamb that followed Gabby home and, for a prank, they toss it into the house where Gabby is sleeping. Roy arrives with Trigger in tow and the Pioneers are delighted to see him. He says it's time to wake Gabby up and has just the way to do it. He grabs his guitar from the backseat and they sing "What's Doin' Tonight In Dreamland." This song alternates tempo from smooth to ruckus. In the end Gabby is awakened and bolts out of bed to meet Roy.

JUMPIN' BEAN

(As sung by the Sons of the Pioneers at the cantina)

transcribed by
SCOTT HOMAN
ERIC VAN HAMERSVELD

words & music by
JACK ELLIOTT

Bb7 F

with your hand.___ (they clap ___

C7 F

___) You'll do the Jump - ing Bean. ___

C7

You'll love it when you do the Jump - ing bean. ___

No se - no - re - ta could be sweet - er when you

F

see her___ jump Jump - in' Bean. The Jump - in'

Bean. (instrumental ___

F C7

F Bb7

___) You'll take the boo - gie beat _

F Bb7
) Then just to beat the band,
F
you beat it with your hand. (they clap
C7 F
) You'll do the Jump - ing Bean.
C7
You'll love it when you do the Jump - in' Bean.
C7
No se - no - ri - ta could be sweet- er when you
F
see her jump Jump - in' Bean. The Jump - in'
Bb7
Bean. The Jump - in' Bean. The Jump - in'
F C7
Bean. The Jump - in' Bean. The Jump - in' Bean. The Jump - in'

Republic Pictures Page 68
"Roll On, Texas Moon" Script Revision: #5

FADE UP ON LONG SHOT OF CANTINA COURTYARD. NIGHT.

At the cantina, due to the continuing animosity, the sheepherders and cattlemen naturally sit on opposite sides of the courtyard. However, Roy and Jill are not immune to a possible budding romance. To Gabby's surprise Jill's lost lamb, which has taken a shine to him, is also in attendance. All the while the Sons of the Pioneers are entertaining the guests with "Jumpin' Bean" that includes a little dancing senorita and clowning around between Pat and Shug. During the song, Jill's prized ram, Hampshire Prince, is killed by the villains.

WON'T YOU BE A FRIEND OF MINE

(As sung by Roy Rogers and Dale Evans in her room at the ranch)

transcribed by
SCOTT HOMAN
ERIC VAN HAMERSVELD

words & music by
JACK ELLIOTT

Republic Pictures Page 93
"Roll On, Texas Moon" Script Revision: #3

CUT TO MEDIUM CLOSE UP OF DALE AT VICTROLA. DAY.

While Jill is cleaning herself up after her car accident and Roy is hanging up her wet clothes, she plays the song "Won't You Be A Friend Of Mine" on her Victrola and sings along. Roy over hears her and comes in through the window to join in. Near the end of the song Bob and Gabby ride up.

ROLL ON TEXAS MOON

(As sung by Roy Rogers and Dale Evans in Gabby's dream)

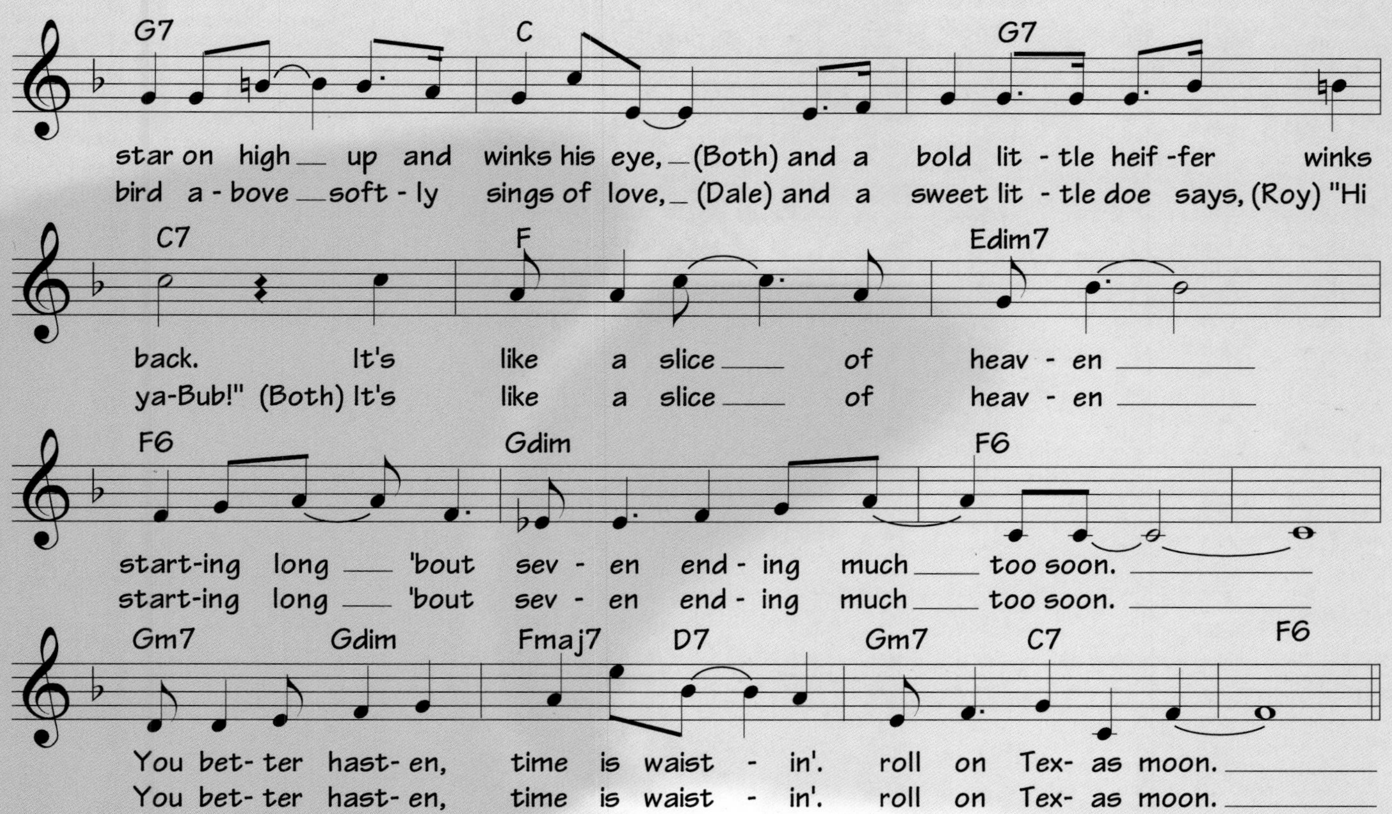

Republic Pictures Page 134
"Roll On Texas Moon" Script Revision: #6

WITH WATERY FX, DISSOLVE FROM EXTREME CLOSE UP OF GABBY SITTING IN A CHAIR IN THE DARK TO HIGH ANGLE CRANE LONG SHOT OF OUTDOOR SCENE IN THE MOONLIGHT. SLOWLY DESCEND TO MEDIUM SHOT OF ROY AND DALE.

Gabby is upset about the rancher/sheepherder situation. He tries to sleep and dreams a happy dream of Roy and Jill singing "Roll On Texas Moon." At the end of the song, as Roy and Jill are getting into a car, it catches fire and Gabby's deam becomes a nightmare which abruptly wakes him.

Produced By
Edward J. White

Directed by
William Witney

Screenplay by
Gerald Geraghty

Starring
Roy Rogers, Dale Evans, Gabby Hayes, Bob Nolan, The Sons of the Pioneers, Trigger

with
Carol Hughes, George Meeker, Lanny Rees, Ruby Dandridge, George Lloyd, Arthur Space, Frank Reicher, George Carleton, The Flying L Ranch Quartet

Prod: #1520 Released: 11 Aug 1946
Black/White - 72min.

Sam Talbot was killed in an accident, or was he? Talbot leaves his ranch to Duke (Rees), his young ward, leaving his niece Jan (Hughes) only $5,000. Roy is the small town newspaper editor and Connie (Dale), who's a St. Louis reporter, are covering the story. Jan enlists Steve (Meeker), her foreman, to help get the ranch and she'll stop at nothing, including killing Duke, to get it.

1. At the reading of Talbot's will, Jan finds out she is not getting the ranch.

2. In a note left by Talbot, Roy and Connie realize that Talbot was murdered.

3. Connie wrote about the possible murder and the sheriff wants the details.

4. At the accident scene, Roy and Connie find Talbot's shattered watch .

5. Roy and Connie are confronted by the crooked coroner while looking for evidence,

6. Jan thinks the coroner will spill the beans, so she shoots him.

7. Duke sees Jan shoot the coroner and tells Roy and Gabby what happened.

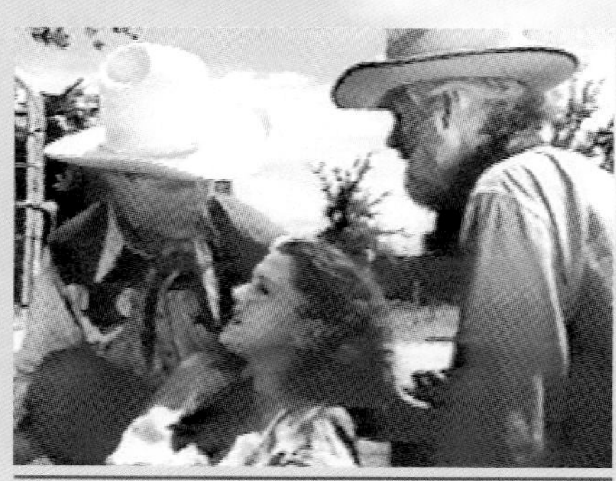
8. Steve, Jan's accomplice, shoots her but she tells Roy everything before she dies.

9. Roy catches up with Steve as he tries to leave on a freight train.

HOME IN OKLAHOMA

Republic Pictures Page 3
"Home In Oklahoma" Script Revision: #2

CUT TO LONG SHOT OF COWBOY AND CATTLE ON OPEN RANGE. DAY.

During the opening credits the chorus sings "Home In Oklahoma." Transition to the Pioneers who sing the song to the end. Part way through, Roy rides in to join the group and the sequence ends on the ranch sign: Talbot Ranch...Hereford Heaven...Oklahoma.

I WISH I WAS A KID AGAIN

(As sung by Roy Rogers in the newspaper office)

Republic Pictures Page 26
"Home In Oklahoma" Script Revision: #3

CROSS DISSOLVE TO MEDIUM LONG SHOT OF ROY AT PRINTING PRESS.

Roy, who is owner of the Hereford Heaven Star newspaper, is busy printing the next edition and singing "I Wish I Was A Kid Again" to pass the time. His assistant, Jimmy, is working with a chicken hatch and gets distracted by Roy singing. The chickens escape and cause havoc as Connie, who is new in town and is also attracted to Roy singing, enters the newspaper office.

THE EVERLASTING HILLS OF OKLAHOMA

(As sung by the Sons of the Pioneers in the ranch house living room)

words & music by
TIM SPENCER

Republic Pictures Page 64
"Home In Oklahoma" Script Revision: #3

CROSS DISSOLVE TO PIONEERS IN RANCH HOUSE LIVING ROOM.

The Pioneers are casually singing "The Everlasting Hills Of Oklahoma" to Connie. Near the end of the song, Roy enters. He's looking for her and is upset that she wrote an article in her newspaper with information that was supposed to be secret.

JAILHOUSE SONG
(As sung by Roy Rogers in the newspaper office)
transcribed by
SCOTT HOMAN
ERIC VAN HAMERSVELD
words & music by
JACK ELLIOTT
Acapella
GLISS
Bb Eb
There once was a gal from St. Lou - ie, ___
F Bb
who went west to vis - it one ___ day.
Eb
A judge that she met liked her so much,
F Bb
he gave her ten years so she'd stay.
Eb Bb
In the jail - house, in the jail -
F Bb
house, he gave her ten years so she'd stay.
Bb Eb
(Dale says: Roy!) She met a real pleas-ant young fel - low, ___
F Bb
and gave him a quick dou - ble - cross.
Bb Eb
She's a - cool - in' her heels in a cell now... (CRASH!)
Republic Pictures
"Home in Oklahoma"
Page 84
Script Revision: #3
CUT TO CLOSE UP OF DALE BEHIND BARS. NIGHT.
Connie is detained by the Sheriff because she would not reveal her source for the Talbot death. Roy, whose newspaper office is next door to the jail, sees her and starts singing "Jailhouse Song." She cuts him off by breaking his window with her shoe.

Republic Pictures Page 91
"Home in Oklahoma" Script Revision: #2

CROSS DISSOLVE TO MEDIUM CLOSE UP. TRUCK BACK LONG SHOT. DAY.

The Breakfast Club is meeting and they start with their club song, the "Breakfast Club Song." The sheriff is there to make sure that Connie understands that he is still suspicious and that she is still being watched.

COWBOY HAM AND EGGS

(As sung by Roy Rogers and the Sons of the Pioneers at the Breakfast Club)

transcribed by
SCOTT HOMAN
ERIC VAN HAMERSVELD

words & music by
TIM SPENCER

Republic Pictures
"Home In Oklahoma"

Page 92
Script Revision: #3

CUT TO LONG SHOT OF PIONEERS GETTING UP FROM TABLE. DAY.

After the Breakfast Club song, Gabby gets up and says that while the gals get the coffee going, Roy and the Pioneers will serve up some "Cowboy Ham and Eggs."

MIGUELITO

(As sung by Dale Evans and Roy Rogers at the Breakfast Club)

transcribed by
SCOTT HOMAN
ERIC VAN HAMERSVELD

words & music by
JACK ELLIOTT

Republic Pictures Page 92
"Home In Oklahoma" Script Revision: #3

CUT TO LONG SHOT BREAKFAST TABLES. DAY.

Roy and Connie are returning to their seats after visiting with the boy, Duke, when Gabby introduces Connie to the club members. Roy tells her that she has to sing for her breakfast. She sings "Miguelito" and drags Roy in to join her. The sheriff keeps his eye on Connie.

HEREFORD HEAVEN

(As sung by the Flying L Ranch Quartet at the Hereford auction)

words & music by
ROY J. TURNER

Republic Pictures
"Home in Oklahoma"

Page 162
Script Revision: #4

FADE UP ON CLOSE UP OF BROCHURE. THEN CROSS DISSOLVE TO LONG SHOT OF CATTLE PEN. DAY.

Roy, Connie, and Gabby show up at the Hereford auction just as the Flying L Ranch Quartet sing "Hereford Heaven" for the entertainment of the attendees.

Produced By
Edward J. White

Directed by
William Witney

Screenplay by
Gerald Geraghty, Julian Zimet

Starring
Roy Rogers, Dale Evans, Gabby Hayes, Bob Nolan, The Sons of the Pioneers, Trigger

with
Paul Harvey, Barry Mitchell, John Bagni, John Phillips, James Taggart, Rex Lease, Steve Darrell, Dove O'Dell, LeRoy Mason, Charles Williams, Eddie Acuff, Clayton Moore

Prod: #1534 Released: 15 Dec 1946
Black/White - 70min.

During the Heldorado Celebration, Roy, a ranger, is asked to stop a money laundering scheme that involves a wealthy playboy, Baxter (Mitchell). Carol (Dale), a friend of Gabby's, has become the honorary deputy sheriff and is determined to help Roy solve the crime. The laundering scheme leads to the murder of Baxter by the big boss, Driscoll (Harvey).

1. Roy pins the honorary deputy sheriff badge on Carol.

2. Baxter is given $250,000 to wash through the gambling casino.

3. Carol is knocked from her horse while following Roy who's after one of the crooks.

4. Baxter has been killed. Carol is taking notes as if she really is a deputy sheriff.

5. Roy and Carol find the car that left tracks at the Baxter murder scene.

6. To keep the villains from receiving more money, Carol rips the claim tags off.

7. During the treasure hunt race, Pat finds a message that says to go help Roy.

8. Roy and Carol encounter the villains at the baggage claim office.

9. Driscoll is caught running out of the claim's office and is arrested.

SILVER STARS, PURPLE SAGE, EYES OF BLUE

(As sung by Roy Rogers in the hotel banquet room)

words & music by
DENVER DARLING

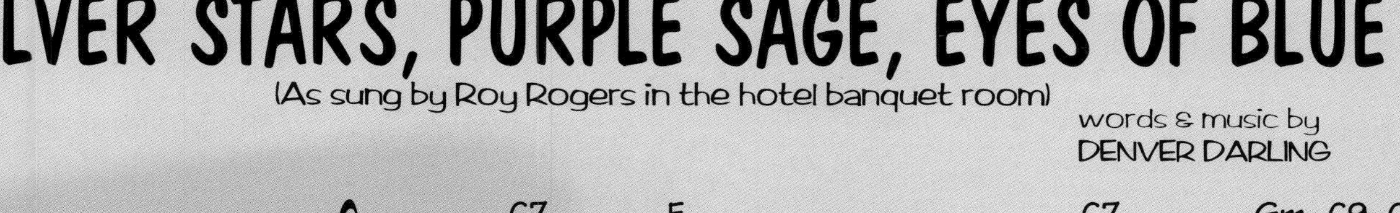

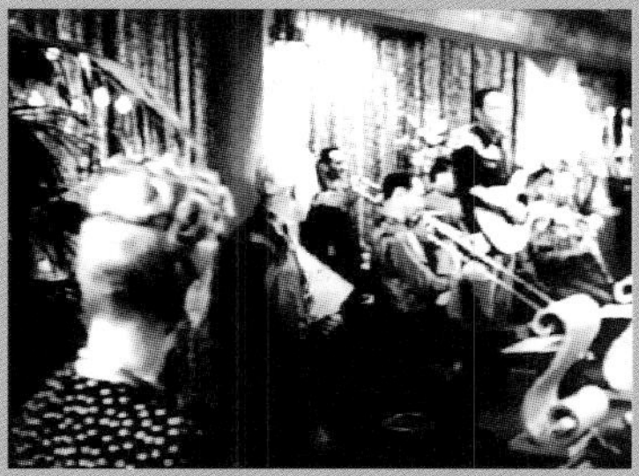

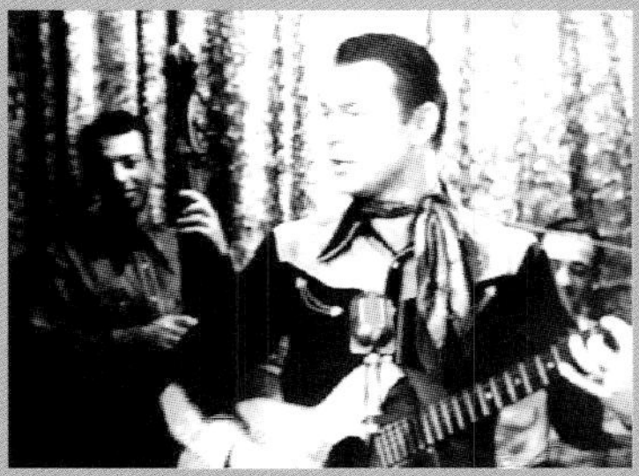

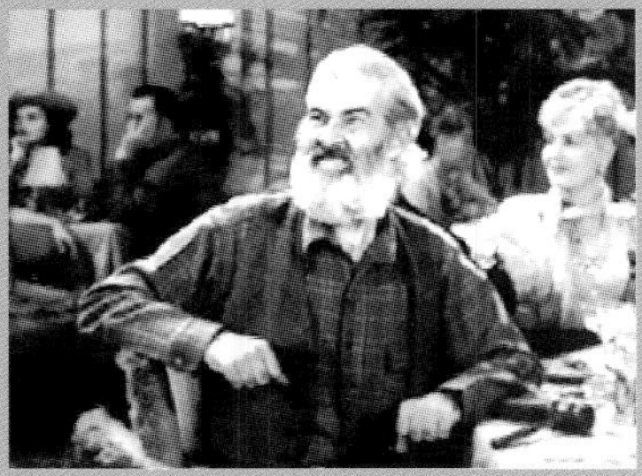

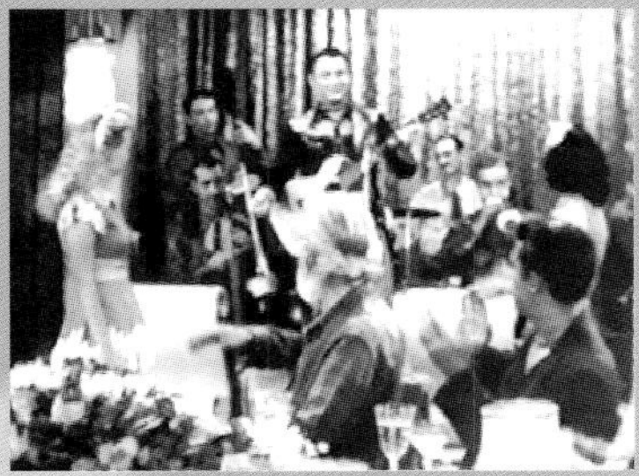

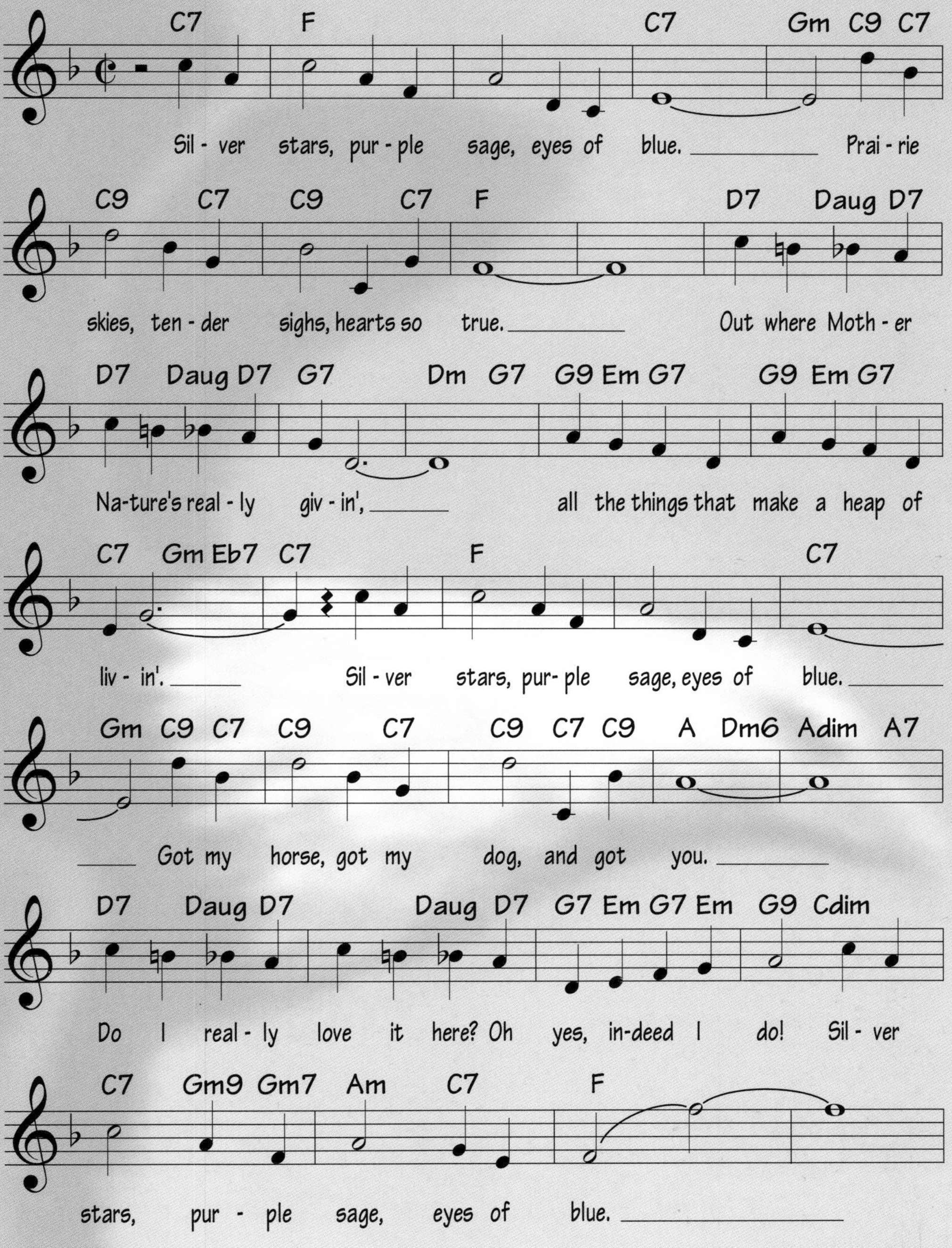

C7 F C7 Gm C9 C7
Sil - ver stars, pur - ple sage, eyes of blue. ____ Prai - rie
C9 C7 C9 C7 F D7 Daug D7
skies, ten - der sighs, hearts so true. ____ Out where Moth - er
D7 Daug D7 G7 Dm G7 G9 Em G7 G9 Em G7
Na-ture's real - ly giv - in', ____ all the things that make a heap of
C7 Gm Eb7 C7 F C7
liv - in'. ____ Sil - ver stars, pur- ple sage, eyes of blue. ____
Gm C9 C7 C9 C7 C9 C7 C9 A Dm6 Adim A7
____ Got my horse, got my dog, and got you. ____
D7 Daug D7 Daug D7 G7 Em G7 Em G9 Cdim
Do I real - ly love it here? Oh yes, in-deed I do! Sil - ver
C7 Gm9 Gm7 Am C7 F
stars, pur - ple sage, eyes of blue. ____

Republic Pictures
"Heldorado"

Page 26
Script Revision: #2

CUT TO LONG SHOT OVER DALE'S SHOULDER OF BANQUET ROOM STAGE.

Roy accidentally mistakes Carol for the hotel's restaurant hat check girl. Later, she hears him singing "Silver Stars, Purple Sage, Eyes of Blue" for the Heldorado committee meeting in the banquet room and goes in to listen. A surprised Roy notices her as she walks by and seems to sing the rest of the song to her.

HELDORADO

(As sung by the cast in the Heldorado Parade)

F G7 C
And the dudes are dressed in their west - ern
G7 C7
best as they join the big pa - rade.
F
A Hel - do - ra - do, a Hel - do - ra - do,
the blues will nev - er do, so lend an ear.
D7 Gm C7 F A7
If you wear a grin, part - ner, you'll be
Dm Gm C7 F
in. Hel - do - ra - do is here.
Bb C7 F
There'll be songs you know when the lights are low,
Bb C7 F
tell - ing tales of trails gone by.
G7 C
And it may - be you'll find a ren - dez -
G7 C7
vous, if the moon gets in your eyes.

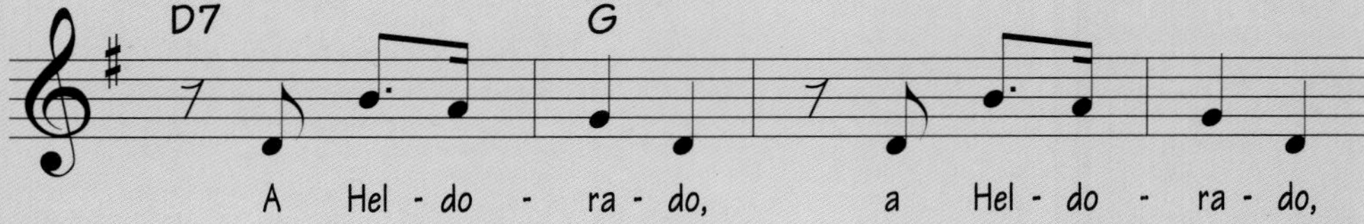

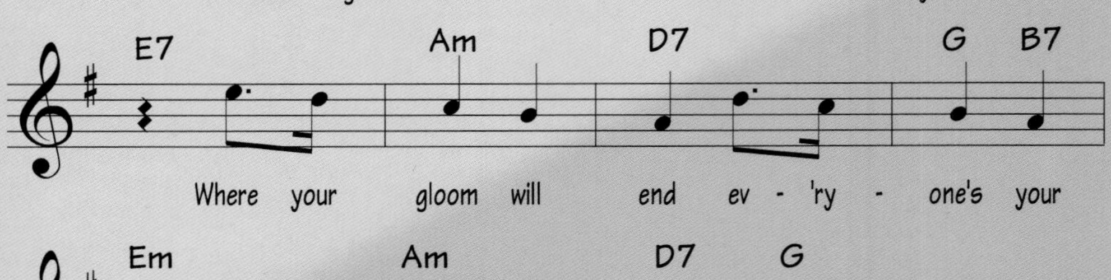

Republic Pictures Page 66
"Heldorado" Script Revision: #3

CUT TO LONG SHOT OF STREET WITH PARADE. DAY.

It's the day of the Heldorado Parade and during a quick photo shoot before the parade begins, Roy, a ranger, and Carol, the honorary sheriff, agree to get along with each other. The parade starts with a marching band followed by Roy, Carol, the Pioneers, Gabby, and various floats. All the participants are singing "Heldorado." Among the bystanders along the street is one of the henchmen disguised with a beard. He is out to shoot Roy but is foiled in his attempt by a little girl running through the crowd who bumps him.

MY SADDLE PALS AND I

(As sung by Roy Rogers and the Sons of the Pioneers at the rodeo)

words & music by
ROY ROGERS

My Saddle Pals And I-2

Ab Bdim Bbm Eb7 Ab Db Dbm Ab
sad - dle pals and I.
verse
Ab C7 Fm
(Roy) We're side by side in the sad - dle, thru
Eb7 Cm Eb7 Ab Adim Eb7
sun - shine and thru rain. We
Ab C7 Fm
ride, ride, ride in the sad - dle
Eb7 Bb7 Eb7 Ebaug
o'er the bar - ren plain.

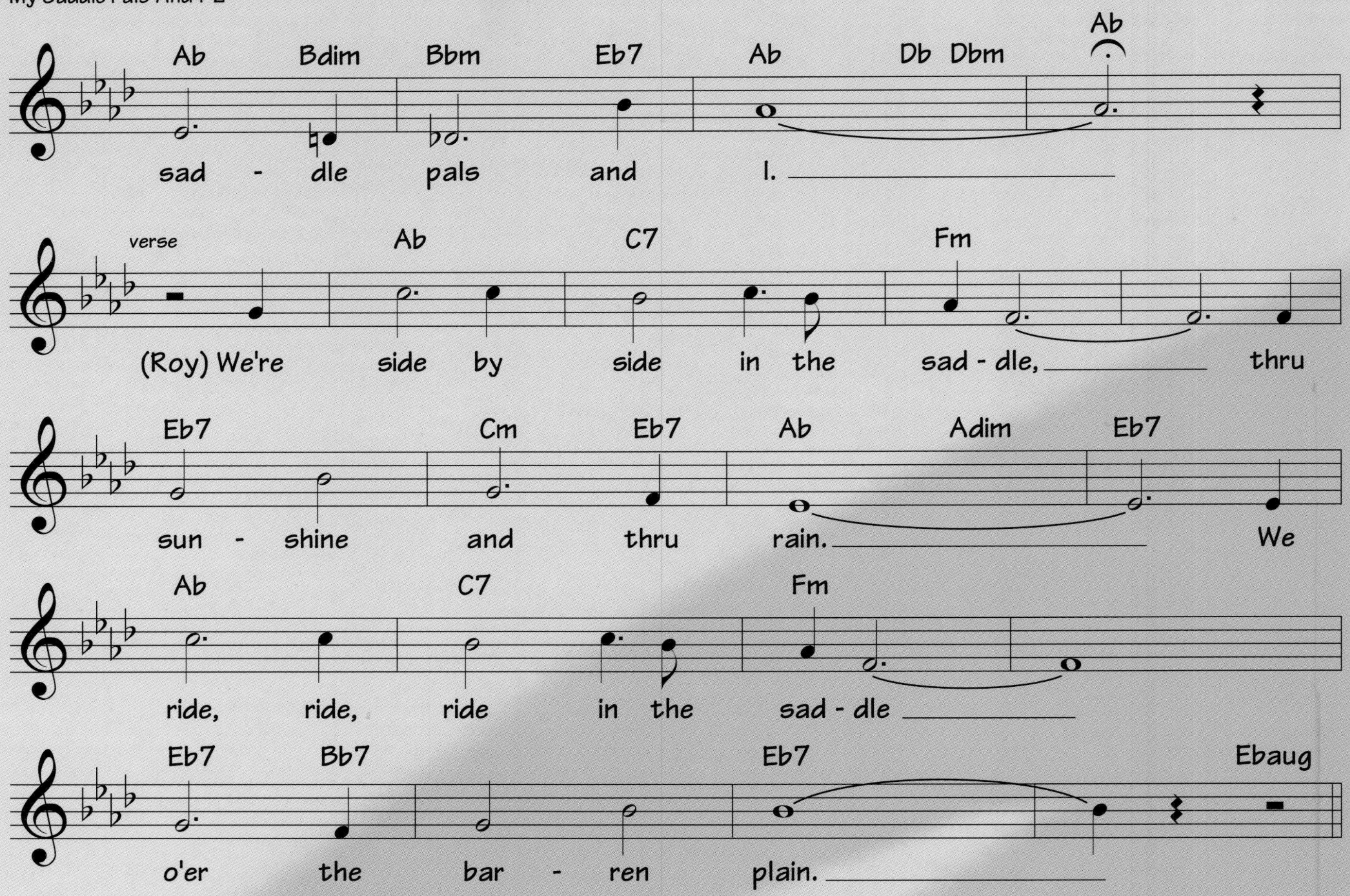

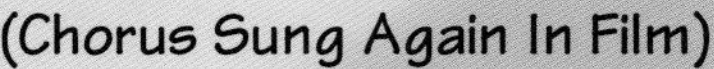

(Chorus Sung Again In Film)

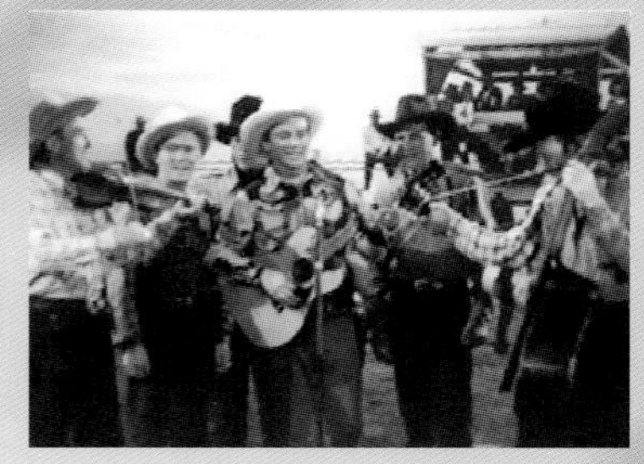

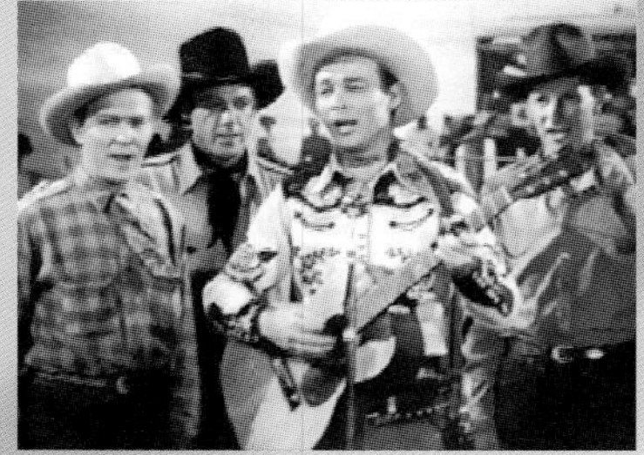

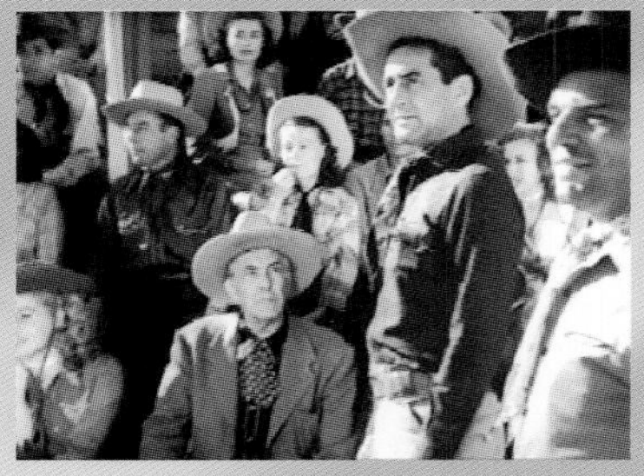

Republic Pictures Page 85
"Heldorado" Script Revision: #2

CUT TO LONG SHOT OF ROY ENTERING RODEO ARENA ON TRIGGER. DAY.

It's the day of the Heldorado Rodeo and the special guest is Roy Rogers. Roy rides in on Trigger and introduces the Sons of the Pioneers. The Pioneers run out to the center of the arena and they all sing "My Saddle Pals And I." While Roy has been occupied singing in the rodeo, the villain's henchmen have killed Alex Baxter. They return to the rodeo and check in with their boss just as Roy and the Pioneers are finishing their song.

GOOD NEIGHBOR

(As sung by Roy Rogers and Dale Evans in the outdoor jail)

Good Neighbor-2
D7
cy. And we should nev - er for - get that we're
Dm G7 C
one big fam - i - ly. So it's plain to see you
can't go wrong. Just stop and help some - one a - long.
Dm G7 Dm G7 Dm G7
Be a good, good, good, good, good, good, be a good, good
C G7 C
neigh - bor. (Roy in Spanish) Si un ami - go ne - ce - si -
ta pla - ta pues pres - te - ce - la por fa - vor
Dm G7 Dm G7 C
sea un buen, buen, buen, buen, buen, a - mi - go.
No tie - ne chis - te es - tar asi sin
na - die que me quie - ra. A mi se -
Dm G7 Dm G7 C
a un buen, buen, buen, buen, buen a - mi - go.
C7
Em - pie - ze a - lla en el sur, con

Good Neighbor-3

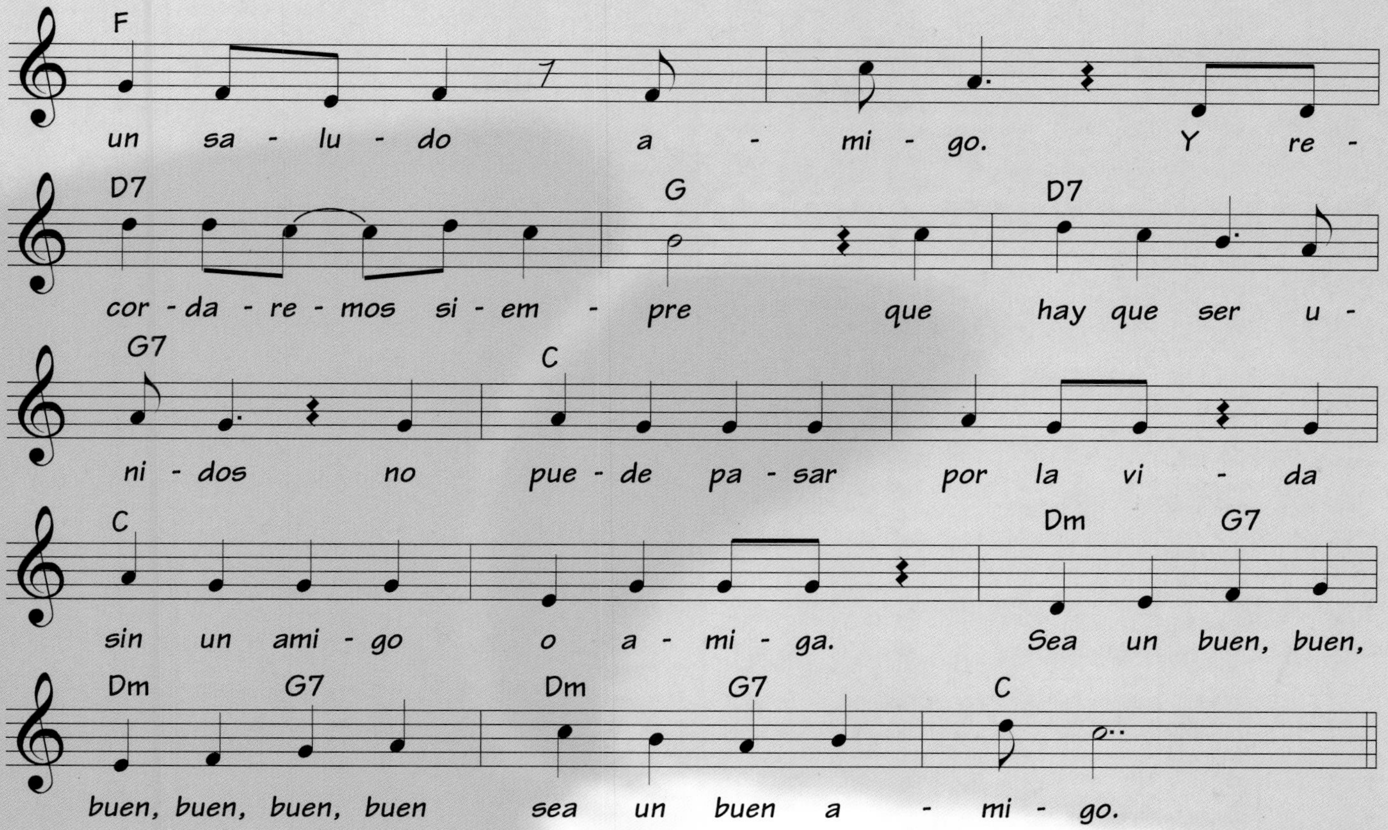
F
un sa - lu - do a - mi - go. Y re -
D7 G D7
cor - da - re - mos si - em - pre que hay que ser u -
G7 C
ni - dos no pue - de pa - sar por la vi - da
C Dm G7
sin un ami - go o a - mi - ga. Sea un buen, buen,
Dm G7 Dm G7 C
buen, buen, buen, buen sea un buen a - mi - go.

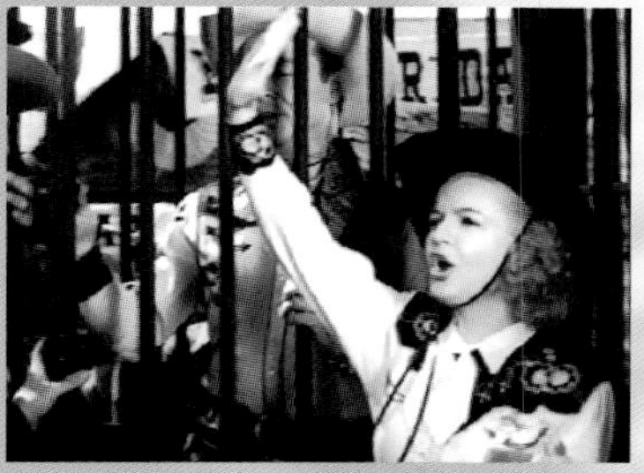

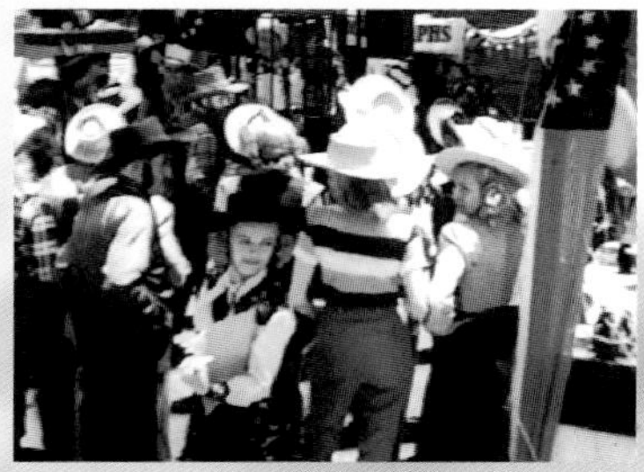

PARKING

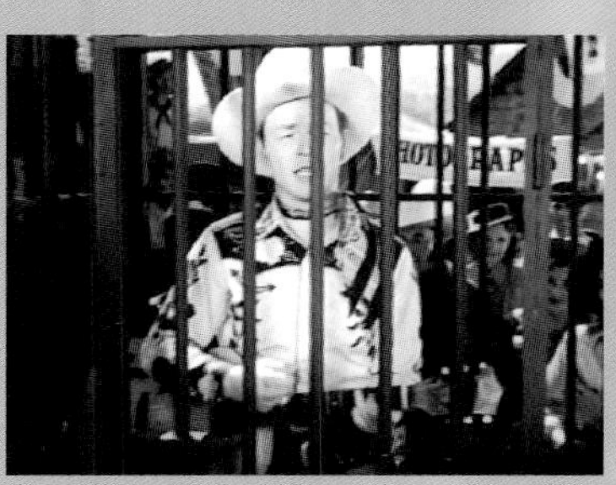

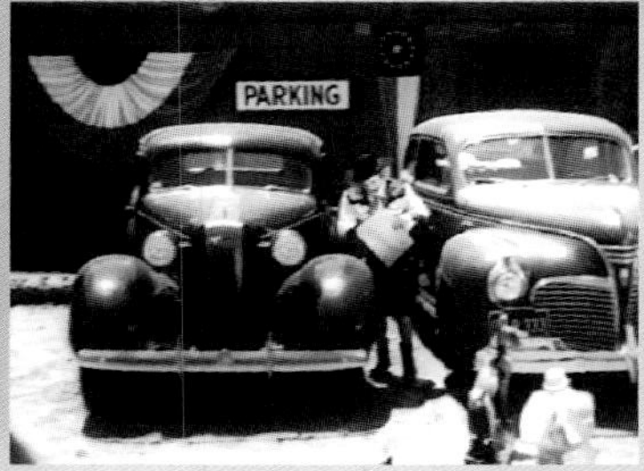

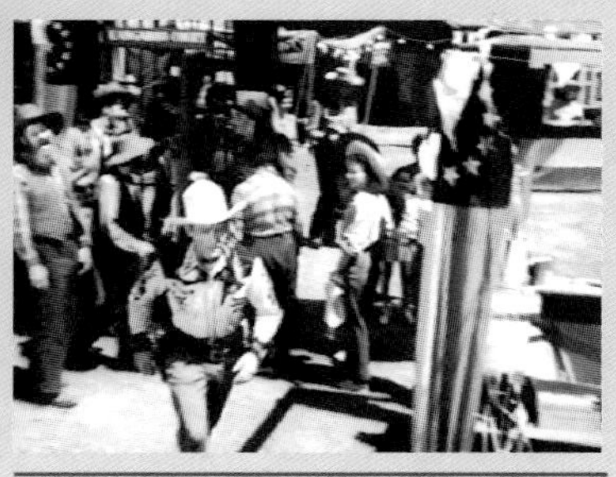

Republic Pictures Page 121
"Heldorado" Script Revision: #5

CUT TO LONG SHOT OF STREET WITH JUDGE, CROWD, AND JAIL. DAY.

Roy and Carol have photos of the tire tracks from the car that was at Baxter's murder scene. On the way to check out various cars, Carol wants time to do some of her own investigating, so she has Roy "arrested" for not having a beard for Heldorado. He has to sing to be released, so he sings "Good Neighbor." Carol sings along. Then while he sings the song in Spanish, she runs away to do her snooping.

YOU AIN'T HEARD NOTHIN' TILL YOU HEAR HIM ROAR

(As sung by the Sons of the Pioneers at the hotel/casino)

transcribed by
SCOTT HOMAN
ERIC VAN HAMERSVELD

words & music by
BOB NOLAN

Bb Ddim Eb Bb
(Pat) On my chest they cracked and they all bounced back and
Eb F7 Bb F7
killed poor Jes - se dead. (Pat) I'm a
(All) You ain't heard noth - in' till you hear him roar.
Bb Eb
high strung lad and my temp - er 'ment's bad and the
F7 Bb F7
least thing makes me sore.
(All) You ain't heard noth - in' till you hear him
Bb Bb Ddim Eb Bb
(Pat) When my teeth I gnash like a light-ning flash the
roar.
Eb Bb
sparks fly ev - 'ry - where. (All) Like a light - ning flash the
F7 Bb Ddim
sparks fly ev - 'ry - where. (Pat) I can roar so loud that the
Eb Edim Bb F7 Bb
thun - der - cloud will burst in the trem-bling air.
(All) You ain't heard noth - in' till you
F7 Bb Eb
(Pat) I'm a high strung lad and my tem - per-'ment's bad and the
hear him roar.
F7 Bb F7
least thing makes me sore.
(All) You ain't heard noth - in' till you hear him

Bb Ddim Eb Bb
roar. (Pat) When they made this land they need-ed a plan for the
Eb Bb
tough-est man to be. (All) They need-ed a plan for the
F7 Bb Ddim
tough-est man to be. (Pat) So the re-ci-pe came and they
Eb Bb F7 Bb
built the frame and then they as-sem-bled me.
(All) You ain't heard noth-in' till you
F7 Bb Eb
(Pat) I'm a high strung lad and my tem-per-'ment's bad and the
hear him roar.
F7 Bb F7
least thing makes me sore.
(All) You ain't heard noth-in' till you hear him
Bb Eb Bb
(Pat) Now, I'm tak-in' this time to ex-plain this rhyme in a
roar.
Eb Bb F7
man-ner un-pro-fane. (All) He's tak-in' his time in a man-ner un-pro-
Bb Ddim
fane. (Pat) But I'm a warn-in' youse guys with a
Eb Edim Bb F7
batch of black eyes, bet-ter smile when you speak my
(All) You

Republic Pictures Page 126
"Heldorado" Script Revision: #3

CUT TO LONG SHOT OF HOTEL LOBBY AREA.

Roy enters the hotel/casino as the Sons of the Pioneers begin singing "You Ain't Heard Nothin' Till You Hear Him Roar," with Pat Brady as the lead. During the song, Roy notices that two of the men he suspects are involved in the Baxter murder are passing a large amount of high dollar cash to one of the hotel employees.

Produced By
Edward J. White

Directed by
William Witney

Screenplay by
Gerald Geraghty

Starring
Roy Rogers, Dale Evans, Bob Nolan, The Sons of the Pioneers, Trigger

with
Olin Howlin, George Meeker, John Laurenz, Rus Vincent, Minerva Urecal, LeRoy Mason, Donna DeMario, Terry Frost, Conchita Leone, Tex Terry

Prod: #1526 Released: 15 Feb 1947
Trucolor - 75min.

Roy has his own oil company and discovers oil on Carlos' (Vincent) ranch and wants to drill. Carlos says his cousin, Rosa (DeMario) owns half the ranch and doesn't want it drilled. Calhoun (Meeker), who owns a gambling ship, also wants the ranch and lures Carlo into losing so he can have him payoff with the ranch. Billie (Dale) owns a tugboat and helps Roy foil Calhoun's scheme.

1. Roy and Alkali (Howlin), Carlos' foreman, discover oil in a cave on Carlos' ranch.

2. Calhoun tells Carlos that he must pay up the $147,000 he owes or lose the ranch.

3. Billie, disguised as cousin Rosa, is rescued by Roy when the crooks try to capture her.

4. Roy and Alkali break in and find Carlos' I.O.U.s in Calhoun's gambling ship office.

5. Calhoun accuses his man, Pete (Laurenz), of leading Roy to the I.O.U.s and kills him.

6. Carlos realizes that Calhoun is behind all the trouble.

7. Calhoun and his men shoot it out with with Roy and the posse.

8. Roy fights with Calhoun and brings him in.

9. In appreciation for all his help, Carlos and his cousin give Roy the oil drilling rights.

RIDE, VAQUEROS, RIDE

(As sung by Roy Rogers and the vaqueros riding on the trail)

transcribed by
SCOTT HOMAN
ERIC VAN HAMERSVELD

words & music by
JACK ELLIOTT

Republic Pictures Page 22
"Apache Rose" Script Revision: #2

FADE UP TO LONG SHOT OF RIDERS AND WAGON ON THE TRAIL. DAY.

Carlos and his vaqueros are helping Roy deliver the oil drilling equipment he has just unloaded from Billie's boat. To pass the time, they sing "Ride, Vaqueros, Ride."

JOSÉ

(As sung by Dale Evans and the Sons of the Pioneers at the restaurant)

transcribed by
SCOTT HOMAN
ERIC VAN HAMERSVELD

words & music by
TIM SPENCER
GLENN SPENCER

Eb Bb7
sé. With a
Eb Bb7
tweest of hees wreest and a bleenk from his eyes, all the
Eb Bb7
sweet se - no - ri - tas are mak - ing with sighs, ev - 'ry
Eb Bb7 Eb
day for Jo - sé. He's a
Abm
root - ta - ti - too, scoot - in',
Eb
root - in', toot - in', shoot - in' ca - bal - le - ro.
Abm
And the way he makes love, Oh! My
Abm Bb7
gol - lies a - bove, eets a shame. Jo -
Eb Bb7 Eb Bb7
sé, keeps hav - ing his way. My gol - ly, he's
Eb Bb7
knock - in' 'em sil - ly with kees - es and stuff. He's not
Eb Bb7
tel - ling them some - theeng, and treat - ing them rough, so they

Eb Bb7
say. Jo - sé, (Dale) down Mex - i - co
Eb Bb7 Eb
way. Gee wheel - i - kers, hees rep - u - ta - tion, it's
Bb7 Eb
good and it's bad he's a real kil - ler dil - ler and
Bb7 Eb Bb7
he can be had (Sons) so they say. Don Jo -
Eb Bb7 Bb7
sé. (Dale) With a twist of his wrist and a
Bb7 Eb
blink from his eyes, oh, sweet se - no - ri - tas are
Bb7 Eb Bb7
mak- ing with sighs (Sons) ev - 'ry day for Jo -
Eb
sé. He's a
Abm
root - ta - ti toot, scoot - in'
Eb
root - tin', toot - in', shoot - in' ca - bal - le - ro.
Abm
(Dale) And the way he makes love, Oh! My

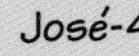

Abm Eb
gol - lies a - bove, it's a shame, (All) Jo -

Eb Bb7 Eb Bb7
sé keeps hav - ing his way. My gol - ly he's

Eb Bb7
knock - in' 'em sil - ly with kees - es and stuff. He's not

Eb Bb7
tel - lin' them some - theeng and treat - ing them rough, so they

Eb Bb7 Eb
say. Jo - sé, Jo - sé.

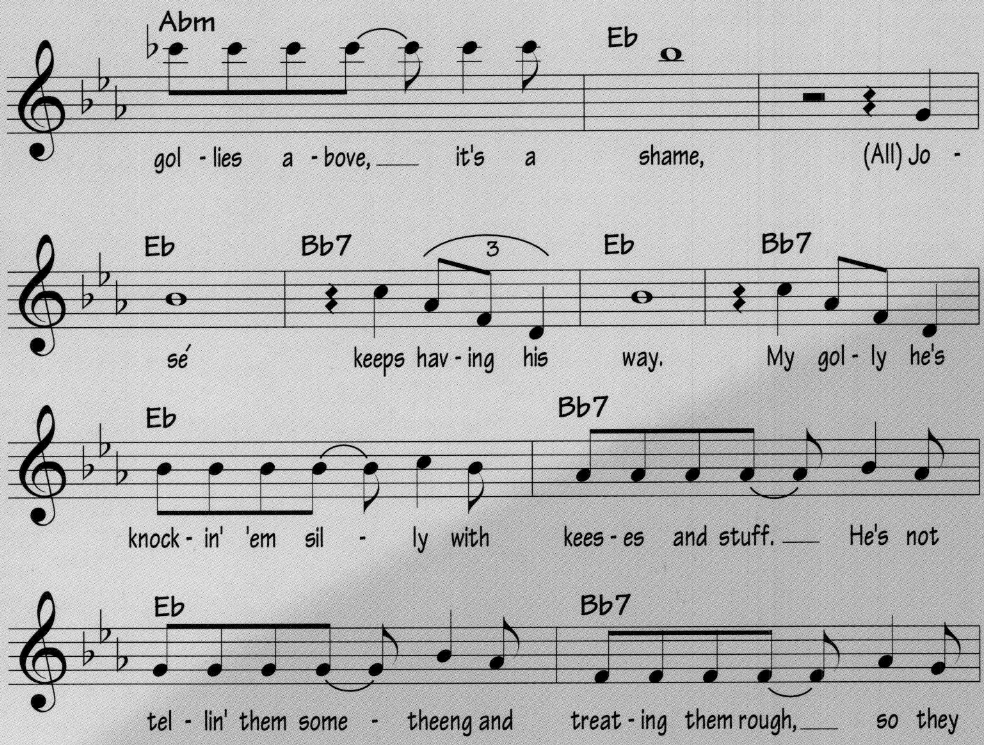

Republic Pictures Page 53

"Apache Rose" Script Revision: #4

CUT TO MEDIUM SHOT OF DALE AT RESTAURANT TABLE WITH OWNER. DAY.

Billie has told her friend, the owner of the restaurant, that she has found a group of Mexican entertainers for him. These "Mexican" entertainers are really her friends, the Sons of the Pioneers, who have tried to disguise themselves with phony mustaches, sombreros, serapes, etc. The restaurant owner wants them to audition. Billie brings them on and they sing "José" in a very bad Mexican accent. During the song Roy rides in and enjoys the music. The restaurant owner gets suspicious when Pat sees Roy, lowers his mustache, and says, "Hi!" Billie quickly steps in between the owner and the Pioneers and sings the last chorus with them to distract him. The restaurant owner isn't buying it.

WISHING WELL

(As sung by Roy Rogers at Dale's rancho party)

Republic Pictures Page 110
"Apache Rose" Script Revision: #3

FADE UP TO LONG SHOT OF ROY AND THE PIONEERS BY THE WISHING WELL IN THE COURTYARD OF CARLOS' RANCHO. DAY.

Someone has tried to kill Rosa, Carlos' cousin and half owner of the rancho. Billie has disguised herself as Rosa to protect her and, in disguise, has asked Roy to entertain at the party for Rosa. Roy, accompanied by the Pioneers, serenades the guests at the party with "Wishing Well." Billie, still in disguise, likes Roy more and more every day. Roy knows she's not Rosa and that she is getting sweet on him. To make her a little jealous, he pretends to sing to another pretty senorita.

THERE'S NOTHING LIKE COFFEE IN THE MORNIN'

(As sung by Dale Evans on the boat)

Gm C7
Just re - ar - range your
F7
point of view. What ap - peals to you? There's
Bb Bb Bb7
noth - in' like cof - fee in the morn - in'. It
Eb Cm Dm G7
hits the spot, all right. No, there's
Cm
noth - in' like ba - con when you're wak - in' and noth -
C7 F7 Bb
- in' like kiss - es at night. Ahh,
Fm Bb7
'neath the moon, all you
Eb
want to do is coo like a kit - ten.
Gm C7
Sun ris - es soon, and
F7
then you'll find ja - va's on your mind. There's

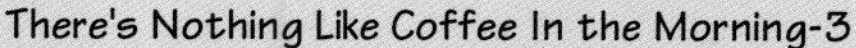

Republic Pictures
"Apache Rose"

Page 147
Script Revision: #3

FADE UP ON LONG SHOT OF DALE'S BOAT. DAY.

To throw off the villains, Roy has pretended to kill Rosa, who was really Billie is disguise. The sheriff locks him up but he escapes from jail with the help of Carlos, Alkali, and the Pioneers. Back on her boat, Billie is making breakfast for Roy and Alkali, who are hiding out in a cave near her anchorage. She sings "There's Nothing Like Coffee In the Morning." At the end of the song, she yells for the boysand they come 'a running.

APACHE ROSE

(As sung by the Sons of the Pioneers in the cave)

transcribed by
SCOTT HOMAN
ERIC VAN HAMERSVELD

words & music by
JACK ELLIOTT

Republic Pictures Page 170
"Apache Rose" Script Revision: #3

FADE UP THE LONG SHOT OF DALE AND THE PIONEERS IN THE CAVE AROUND A CAMPFIRE. NIGHT.

Roy is meeting the Pioneers at the cave near Billie's boat so that they can follow one of the villain's men out to the gambling ship. While the Pioneers wait for Roy, they sing "Apache Rose" for Billie. Roy rides in on Trigger near the end of the song.

Produced By
Edward J. White

Directed by
William Witney

Screenplay by
Sloan Nibley

Starring
Roy Rogers, Dale Evans, Andy Devine, Bob Nolan, The Sons of the Pioneers, Trigger

with
John McGuire, Olaf Hytten, David Sharp, Fritz Leiber, Hank Patterson, Eddie Acuff, Fred S. Toones, James Linn, Ray "Doc" Adams, Whitey Christy, Charles Sullivan, Ray Turner, Eddie Parker, Fred Graham

Prod: #1525 Released: 15 May 1947
Trucolor - 78min.

Roy, a border investigator, and Cookie Bullfincher (Devine), the local sheriff, are out to solve a mystery concerning a mine that straddles the border between the U.S. and Mexico. The mine is owned by Gridley (McGuire). Writer, Lee Madison, A.K.A. Helen (Dale) arrives to get material for her new book. A Mr. Bates (Hytten) is looking for a missing George Lancaster. He makes Cookie nervous.

RR

1. Roy confronts Gridley about the killing of his foreman, Gus (Sharp).

2. Everyone expected Lee Madison to be a man. She decides not tell them "he's" a she.

3. At the mine, Roy is beaten by Ulrich (Sharp), Gridley's man.

4. Mr. Bates, an Englishman, asks Roy and Cookie about a George Lancaster.

5. Roy finally learns that Lee, going by the name of Helen, is really Madison.

6. Bates is attacked by two of Gridley's men and left for dead.

7. The entrance to a mine in Mexico that connects with Gridley's is discovered.

8. Roy fights Gridley and Ulrich. Gridley goes over the cliff and Roy brings Ulrich in.

9. Cookie is the missing Lancaster and the heir to the Earl of Lancaster's estate.

BELLS OF SAN ANGELO

(As sung by Roy Rogers, the Sons of the Pioneers, Andy Devine, and the Padre while riding on the trail)

transcribed by
SCOTT HOMAN
ERIC VAN HAMERSVELD

words & music by
JACK ELLIOTT

F7 Bb
tell of an old, but a true love, the
C7 Cm F7
love that I keep in my heart. For the
Bb Cm F7
bells of San An - ge - lo call to me, "Come
Cm F7 Bb
back. Come back." they sing. I know that my
Cm F7 Cm
heart ev - er there will be when the bells of San
F7 Ddim G7 Cm
An - ge - lo ring, when the bells of San
F7 Bb Fm
An - ge - lo ring. (In Spanish) Di - le que
Bb7 Eb G7
nun - ca me de - je, que nun - ca se
Cm F7
va - lla de aqui. Di - le que
Bb C7
so - to la muer - te me lla - ma pon -

Republic Pictures Page 2
"Bells of San Angelo" Script Revision: #2

FADE UP MEDIUM LONG SHOT OF BELLS. DAY.

Through the opening titles, Roy, Cookie, the Sons of the Pioneers, and the Padre (riding on a donkey) sing "Bells of San Angelo" while riding the trail to the mission .

HOT LEAD

(As sung by Pat Brady and the Sons of the Pioneers in the wagon on the trail)

transcribed by
SCOTT HOMAN
ERIC VAN HAMERSVELD

words & music by
TIM SPENCER

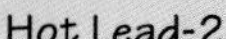

Bb F
ups and let it hail, hot lead,___ (gun shots) hot

C7
lead.___ (gun shots) Found a - noth - er three or four, I just

ups and let it pour, hot lead, (gun shots) hot shot

F Bb
lead. (gun shots) (Sons) The west is wild and wool - ly, and it's

F Bb
tough - er than a boot. Shoot - in' irons are al - ways

Bb F C7
itch - in', ach - in' fer some - one to shoot. (Pat) Let a

F Bb
ban - dit come in sight, I'll just up and pours 'em

F C7
white hot lead. (gun shots) Ho - o - o - o - ot - th

GLISS F
th - th le - ad! (Sons yell: Hot Lead!)

Republic Pictures Page 31
"Bells of San Angelo" Script Revision: #3

CUT TO EXTREME LONG SHOT OF WAGON ON TRAIL. DAY.

Roy and the Pioneers want to give Lee Madison, a dime-novel western writer, a real west reception in the form of a holdup. While Roy hides out in the hills, the Pioneers meet the bus. When Helen, who is really Lee Madison and keeps it to herself, gets off they think they've missed "Mr." Madison. She's on her way to the lodge, so they offer her a ride. On the way they sing "Hot Lead." At the end of the song, Roy, who doesn't know that "Mr" Madison isn't on the wagon, stages the holdup ruse.

COWBOY'S DREAM OF HEAVEN

(As sung by Roy Rogers and the Sons of the Pioneers at the lodge)

F7

strum - min' out ____ a west - ern mel - o - dy ____

Bb7

____ (All) in that cow - boy's dream of

Eb

heav - en. (Roy) While on a dis - tant hill a coy -

F7

- ote's croon - in' out the harm - o -

Bb7 Eb

ny (All) in that cow - boy's dream of

Ab

heav - en. (Roy) He may be wea - ry____ from

Eb Cm

rid - in' all ____ the day. (All) But when the sha - dows

F7 Bb7

fall a - round you're sure to hear him

Eb

say, (Roy) "Give me a lit - tle bit ______ of

F7

range land and per - haps a pal or

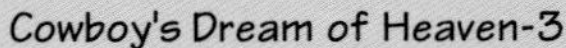

Republic Pictures Page 55
"Bells of San Angelo" Script Revision: #4

CUT TO CLOSE UP OF ROY SINGING WITH THE PIONEERS IN THE BACK.

Lee Madison is supposed to be at the lodge for a party in his honor but he hasn't shown up yet. Meanwhile, Roy and the Pioneers are entertaining the guests with "Cowboy's Dream of Heaven." During the song, Roy notices two men from the mining camp arrive and it bothers him. Helen is also there and his attention is quickly shifted to her. He and the others still don't know that Helen is Lee Madison, a girl.

I LOVE THE WEST

(As sung by Dale Evans at the lodge)

transcribed by
SCOTT HOMAN
ERIC VAN HAMERSVELD

words & music by
JACK ELLIOTT

I Love the West-2
accel. G Em Am D7
sun keeps shin - in' and the gals are pin - in', where the
G Em Am D7
light is light - er and the boys are bright - er. That's
Am D7 G C
why I love the west. Where the he - ro,
G Am
strong and si - lent, keeps the lit - tle
D7 G n.c. Em
gal from harm. Fight - in' twen - ty
n.c. Em
thou - sand In - di - ans, or pay - ing off the
A7 Gb
mort - gage on the farm. Yes, I love the
Bbdim Am7 Am7(b5)
west. For ev - 'ry - thing's best in the west, where the
accel. G Em Am D7
days are hot - ter and the nights are cold - er, where the
G Em Am D7
young are young - er and the old are old - er, where the

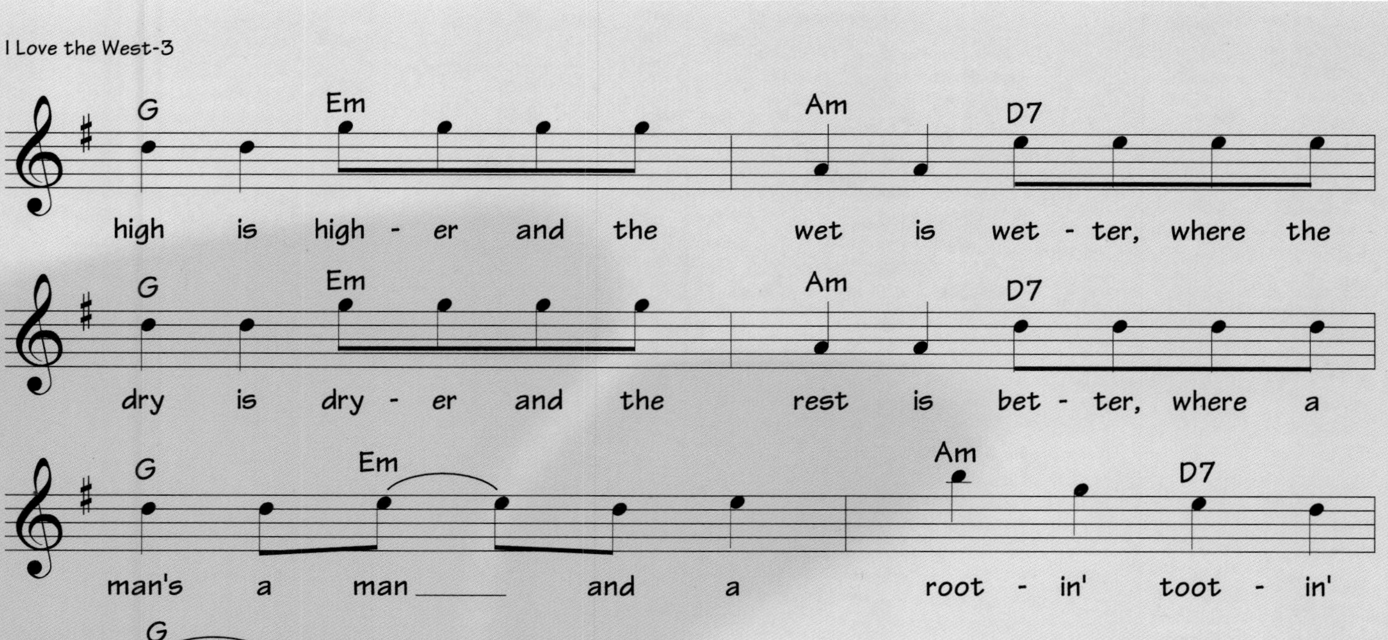

Republic Pictures Page 74
"Bells of San Angelo" Script Revision: #3

CUT TO LONG SHOT OF ROY, DALE, ANDY AND THE PIONEERS.

Helen now knows that it was Roy who staged the phony holdup, but Roy still doesn't know that Helen is really Lee Madison. Bob Nolan says that the Pioneers are rehearsing a song that Madison wrote, "I Love the West." Roy makes fun of it and Helen, still not telling that she's Madison, wants to sing the song. She begins with a dramatic approach to which Roy feigns sickness. Then she straps on a six-gun and continues with an upbeat version that ends with her accidentally shooting a mounted moose head.

EARLY IN THE MORNING
(As sung by Roy Rogers and Dale Evans at the fox hunt)
transcribed by
SCOTT HOMAN
ERIC VAN HAMERSVELD
words & music by
JACK ELLIOTT
n.c.
(horn
) (Toones) Gee, but I like to get up
ear - ly in the morn - in', there are
such a lot of things to do. (Dale) To
watch the sun come steal - in', (Roy) ov - er mis - ty hills re -
veal - in' (Roy/Dale) ti - ny dia - monds spark - lin' on the
dew. It's great just to be
liv - in' from the dawn - in'. Ev - 'ry -
thing is clean and bright and new. Gee, but I
like to get up ear - ly in the morn -
in' so I can spend a long - er day with

Republic Pictures
"Bells of San Angelo"

Page 132
Script Revision: #4

CUT TO MEDIUM SHOT OF COOK STANDING BY THE CHUCKWAGON. DAY.

At the lodge, a fox hunt is organized for the British guest, Mr. Bates. Early in the morning, a chuckwagon is set up and breakfast is underway. Roy and Lee arrive on horseback. (They have become friends after Roy finally learned that Helen is really Lee Madison.) Practicing with the starting horn, Mr. Bates blows the start-the-hunt notes. Roy and Lee chime in, singing "Early In the Morning" while Cookie takes the "fox," which is really a racoon with a ribbon bow, out to be caught.

LAZY DAYS

(As sung by the Sons of the Pioneers on the front porch of the lodge)

Republic Pictures Page 185
"Bells of San Angelo" Script Revision: #4

CUT FROM EXTERIOR DALE RIDING AWAY ON TRIGGER TO EXTERIOR FRONT OF LODGE PORCH. DAY.

The Pioneers are loafing on the front porch of the lodge singing "Lazy Days." At the end of their song, Trigger runs in without a rider and rears up a couple of times to get their attention. They understand that there must be a problem and run to their horses to follow Trigger.

Produced By
Edward J. White

Directed by
William Witney

Screenplay by
Sloan Nibley, John K. Butler

Starring
Roy Rogers, Dale Evans, Estelita Rodriguez, Foy Willing and the Riders of the Purple Sage, Trigger

with
Martin Garralaga, Lucien Littlefield, Robert Emmett Keane, Robert Bice, Douglas Fowley, David Sharpe,

Prod: #1627 Released: 4 Apr 1949
Trucolor - 67min.

Roy and the Riders are game wardens. Roberts (Fowley) wounds Oliver (Bice) after they escape prison. Roberts visits Masters (Keane), Oliver's uncle, and demands to be part of a plan to get oil from Masters' brother, Russell (Littlefield). Russell and Dr. Kay Parker (Dale), run a fish hatchery. Masters kills his brother, and Oliver returns to help Roy get Roberts.

1. Oliver and Roberts argue, culminating in Roberts knifing Oliver.

2. Roberts visits Masters demanding to get in a swindle to get oil from his brother.

3. Roy mistakenly thinks that Kay is a fish poacher.

4. Roberts and Masters hook up explosives to test the lake for oil.

5. Masters shoots holes in his brother's boat, sinking it and drowning him.

6. At the reading of the will, the hatchery is given to Kay.

7. Roy has Kay arrested for Russell's murder to keep her safe.

8. Oliver returns and makes a deal with Roy to get Roberts.

9. Roy catches Roberts at the hatchery and arrests him for murder.

TWO GUN RITA

(As sung by Estelita Rodriguez and the prisoners at the jail)

transcribed by
SCOTT HOMAN
ERIC VAN HAMERSVELD

words & music by
JACK ELLIOTT

Edim Bb
pi - ty. 'Cause they ain't a - round for
F7 Bb F7
long to swear much more. (Prisoners) She can
Bb Bb7 Eb
ride and rope and wres - tle good as an - y man you
Edim Bb
know. (Estelita) And when it comes to ro - mance, I am
Cm F7 Bb
tops. Oh, I've al - ways got a
Bb7 Eb
new love. (Prisoners) But she ne - ver leaves a
Edim Bb
blue love (Estelita) 'cause when I drop him,
F7 Bb
bang, he real - ly drops. I'm Two Gun
Bb7 Eb Bb
Ri - ta from down in Gow - er Gulch, an
Cm
or - ne - ry crit - ter with a for - ty - four.
F7 Bb Bb7
(Prisoners) She should real - ly get com - mis - sions from her

Eb Edim Bbm
friend, the town mor - ti - cian. (Estelita) 'Cause I send a lot of
F7 Bbm F7 Bb
busi - ness to his door. (Prisoners) But it's sad to tell, poor
Bb7 Eb Edim
Ri - ta up and fin - 'ly met her match, a
Bb Cm
strang - er by the name of Rang - er Bill.
F7 Bb Bb7
(Estelita) When I saw I could - n't scare him, then I
Eb Edim Bb
knew I had to dare him (Prisoners) to a shoot - in' match where
F7 Bb
they both fire at will. Well,
Bb7 Eb
Two Gun Ri - ta, from down in Gow - er
Bb
Gulch, ain't gon - na use her two guns an - y -
Cm F7 Bb
more (Estelita) 'Cause my past is dead and
Bb7 Eb Edim
bur - ied, Rang - er Bill and I got mar - ried. And

Republic Pictures Page 23
"Susanna Pass" Script Revision: #2

FADE UP TO LONG SHOT OF JAIL EXTERIOR. ROY RIDES IN. NIGHT.

Carlos and his daughter, Rita (Estelita Rodriguez), are taking care of the prisoners. She is guarding them while her father is fixing dinner. Roy, the acting sheriff, arrives just as Estelita and the prisoners sing "Two Gun Rita."

SUSANNA PASS

(As sung by Roy Rogers, Dale Evans, and the Riders of the Purple Sage at dinner)

transcribed by
SCOTT HOMAN
ERIC VAN HAMERSVELD

words & music by
JACK ELLIOTT

Republic Pictures Page 62
"Susanna Pass" Script Revision: #3

CUT TO LONG SHOT OF OUTDOOR PATIO. NIGHT.

Roy, Kay, and the Riders of the Purple Sage sing "Susanna Pass" as they leisurely set the table for dinner. They are unaware that the villains are setting up a blasting charge to test for oil under the lake which will kill the hatchery fish.

A GOOD, GOOD MORNING

(As sung by Roy Rogers, Dale Evans, and the Riders of the Purple Sage at the fish hatchery)

E A
(Foy) Good to be a - live, ain't you the luck - y
C#7 F#7 B7
one. (All) Things just got - ta go right.
E
I'm gon - na shake your hand and hol - ler good, good morn -
F# B7
- in'. That's the thing that ev - 'ry one should do.
E
I'm gon - na lift my voice for it's a new day born -
F#m B7 E
- in'. A good, good morn - in' to you.
E7 GLISS A GLISS
(Dale) O - pen up your heart and let it look at the sun.
E F#m B7 3 E
(All) Broth - er, ain't that a sight.
GLISS A
(Dale) Good to be a - live, ain't you the luck - y
C#7 F#7 B7
one. (All) Things just got - ta go right.
E
I'm gon - na shake your hand and hol - ler good, good morn -

Republic Pictures
"Susanna Pass"

Page 112
Script Revision: #4

FADE UP TO LONG SHOT OF INSIDE OF FISH HATCHERY WITH POINT OF VIEW THROUGH RUNNING WATER.

At the fish hatchery, Roy and the Riders of the Purple Sage are helping Kay by bringing in barrels of young fish while singing "A Good, Good Morning."

BRUSH THOSE TEARS FROM YOUR EYES

(As sung by Roy Rogers and the Riders of the Purple Sage at the Ranger Station)

words & music by
OAKLEY HALDEMAN
AL TRACE
JIMMY LEE

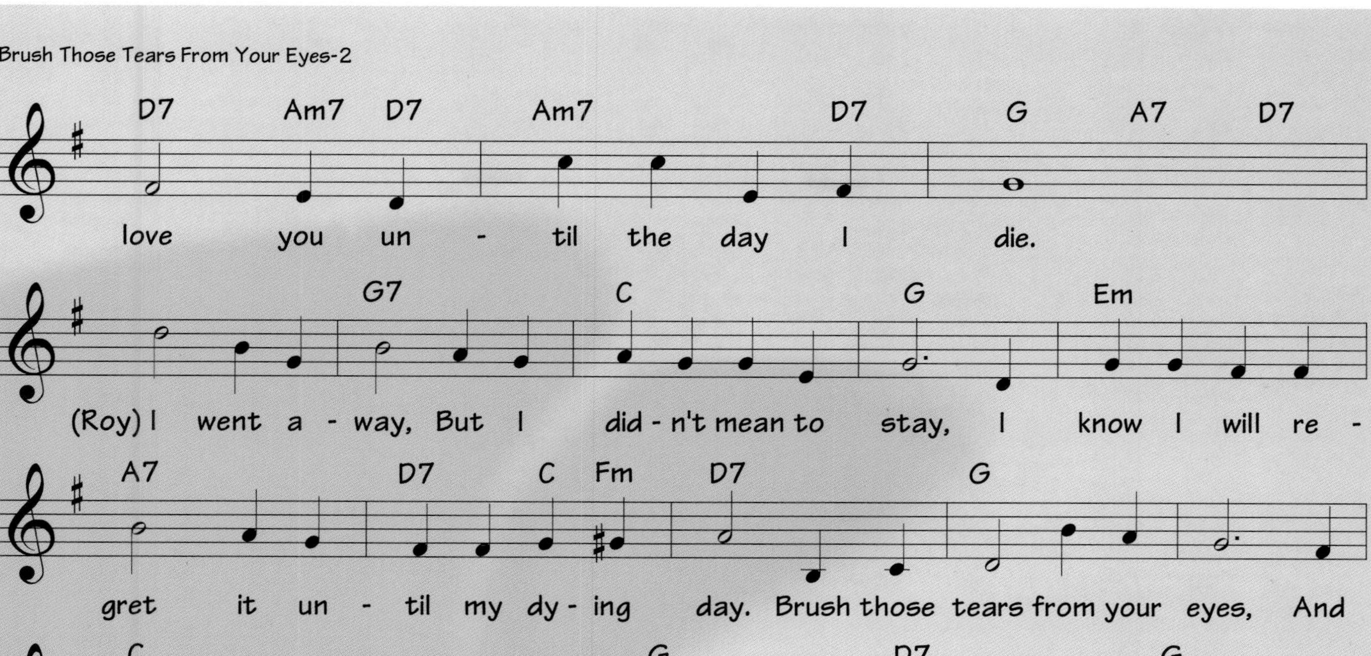

Republic Pictures Page 154
"Susanna Pass" Script Revision: #2

FADE UP ON RANGER LOOKOUT SIGN. SLOWLY PAN LEFT. CUT TO LONG SHOT OF ROOM WITH POINT-OF-VIEW THROUGH THE UPPER AND LOWER BUNKBED.

Roy and the Riders of the Purple Sage are relaxing at the ranger station waiting for Kay to arrive. She has been locked in jail to protect her life and is now going to escape across the border with the help of Roy, the Riders and Rita. While Roy feeds treats to the dog, they all sing "Brush Those Tears From Your Eyes."

Produced By
Edward J. White

Directed by
William Witney

Screenplay by
Sloan Nibley, John K. Butler

Starring
Roy Rogers, Dale Evans, Pat Brady, Foy Willing and the Riders of the Purple Sage, Trigger

with
Monte Montana, Elizabeth Risdon, Bryon Barr, James Cardwell, Roy Barcroft, Emmett Vogan

Prod: #1628 Released: 9 Sep 1949
Trucolor - 67min.

McKenzie (Barcroft), along with his men Steve (Barr) and Luke (Wilke), are trying to sell diseased cattle. Local men, Roy, the Riders and Pat, along with Ruth (Dale), the new teacher, are trying to solve several murders including a vet, and uncover the sick cattle-sale plot. Dolly (Risdon), Steve's mother, tries to persuade him to surrender before he gets killed.

1. Steve stops the bus to kill the vet, Dr. Fredericks (Vogan).

2. Steve escapes in a trail camp wagon while Roy is fighting with the trail boss.

3. Pat, a grocer and bounty hunter want-a-be, tells Roy about the rewards he's after.

4. Steve demands money from McKenzie to keep his mouth shut about the cattle.

5. Steve fights against Roy and the posse while forcing his mother to drive.

6. Roy and Pat find a sick calf.

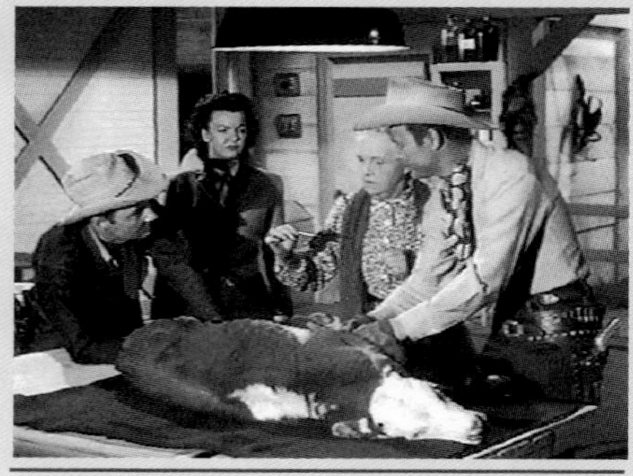

7. They discover that the calf has hoof and mouth disease.

8. Pat is wounded in the knee as he and Roy fight off the outlaws.

9. Steve surrenders just before he collapses and dies.

ALPHABET SONG

(As sung by Roy Rogers, Pat Brady, and the Riders of the Purple Sage at the school house)

transcribed by
SCOTT HOMAN
ERIC VAN HAMERSVELD

words & music by
DALE BUTTS
SLOAN NIBLEY

rubato

Db C Db Gb

(Foy) As I look a - round, (Riders) it brings back

Db Ebm Adim Db

mem - o - ries of days gone by.

Eb7

(Foy) It was in this very room we'd sit and

Ab7 Eb7

play. (Riders) And this is what the teach - er would

in tempo

Ab7 Db Gb

say. "A B C D E F

Db Ebm Db Ab7 Db

G H I J K L M N O P,

Gb Db Ebm

L M N O P Q R S T U V

Db Ab7 Db

dou - ble - U X Y Z." (trumpet instrumental

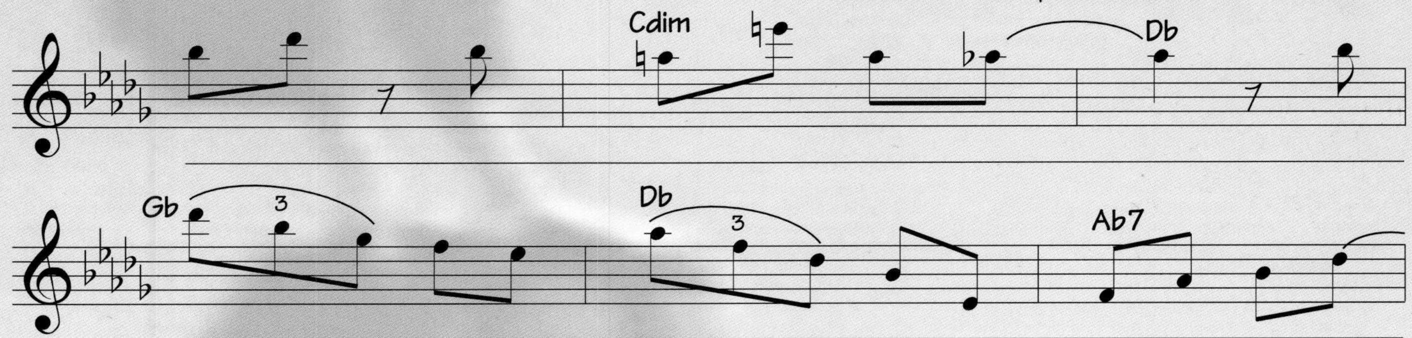

Cdim Db

Gb 3 Db 3 Ab7

Db
3
Gb
Db
Ab7
Db
Gb
Fm
) (Roy) Now you must know your
Ebm
Db
les - sons well or you'll wear a dunce cap like a
Db
Db7
Gb
Fm
Ebm
fool. (Riders) If you're a dunce, don't mind the bell
Db
Eb7
Ab7
the teach - er will keep you af - ter school.
Db
Gb
Db
till you learn: A B C D E F G
n.c.
H I (Riders say: J K?) (drum: boom, boom, boom, boom)
Ab7
Db
(Riders) L M N O P, L M N O P Q
Gb
Db
Ebm
Db
Ab7
R S T U V dou - ble - U X Y
Db
rubato
Db7
Gb
Z. (Roy) Lit - tle Juan Go - mez, he did - n't
Gbm
Db
Ab7
Db
do so well though he was so smart.

Alphabet Song-3
Db Db7 Gb
He knew how to read and he knew how to spell.
Gbm Db Ab7 Db
But it broke his heart when the
Ab Eb7 Ab
tech - er said, "Re - cite the al - pha - bet." Just
Ab Eb7 Ab
how he'd sound I'll nev - er for - get:
Db Gb Db Ebm
(Roy in Spanish) A BE CE DE E - FE GE HA - CHE
Db Ab7 Db Gb
JO - TA KA E - LE ME - NE. Si no a
Fm Ebm Db
pren des tu lec - ción, la go - rra de ton -
Db Db7 Gb
to ya te pon - gan. (Riders) If you're a
Fm Ebm Db Eb7
dunce, don't mind the bell the teach - er will
Ab7 Db
keep you af - ter school till you learn: A B
Gb Db Ebm Db Ab7
C D E F G H I J K L M N O

Republic Pictures Page 37
"Down Dakota Way" Script Revision: #2

CROSS DISSOLVE TO LONG SHOT OF SCHOOL HOUSE EXTERIOR. DAY.

The Riders of the Purple Sage are meeting Roy at the old school house. They see old musical instruments lying around and sing the "Alphabet Song." Roy and Pat, with his dogs, arrive and join in. Ruth, the new teacher, arrives and is upset that they trespassed.

THE COWBOY'S DREAM

(As sung by Roy Rogers, Dale Evans, Pat Brady and the Riders of the Purple Sage at church)

words & music by
TRADITIONAL

Republic Pictures
"Down Dakota Way"

Page 87
Script Revision: #3

CUT TO LONG SHOT CHURCH INTERIOR. DAY

It's Sunday and at church Ruth plays the organ and sings "The Cowboy's Dream" along with Roy, Pat, and the Riders of the Purple Sage. Steve's mother, who is still under arrest, is with the sheriff in the congregation. Steve shows up during the song and motions for the sheriff and his mother to step outside. He wants to give the sheriff bail money to get his mother out of jail.

CANDY KISSES

(As sung by Dale Evans and the Riders of the Purple Sage at the General Store)

words & music by
GEORGE MORGAN

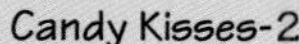

G7 C C7 F
(Riders) I built a cas - tle ___ out of dreams, dear, ___ I thought that

C D7 G7
you ___ were build - ing one too. ___ Now my

C C7 F
cas - tles ___ all have fall - en, ___ and I am

C G7 C
left ___ a - lone ___ and blue. ___

C7 F
___ (Dale) Once my heart was ___ filled with

C D7
glad - ness. ___ Now there's sad - ness, ___ on - ly

G7 C
tears. ___ (Dale) Can - dy kiss - es ___

C7 F
___ wrapped in pa - per ___ mean more to

C G7 C
you ___ (All) than mine do, dear.

Republic Pictures Page 112
"Down Dakota Way" Script Revision: #4

FADE UP LONG SHOT OF STREET. PAN TO STORE SIGN. CUT TO MEDIUM SHOT THROUGH WINDOW INTO STORE. EVENING.

Ruth and the Riders of the Purple Sage are in Pat's General Store singing "Candy Kisses" when Roy and Pat arrive with a sick calf.

Produced By
Edward J. White

Directed by
William Witney

Screenplay by
Sloan Nibley

Starring
Roy Rogers, Dale Evans, Pat Brady, Foy Willing and the Riders of the Purple Sage, Trigger, Trigger Jr.

with
Estelita Rodriguez, Douglas Evans, Frank Fenton, Greg McClure, Dale Van Sickel, Clarence Straight, Jack Sparks, Chester Conklin, Karl Hackett

Prod: #1830 Released: 15 Nov 1949
Trucolor - 67min.

Middleton (Evans) has a diamond smuggling operation that uses wild horses crossing the border. Roy arrives to rent Stormy's (Dale) ranch as a base to catch wild horses. Trigger is accused of killing one of Middleton's men. To keep Trigger from being destroyed, Roy takes the blame and goes to prison. He returns from prison and catches the smugglers.

1. The smugglers use a false horseshoe to transport diamonds.

2. Hart (Van Sickel) delivers the diamonds to his boss, Middleton.

3. Stormy welcomes Roy and Pat to her Circle B ranch.

4. Trigger is to be destroyed, but Roy quickly takes the blame to save him.

5. With Roy in jail, Trigger is auctioned off to Middleton.

6. To get the outlaws, Roy "escapes" and the sheriff gets Middleton to help catch him.

7. Roy returns and finds that Trigger's son, Trigger Jr., has been born.

8. With Roy on Trigger Jr. and Pat in his Jeep, they capture the smugglers.

9. Trigger has been with the wild horses, and Roy, with Trigger Jr., get him back.

THERE'S ALWAYS TIME FOR A SONG

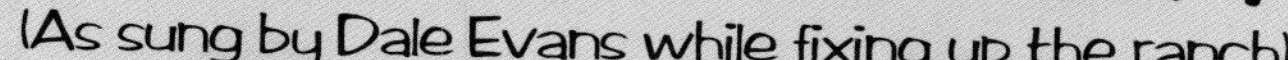

transcribed by
SCOTT HOMAN
ERIC VAN HAMERSVELD

words & music by
FOY WILLING
SID ROBIN

G E7
It makes no diff - erence where you are, la da da

A7 Am Ab7
de da. Just hang your heart next to a star, la da da

G G#dim
de da. You'll al - ways find when things are go - ing

Am Ab7 G D7
wrong, there's al - ways time for a song. What does it

G E7 A7
mat - ter, work or play, la da da de da. It makes no

Am Ab7 G
diff-erence, night or day, la da da de da. Just keep a

G#dim Am Ab7
hum - min' as you go a - long, ______ there's al - ways time for a

G Bm Bbdim Bm E7
song. You need no spe - cial sea - son. De -

Am D7 G F#m(-5) B7
cem - ber's as good as May. Just sing for an - y

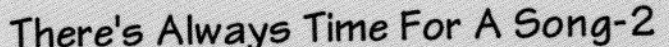

Em A7 D7

rea - son and love will come your way. If you keep

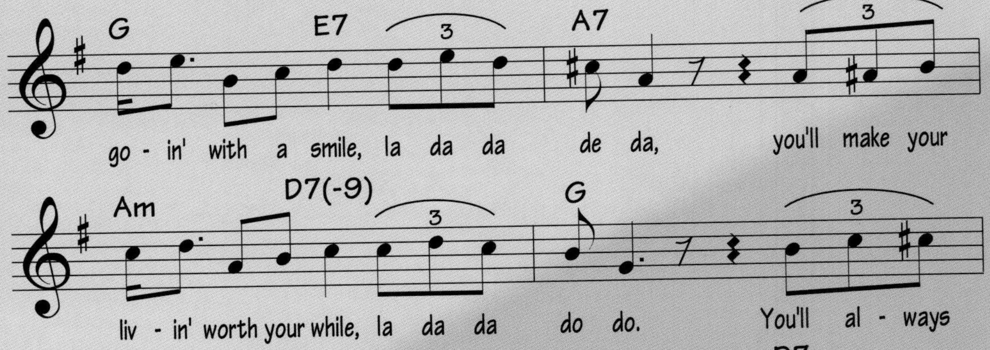

G E7 A7

go - in' with a smile, la da da de da, you'll make your

Am D7(-9) G

liv - in' worth your while, la da da do do. You'll al - ways

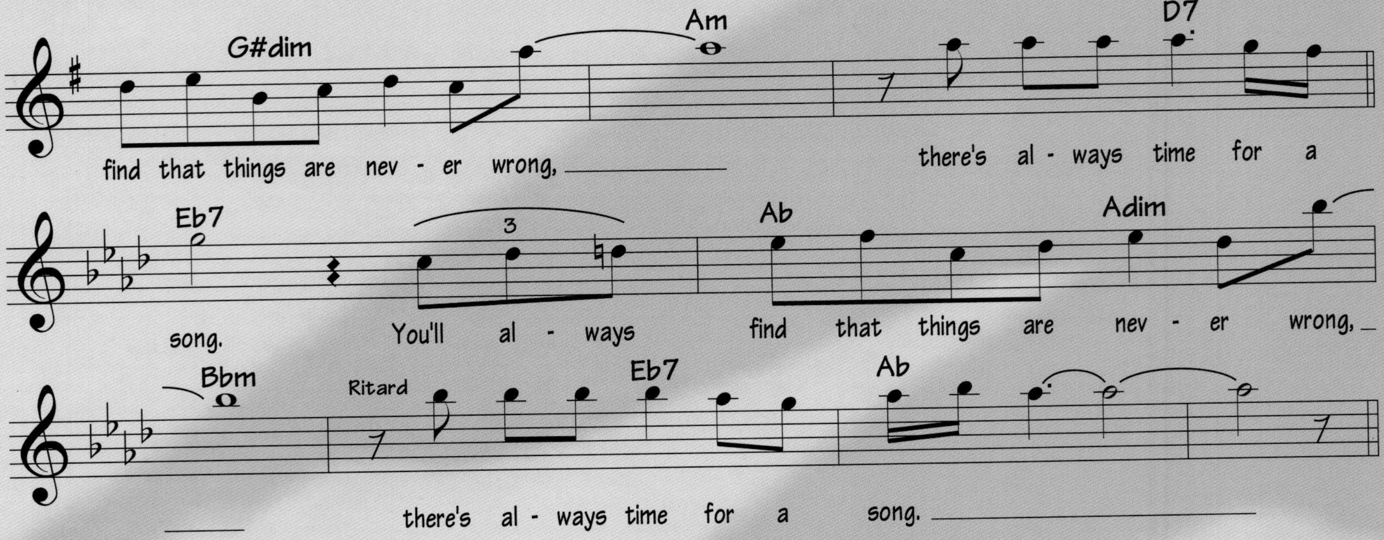

G#dim Am D7

find that things are nev - er wrong, ______ there's al - ways time for a

Eb7 Ab Adim

song. You'll al - ways find that things are nev - er wrong, ______

Bbm Ritard Eb7 Ab

there's al - ways time for a song. ______

Republic Pictures
"The Golden Stallion"

Page 26
Script Revision: #2

CUT TO CLOSE UP OF RANCH SIGN. CUT TO MEDIUM LONG SHOT AND PAN RIGHT ACROSS THE RANCH HOUSE PORCH. DAY.

Stormy and Peppi (Estelita Rodriguez) are fixing up Stormy's father's ranch, the Circle B, to lease it. While doing the chores around the ranch house, Stormy sings "There's Always Time For A Song."

THE GOLDEN STALLION

(As sung by Roy Rogers, Dale Evans, Pat Brady and the Riders of the Purple Sage at the ranch)

words & music by
SID ROBIN
FOY WILLING

Republic Pictures Page 38
"The Golden Stallion" Script Revision: #3

FADE UP ON SUNRISE GRAPHIC. DISSOLVE TO LANDSCAPE WITH WINDMILL. DISSOLVE TO MEDIUM SHOT OF HORSE OUTSIDE THE RANCH HOUSE. DAY.

Roy has leased Stormy's ranch in order to have a base of operations to catch wild horses that travel back and forth across the border. While preparing to ride out to search for the horses, Roy, Stormy, Pat and the Riders of the Purple Sage sing "The Golden Stallion."

DOWN MEXICO WAY

(As sung by Estelita Rodriquez at the celebration party)

words & music by
JULE STYNE
SOL MEYER
EDDIE MAXWELL

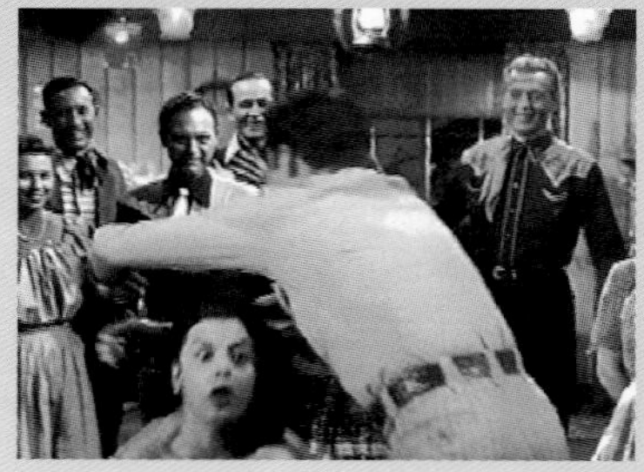

E/B B7 E F#m7
gay _____ a - way ___ and ser - en - ade _

B7 E7 A
___ your la - dy. And ___ your life will be com - plete, _____

___ your heart will beat _____ when se - nor - i - tas teach _

Bm7
___ you to play. So take a chance. _____

E9 Bm7 E9 Bm7(b5)
___ and start to dance _____ you'll find ro - mance down Mex -

E9 A
- i - co way. Ai _____ yai, ai yai. _____

Bm7
(Riders: Ai _____ yai. Ai yai. _____) So take a chance _____

E9 Bm7 E9 Bm7(b5)
___ and start to dance. _____ you'll find ro - mance down Mex -

E9 A
- i - co way. Down Mex - i - co way.

Republic Pictures Page 78
"The Golden Stallion" Script Revision: #4

CUT TO MEDIUM SHOT OF ESTELITA SURROUNDED BY GUESTS IN THE RANCH HOUSE MAIN ROOM. EVENING.

To celebrate the return of Trigger, a party is held at the ranch. After a square dance, Peppi grabs Pat to join her as she sings "Down Mexico Way." Pat is in love and at the end of the song he tries to give her a kiss, but she ducks out just in time.

NIGHT ON THE PRAIRIE

(As sung by Roy Rogers, Dale Evans, Pat Brady, Estelita Rodriguez, and the Riders of the Purple Sage at the campsite)

transcribed by
SCOTT HOMAN
ERIC VAN HAMERSVELD

words & music by
NATHAN GLUCK
ANNE PARENTEAN

G7 Dm G7
(Roy) Ev - er a - lone, never a home (All) And
C G7 Adim C Ebdim C7 E
when the long, long day is done, I'm
F Am F F7
dream - in' a - lone (Roy/Dale) in the moon - light, when
Bb Bdim F
night falls on the prai - rie.
C7sus C7 C7sus C7
But my thoughts will stray, ev - er far a - way,
F Bb F F7
dream - in' of you. (Estelita in Spanish) A
Bb F
so - las yo vo - y no se que ha - cer.
Gm C7 F
sin rum - bo vo - y que im - por - ta
G7 Dm G7
so - lo es - to - y. sin mi que - rrer. (All) And
C G7 Adim C Ebdim C7 E
when the long, long day is done, I'm
F Am F F7
dream - in' a - lone in the moon - light, when

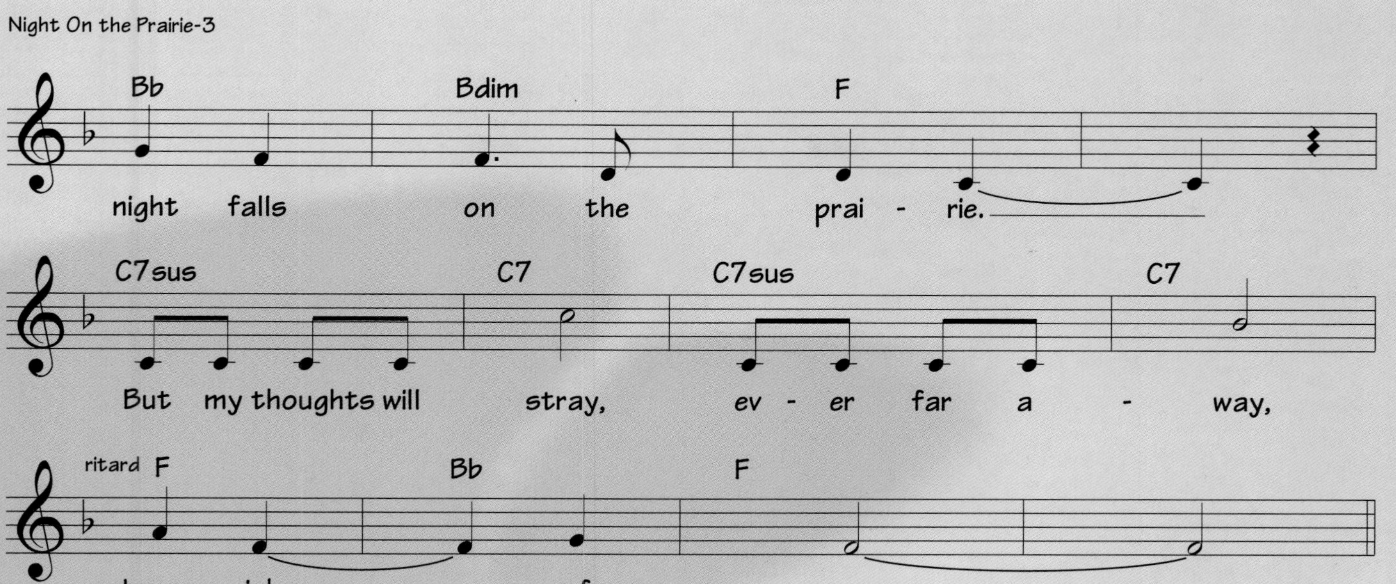

Republic Pictures Page 143
"The Golden Stallion" Script Revision: #4

CROSS DISSOLVE TO LONG SHOT OF PEOPLE AROUND CAMP FIRE. NIGHT.

Roy has "escaped" from jail and is hiding out with Stormy, Pat, Peppi, and the Riders of the Purple Sage. While they leisurely sing "Night On the Prairie" around the campfire, the sheriff and his posse are closing in on them to capture Roy. This is all just part of a plan that Roy and the sheriff have cooked up to catch the villains off guard.

Produced By
Edward J. White

Directed by
William Witney

Screenplay by
Sloan Nibley

Starring
Roy Rogers, Dale Evans, Pat Brady, Foy Willing and the Riders of the Purple Sage, Trigger

with
Grant Withers, Leo Cleary, Clifton Young, Robert Bice, Stuart Randall, John Hamilton, Edmund Cobb, Eddie Lee, Rex Lease, Lane Bradford

Prod: #1629 Released: 8 Jan 1950
Trucolor - 67min.

Roy, an insurance investigator, is out to solve the murder of uranium mine owner, Perez. To hide his identity, Roy joins the Riders as a linemen for the local power company. Pam (Dale) also works for power company. The investigation leads to an operation headed by Bennet (Withers) and Roy's old friend, Dr. Harding (Cleary), who are selling uranium to a foreign power.

1. The Riders find Perez's body floating in reservoir.

2. Insurance men Linden (Hamilton) and Rafferty (Cobb) ask Roy for help.

3. While the doctor works on Pat, Roy tells them he's looking for a job.

4. Pam's car breaks down. Roy stops to help She thinks he's an outlaw and steals Trigger.

5. Roy and Pat find the mine workers tied up in a shed.

6. While under pain drugs after being shot, Pat tells about Roy's investigation.

7. Roy suspects the doctor and is caught trying to open his safe.

8. The foreigners arrive to get the uranium, and Roy with the posse round them up.

9. Roy chases outlaw Ross (Young) up a high-tension tower.

GOT NO TIME FOR THE BLUES

(As sung by Dale Evans, and the Riders of the Purple Sage at the electical high-tension tower)

transcribed by
SCOTT HOMAN
ERIC VAN HAMERSVELD

words & music by
FOY WILLING
SID ROBIN

Got No Time For the Blues-2
B7 E7 A
got no time for the blues. (Dale) It's
D A E7
Spring all the year, from June right
A D
through to May. No time
A B7
to shed a tear, (All) ev - 'ry day's a
E7
hol - i - day. (Foy) If you
A
find some - bo - dy frown - in', Broth - er,
D
just set him straight. (Dale) Tell him that he bet - ter
D7
change his ways, it's get - ting late.
A
Hi, Part - ner! Help me spread the good news,
B7 E7 A
(All) that we've got no time for the blues.

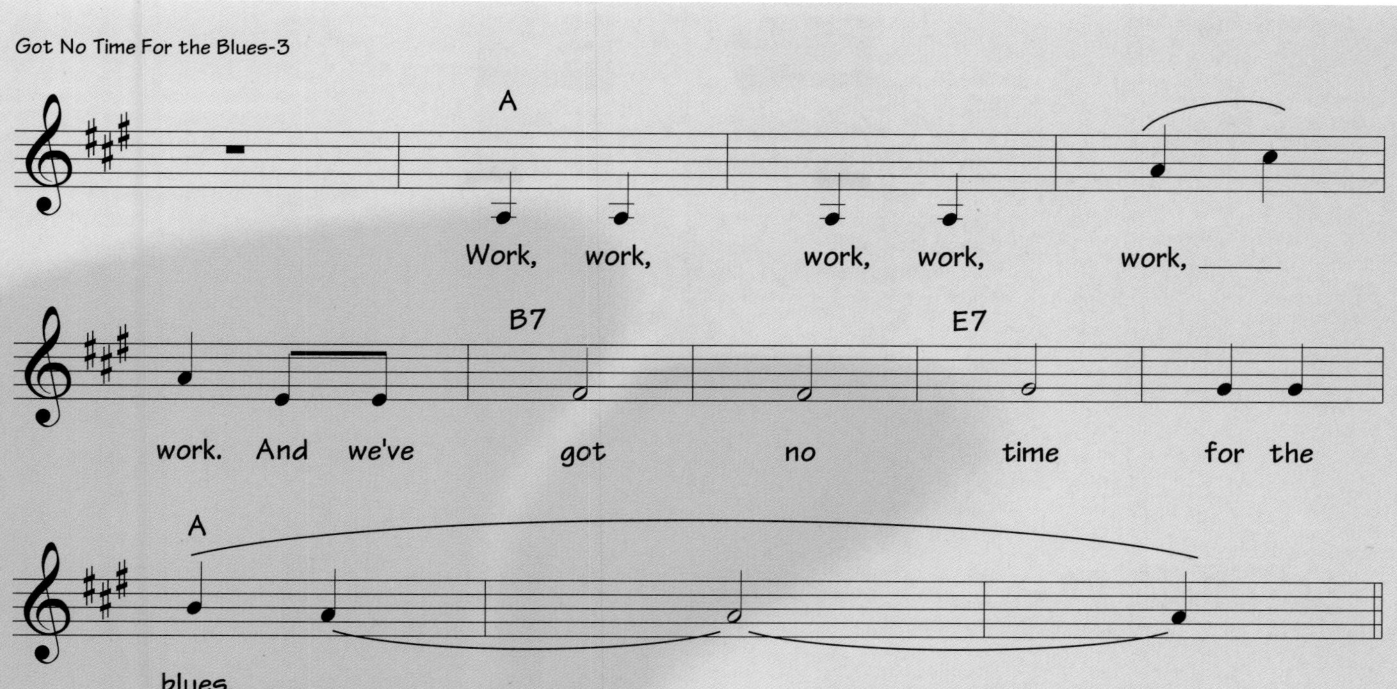

Republic Pictures Page 48
"Bells of Coronado" Script Revision: #2

CUT TO CLOSE UP OF RADIO. DAY.

The Riders of the Purple Sage, as linemen for the power company, are at their job site and have just rigged up power for their radio. Foy switches it on and they sing "Got No Time For the Blues" along with the music. During the song Pam drives up with their pay envelopes and joins in the song with them.

BELLS OF CORONADO

(As sung by Roy Rogers, Dale Evans, Pat Brady and the Riders of the Purple Sage on the trail)

Republic Pictures Page 91
"Bells of Coronado" Script Revision: #3

CROSS DISSOLVE TO LONG SHOT AT LOW ANGLE ALONG SIDE THE TRAIL. DAY.

Roy has a lineman job with the power company and he, the Riders of the Purple Sage, and Pat Brady are off to the jobsite. It's such a pretty morning that Pam decides to join the guys on their ride. Along the way they sing the "Bells of Coronado."

SAVE A SMILE

(As sung by Roy Rogers, Dale Evans, and
the Riders of the Purple Sage at the doctor's office)

transcribed by
SCOTT HOMAN
ERIC VAN HAMERSVELD

words & music by
FOY WILLING
SID ROBIN

Republic Pictures
"Bells of Coronado"

Page 149
Script Revision: #3

FADE UP ON GRAPHIC OF TOWN AT NIGHT. CROSS DISSOLVE TO FRONT OF DOCTOR'S OFFICE. NIGHT.

Pat has been shot by one of the outlaws. While recovering at the doc's office, which is also his house, Roy, Pam and the Riders of the Purple Sage throw him a party. They pass out cake and, just as they begin singing "Save A Smile," the doctor arrives.

Produced By
Edward J. White

Directed by
William Witney

Screenplay by
Sloan Nibley

Starring
Roy Rogers, Dale Evans, Pat Brady, Foy Willing and the Riders of the Purple Sage, Trigger

with
Estelita Rodriguez, Russ Vincent, George Meeker, Fred Kohler, Jr., Edward Keane, House Peters, Jr., Pierce Lyden, Don Frost, William Lester, Joseph Garro, Bob Wilke, Bob Burns

Prod: #1831 Released: 22 Mar 1950
Trucolor - 67min.

Judge Wiggens (Keane) has a halfway house for parolees. Ricardo (Vincent), a recent parolee, is abducted by Brunner's (Meeker) men to clean two counterfeit gold certificate plates. Threats on his sister, Lola (Estelita), makes him cooperate. Roy, Pat, the Riders, and Pat Callahan (Dale), the acting sheriff, must track down the counterfeiters.

1. Ricardo, a paroled counterfeiter, is taken at gun point by two of Meeker's men.

2. Roy has found a letter from the missing Ricardo stating that his sister is arriving.

3. Lola is almost kidnapped but Roy arrives and chases the villains away.

4. Clifford makes a deal with Brunner to buy the gold certificates.

5. Brunner forces Ricardo to cooperate by reminding him that they can kill Lola.

6. Roy fights Brunner's man, Mason but Brunner intervenes before he can talk.

7. Roy is accused of killing one of Brunner's men but escapes before he's arrested.

8. Roy rescues Lola and Ricardo from the burning wagon.

9. Brunner is attacked by a mountain lion and killed.

ROOTIN' TOOTIN' COWBOY

(As sung by Roy Rogers and the Riders of the Purple Sage at the chuck wagon)

transcribed by
SCOTT HOMAN
ERIC VAN HAMERSVELD

words & music by
FOY WILLING
SID ROBIN

Eb Edim F7
rest. He's a root - in' toot - in'
Bb Bb7
cow - boy from the west.
Eb Bb
(Roy) Ev - 'ry night while the moon is shin - ing
F7
bright, he slow - ly jogs a -
Bb Bb7 Eb
long. To the
Bb
beat of his faith - ful po - ny's feet,
C7 F7
he sings his cow - boy song.
Bb
(All) If he likes his west - ern cook - in',
B
and his gal is sure good look - in',
Bb F7
Sun - day he wears a fan - cy vest.
Bb D7
It's a cinch that you guessd the

Republic Pictures
"Twilight In the Sierras"

Page 8
Script Revision: #3

CUT TO LONG SHOT OF CHUCK WAGON ON OPEN RANGE. DAY.

The Riders of the Purple Sage, along with Pat Brady and Ricardo (a parolee), are tending sheep on Judge Wiggens ranch. To pass the time they sing "Rootin' Tootin' Cowboy." Roy and Williams (another parolee) ride up and Roy joins in the song.

PANCHO'S RANCHO

(As sung by Pat Brady, Estelita Rodriguez, and the Riders of the Purple Sage while riding in the wagon)

transcribed by
SCOTT HOMAN
ERIC VAN HAMERSVELD

words & music by
FOY WILLING
SID ROBIN

D7 G
nights were made for love.
D7 G
(All) Pan - cho's Ran - cho,
D7 G
that's where I will be.
D7 G
Pan - cho's Ran - cho,
D7 G
that's the place for me. (Estelita) There's ma -
G
ra - cas in the air. Some mu - ch - chos ev - 'ry
D7
where, (Pat) and a se - no - ri - ta sweet.
You'll find ev - 'ry girl and boy lives a
life of song and joy. (Estelita) And there's mu - sic
G
in the street. You will

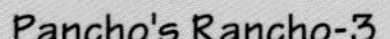

G
hear the vi - o - lins, cas - ta - nets, and man - do -

E7 Am
lins. Mel - o - dies from high a - bove.

It's the place to sing and dance. It's the

G D7
place to find ro - mance. ____ It's the place to

G D7
fall in love, (All) Pan - cho's

G D7
Ran - cho. ____ That's where I will

G D7 G
go. ____ Pan - cho's Ran - cho, ____

D7 G
____ down in Mex - i - co. ____

Republic Pictures Page 58
"Twilight In the Sierras" Script Revision: #2

CUT TO LONG SHOT OF WAGON ON THE TRAIL COMING TOWARD CAMERA. DAY.

After rescuing Lola from two villains in a runaway wagon, Roy flags down Pat, Pat Brady, and the Riders of the Purple Sage who are on their way to the ranch. He wants them to take Lola with them while he and Dale go look for the villains that fell off Lola's wagon. Along the way Pat Brady, Lola, and the Riders sing "Pancho's Rancho."

IT'S ONE WONDERFUL DAY

(As sung by Dale Evans, Roy Rogers, Pat Brady, and the Riders of the Purple Sage at the lodge)

transcribed by
SCOTT HOMAN
ERIC VAN HAMERSVELD

words & music by
FOY WILLING
SID ROBIN

G C

song. (Pat/Riders) Hoo - ray for

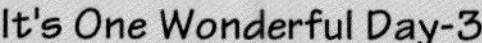

D7

gor - geous, (Dale) de - light - ful, (Roy/Dale) one won - der - ful,

G

won - der - ful day. ___ It's one

C

won - der - ful day and I'll keep it that

way. Yes, it's been like that right from the

G7 C

start. You can bet that it

G7

comes from the heart. It's a

ra - di - ant, fright - ful, a gor - geous, de -

C

light - ful, one won - der - ful, won - der - ful day.

Republic Pictures Page 78
"Twilight In the Sierras" Script Revision: #2

FADE UP TO CLOSE UP OF COOKING EGGS. CUT TO LONG SHOT OF LODGE LIVINGROOM.

The gang is going out to hunt for a marauding mountain lion. While they're eating breakfast, Pat, Roy, Pat Brady, and the Riders of the Purple Sage sing "It's One Wonderful Day."

TWILIGHT IN THE SIERRAS
(As sung by Roy Rogers, Dale Evans, Pat Brady, and the Riders of the Purple Sage at the ranch)
transcribed by
SCOTT HOMAN
ERIC VAN HAMERSVELD
words & music by
FOY WILLING
SID ROBIN
(Roy) When it's twi - light in the Si - er - ras, watch the gol - den haze
sink - ing in the west, (Riders) in the west. (Roy) Pur - ple sha - dows in the Si - er - ras, when the earth and sky
all turn to rest.
(Roy/Dale) Eve - ing spreads its vale on the trail with sil - ver dew.
Add - ing so much to a
world that's bright and new. (Roy) When it's

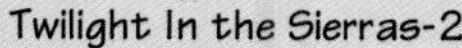

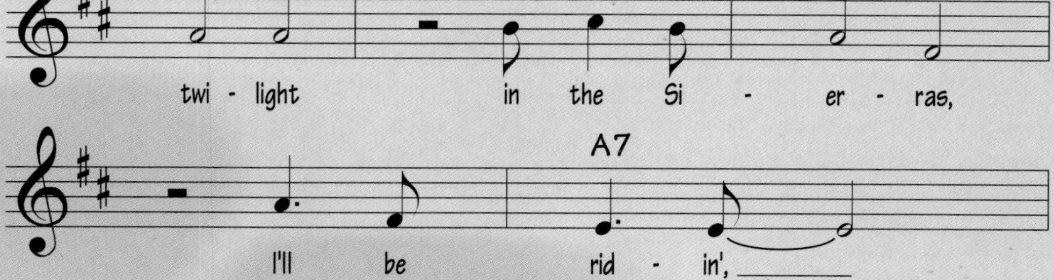

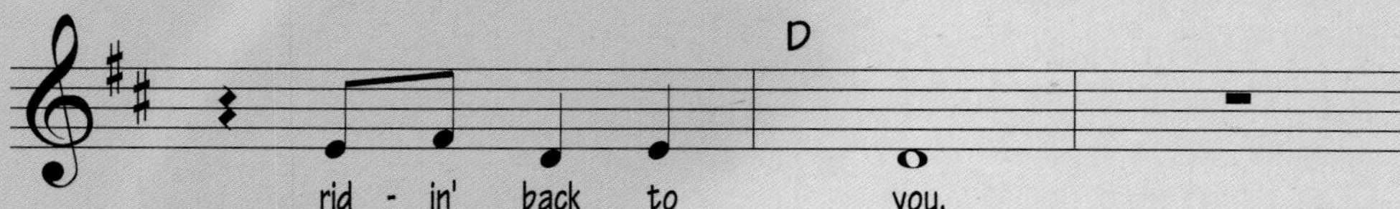

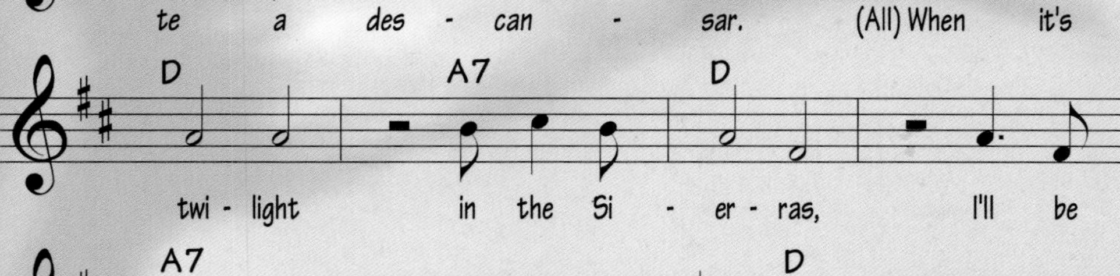

Republic Pictures
"Twilight In the Sierras"

Page 125
Script Revision: #3

FADE UP TO EXTERIOR OF RANCH. CUT TO MEDIUM LONG SHOT OF DALE. CUT TO LONG SHOT OF LIVING ROOM. NIGHT.

In a plan to catch the villain, Brunner, Roy has been paroled to the judge. Roy, Pat, Pat Brady, the Riders of the Purple Sage, and the sheriff are at the ranch waiting for Brunner to arrive to sign Roy's arrest complaint. While waiting, Roy, Pat and the Riders sing "Twilight in the Sierras."

Produced By
Edward J. White

Directed by
William Witney

Screenplay by
Gerald Geraghty

Starring
Roy Rogers, Dale Evans, Pat Brady, Gordon Jones, Foy Willing and the Riders of the Purple Sage, Trigger, Trigger Jr.

with
Grant Withers, Peter Miles, George Cleveland, Frank Fenton, I. Stanford Jolley, Jack Ingram, Stanley Andrews, Dale Van Sickle, Tom Steele, the Raynor Lehr Circus

Prod: #1834 Released: 30 Jun 1950
Trucolor - 68min.

Roy's Western Show is staying at Harkrider's ranch run by the Colonel (Cleveland), and his daughter, Kay (Dale), and his son, Larry (Miles). Mason (Withers) has an extortion operation, the Range Patrol, that includes a killer white horse that gives trouble to ranchers. When the killer horse attacks and blinds Trigger, Roy goes into action.

1. During a violent wind storm, Roy and his show arrive at the Harkrider's ranch.

2. The Colonel really doesn't want the show at his ranch because of past memories.

3. Trigger Jr. is captured by the Range Patrol and Roy comes to the rescue.

4. Roy turns down Mason's offer of the Range Patrol services.

5. Roy tangles with the killer white horse that becomes knows as the Phantom.

6. The Western Show practices their trapeze circus act.

7. Trigger fights with the white horse and goes blind from a blow to the head.

8. The Phantom Horse attacks the Colonel, knocking him from his wheelchair.

9. Roy captures Mason and has to kill the vicious white horse.

THE BIG RODEO

(As sung by Roy Rogers, Pat Brady, and the Riders of the Purple Sage at the horse auction)

transcribed by
SCOTT HOMAN
ERIC VAN HAMERSVELD

words & music by
FOY WILLING
SID ROBIN

F
west, how cow - boys earn their pay,
G7
rid - in' broncs ___ and rop - in' calfs, ___ the
C E
best time ___ of the day. So, lis - ten to our
F
sto - ry ___ of the west in all ___ its
C G7 C
glo - ry. (All) Yip - pe A, A, A, Yip - pe - o.
C
(Riders) Ro - de o, ___ (Pat yells: Who, Ha. How!) (Roy) ride 'em cow - boy.
G7
(Riders) Ro - de - o, ___ (Pat yells: He, He Yow!) (Roy) hold 'em down.
C
(Riders) Ro -de - o, ___ (Pat yells: Heee, Yaow!) (Roy) ride 'em cow - boy.
G7 C
(Riders) Yip - pe A, A, A, Yip - pe - o.
E
(Roy in Spanish) Lo quie - res por a - quí. ___ Lo

Republic Pictures Page 43
"Trigger, Jr." Script Revision: #3

CROSS DISSOLVE TO SIGN AND TILT DOWN TO READ. PAN STAGE LEFT AND TRUCK BACK TO LONG SHOT OF HORSE CORAL.

Roy, Kay, the Colonel, Pat Brady, and the Riders of the Purple Sage are at a government horse auction. Kay and her father, the Colonel, are there to bid. Roy, Pat and the Riders are there to promote their upcoming Western Show by entertaining the crowd with "The Big Rodeo." Also at the auction is Mason, the head of the Range Patrol, which is really an extortion racket aimed at the local ranchers.

MAY THE GOOD LORD TAKE A LIKIN' TO YOU

Ab Abm Adim Eb
dream come true with a ma - kin' you've
Db7 C7
no - thin' to do. It's 'cause the
F7
good Lord has tak - in' a
Fm7 Bb7 Eb C
lik - in' to you. (Dale) May the good Lord
take a lik - in' to ya. May He
D7 G7
ride be - side you all the way.
C C7
May He be your pal in your
F Fm C
life's cor - ral. And be part of your team
D7 G7
when you las - so your dream. May the
C
good Lord take a lik - in' to ya.
D7
May your wish - es nev - er go a -

May the Good Lord Take A Likin' To You-3
G7 C C7
stray. And if some - day you find a
F F#dim C
love that's true, with a find - in' you've
Bb7 A7
no - thin' to do. It's 'cause the
D7
good Lord has tak - in' a
G7 C Eb
lik - in' to you. (All) May the good Lord
Ab Eb
take a lik - in' to ya. May He
F7 Bb7
spread His bless - ings on your trail.
Eb Eb7
May He be your guide an - y -
Ab Abm F7
where you ride. And be al - ways your
Bb7
hope when you're need - in' Him most. (Dale) May the
Eb
good Lord take a lik - in' to ya. (Riders) Hap - py

Republic Pictures
"Trigger, Jr."

Page 95
Script Revision: #3

FADE UP ON CLOSE UP OF LARRY. IMMEDIATELY TRUCK BACK TO LONG SHOT OF GROUP AROUND DINING ROOM TABLE.

It's Kay's little brother Larry's birthday party. Their father, Roy, Kay, the Riders of the Purple Sage and Splinters (Jones) are gathered around the dining room table for the cake cutting. Before Larry blows out the candles, Roy, Kay and the Riders sing "May the Good Lord Take A Likin' To You."

STAMPEDE

(As sung by Roy Rogers, and the Riders of the Purple Sage during the stampede nightmare)

transcribed by
SCOTT HOMAN
ERIC VAN HAMERSVELD

words & music by
DAROL RICE
FOY WILLING

Stampede-2
Dm Gm A7
thun - der. There's wind and
Dm
rain. Stam - pede. (Riders) Stam -
pe - de. (Roy) Ten thou - sand cat - tle on the
run. Pray for an ear - ly morn - ing
Dm A7
sun. (Riders) Light - ning stabs the skies. Cat - tle
Bb A7 Dm
drop and nev - er rise. Stam - pede.
(Roy) Ten thou - sand cat - tle in
flight. The dev - il's a'rid - ing herd to -
night. (Riders) Thun - der of the
A7 Bb A7
hooves, (All) and the fu - ry from the skies,
Dm
(Roy) don't get out in front or eve - ry man

Stampede-3
dies. (Riders) Stam - pede.
Bb7
(Roy says: Coal black clouds like funeral shrouds, roll down
Cdim
their icy breath, and we faced a fright this raging
Bbdim
Fm
night, with odds on the side of death. For a
Bdim
Gbm
stampeding herd, when it's panic stirred, it's a thing for the
Dbdim
Gm
cowboy to shun. 'Cause no mortal man ever holds
Bdim
A7
command, when the cattle are on the run.) (Riders) Stam - pede. (Roy) The
Dm
ris - ing of the wind sends out its wail.
Driv - ing cat - tle down an end - less trail.
Dm
A7
Bb
(Riders) Roll - ing thun - ders boom, send - ing cat - tle to their
A7
Dm
doom. Stam - pede.

Republic Pictures
"Trigger, Jr."

Page 125
Script Revision: #5

FX DISSOLVE FROM CLOSE UP OF SLEEPING BOY TO CLOSE UP OF CAMPFIRE. TRUCK BACK TO LONG SHOT OF ME AROUND CAMPFIRE IN THUNDERSTORM. NIGHT.

Larry, also known as Duke, is in the barn staying with the blind Trigger and his calf during a thunderstorm. He drifts off to sleep and has a nightmare about Roy and the Riders singing "Stampede" on a cattle drive in the middle of their own raging thunderstorm.

Produced By
Edward J. White

Directed by
William Witney

Screenplay by
Eric Taylor

Starring
Roy Rogers, Dale Evans, Pinky Lee, the Roy Rogers Riders, Trigger

with
Douglas Fowley, Ric Roman, Leonard Penn, Willie Best, Lillian Molieri, Charlita, Pat Brady, Frank Richards, George Lewis, Marguerite McGill

Prod: #1840 Released: 15 Oct 1951
Black/White - 67min.

Roy's transportation company has been hired by Doris (Dale) to take her prized racehorse, Miss Glory, to Mexico. The gypsy, Josef (Roman), and a gang lead by Denning (Richards), working for Norris (Fowley), Doris's ranch manager, steal the horse and plan to race her back in the U.S. Roy suspects foul play and, with Pat and Pinky, they go after the horse thieves.

1. Roy with Trigger, race Doris, on Miss Glory.

2. Gypsy fortune teller Rosina (Charlita) warns Roy and Doris of danger ahead.

3. The outlaws attack Roy's truck and steal Miss Glory.

4. Roy is kept busy fighting while Josef gets Miss Glory out of the gypsy camp.

5. Norris tells Doris that Miss Glory's insurance is not good in Mexico. She'll lose the ranch.

6. Chasing a suspicious gypsy wagon, Roy transfers from a police car to Trigger.

7. Miss Glory is discovered hiding under a painted disguise.

8. The outlaws lock Roy and Doris in a stall. Pinky frees them.

9. Trigger keeps Denning occupied until Roy arrives to capture him.

MY HOME IS OVER YONDER

(As sung by Roy Rogers, Pat Brady, Wille Best, Dale Evans, and the Roy Rogers Riders while loading horses)

transcribed by
SCOTT HOMAN
ERIC VAN HAMERSVELD

words & music by
JACK ELLIOTT

Bb Bdim

not a fence can't hold him in when

Gm C7 F

he be - gins to say, (All) "My

home is o - ver yon - der. My

home is ov - er yon - der. I'd

like to stay and I may some - day, but

now I'm head - in' yon - der. I

Eb F

feel the urge to wan - der, to

Eb F

wan - der and to won - der." (Roy/Dale) I'll

sleep the night 'neath the pale moon - light. My

home is o - ver yon - der.

Bb

(RR Riders) Yon - der. (Dale) Well, I bought a shack down

Bdim F
Tex - as way, and staked a claim up north.
F7 Bb
I nearly - ly run my -
Bdim Gm C7
self to death a cha - sin' back and
F Bb
forth. (Pat) Just now and then I'd
Bdim F
tell some gal that she's the one for
F7 Bb
me, that I'll be a - wait - in'
Bdim Gm C7
fer her hand, to write me R F
F
D. (All) My home is o - ver yon - der. My
home is o - ver yon - der. (Roy/Dale) I'd
like to stay and I may some - day, but

F

now I'm head - in' yon - der. ____ I

Eb F

feel the urge to wan - der, to

Eb F

wan - der and to won - der. (Roy/Dale) I'll

sleep the night ____ 'neath the pale moon - light. (All) My

home is o - ver yon - der. ____ (Basso) My

home is o - ver yon - der. ____ (All) Yon - der.

Republic Pictures Page 17
"South of Caliente" Script Revision: #2

CUT TO MEDIUM SHOT OF WILLIE WITH HORSE. DAY.

Roy and his pals have been hired to move Doris's horses to the border for sale. To help sooth one of the horses, a skittish throughbred, Willie starts singing "My Home Is Over Yonder." Roy, Doris, Pat, and the Roy Rogers Riders join in.

GYPSY TRAIL

(As sung by Roy Rogers, Dale Evans, and Charlita at the gypsy camp)

transcribed by
SCOTT HOMAN
ERIC VAN HAMERSVELD

words & music by
JACK ELLIOTT

Gypsy Trail-2
G7 atempo Cm G7
know. (All) There be - neath the stars
Cm
you will hear their soft gui - tars.
C7 Fm
Then while sha - dows play,
they will laugh and love and dance the
G7 Cm
night a - way.
freely G7 Cm
(Dale) No one but a gyp - sy ev - er
G7 Cm
knows just where to find them.
Fm Ab G7
No one ev - er sees them come or go.
G7 Cm
It's a hid - den ron - dez - vous where
G7 Cm
cares are left be - hind them. Down the
Ab
se - cret trail that on - ly gyp - sies

G7 atempo Cm G7
know. (Roy/Dale in Spanish) Al ______ a - tar - de - cer

Cm
se o - ye el can - to del pla - cer

C7 Fm
y ______ con e - mo - ción

bai - lan, ćan - tan los gi - ta - nos

G7 Cm
su can - ci ón.

Fm
(Dale) We will laugh and love and dance the

G7 GLISS Cm
night ______ a - way.

Republic Pictures
"South of Caliente"

Page 68
Script Revision: #3

CUT TO MEDIUM SHOT OF CHARLITA. TRUCK BACK TO REVEAL LONG SHOT OF GYPSY CAMP. NIGHT.

Roy, Doris, and a local policeman are on their way to the gypsy camp to find out about the stolen horses. The horse thief leader knows they are coming and orders the gypsies to act natural and play their music. As the group arrives Rosina (Charlita) begins singing "Gypsy Trail" and pulls both Roy and Dale in to accompany her.

YASHA THE GYPSY
(As sung by Pinky Lee at the gypsy camp)
transcribed by
SCOTT HOMAN
ERIC VAN HAMERSVELD
words & music by
LEE WAINER
2/4
Em
I'm Ya - sha the gyp - sy, the
gyp, gyp, gyp, gyp, gyp - sy. Oh,
E7
Am
I'm the hot - test gyp - sy in the land.
B7
To keep my - self in
shape, I eat the hot - test food I
Em
B7
can. It hiss - es as it
siz - zles till it melts the fry - ing
Em
Am
pan. I eat it up and
Em
then I wash it down with ker - o -
Am
GLISS
Em
sene. That's why my face turns

Republic Pictures
"South of Caliente"

Page 82
Script Revision: #4

CUT TO MEDIUM LONG SHOT OF PINKY AND GYPSY. NIGHT

Pinky arrives at the gypsy camp disguised as a gypsy. Over-hearing talk about stealing horses, he's challenged by one of the men. He tries to cover himself by breaking out into the song "Yasha the Gypsy" to explain himself. Realizing this is not working, at the end of the song he beats a retreats on his mule.

WON'T YOU BE A FRIEND OF MINE

(As sung by Roy Rogers and Pinky Lee at the border crossing)

Republic Pictures
"South of Caliente"

Page 122
Script Revision: #3

CROSS DISSOLVE TO LONG SHOT OF BORDER CROSSING. TRUCK INTO MEDIUM LONG SHOT OF PINKY. DAY.

Having sent a truck load of horses into Mexico, Roy and Pinky stay to watch the border for any sign of the gypsy girl. While waiting they pass the time by singing "Won't You Be A Friend of Mine" accompanied by an unseen chorus, the Roy Rogers Riders.

Produced By
Edward J. White

Directed by
William Witney

Screenplay by
Albert DeMond, Eric Taylor

Starring
Roy Rogers, Dale Evans, Pinky Lee, Pat Brady, the Roy Rogers Riders, Trigger

with
Estelita Rodriguez, Ken Terrell, Roy Barcroft, Eduardo Jimenez, Anthony Caruso, Emmett Vogan, Maurice Jara

Prod: #1841 Released: 15 Dec 1951
Black/White - 68min.

Lopez (Jara), a Border Patrol officer, is killed while witnessing Bradford (Caruso) and Sloan (Barcroft) smuggle cattle from Mexico to the U.S. Roy, Pat and the Riders, who are also Border Patrol officers, are investigating the trouble. Things heat up and Bradford kidnaps Pancho (Jimenez), Lopez's son. Cathy (Dale) is reporting the events for the local paper.

1. Roy meets Lopez and his son Pancho.

2. Using a dust storm for cover, the smugglers herd cattle across the border.

3. Lopez tries to arrest the smugglers but they shoot him.

4. Cathy is hired as reporter for the local Rancher's Journal.

5. Bradford and Sloan kidnap Pancho in order to trade him for their man, Tony.

6. Pinky shows Roy a picture he took which shows the villains in town.

7. Roy fights with Sloan, a gun Sloan is holding goes off, and Sloan is killed.

8. The Border Patrol races in, guns blazing, to stop the smugglers.

9. Roy shoots Bradford who falls into the herd and is trampled to death.

YOU NEVER KNOW WHEN LOVE MAY COME ALONG

(As sung by Pinky Lee and Estelita Rodriguez at the office)

transcribed by
SCOTT HOMAN
ERIC VAN HAMERSVELD

words & music by
JACK ELLIOTT

Eb7 Ab7
GLISS
4
4
Gree. (Estelita) You've got to
Db
wear a smile up - on your face. Got to
Eb7
learn to sing a song, 'cause you
Ab7
nev - er know when love may come a -
Db Ab7
long, a - long. You've got to
Db
keep from Mis - ter Gloo - my's place, ev - en
Eb7
when the world seems wrong, 'cause you
Ab7
nev - er know when love may come a -
Db
long. You've got to
Ab
keep your weath - er eye o -
Bbm Ebm
pen for the la - dy known as
UNCLAIMED
FREIGHT

Republic Pictures
"Pals of the Golden West"

Page 46
Script Revision: #2

CUT TO LONG SHOT OF BUILDING FRONT. DAY.

While Pinky is sweeping up at the Borrasco Bulletin & Freight Office, he sings "You Never Know When Love May Come Along." Elena (Estelita Rodriguez), the owner of the Bulletin and the object of Pinky's affection, joins in with him.

PALS OF THE GOLDEN WEST

(As sung by Roy Rogers, Pat Brady, and the Roy Rogers Riders at the border patrol camp)

transcribed by
SCOTT HOMAN
ERIC VAN HAMERSVELD

words & music by
JACK ELLIOTT

Eb

tough, and some - one wants it rough, then,

F7 Bb7 Eb Bb7

bro - ther, there is heck to pay. So,

Eb F7

here's to all the boys a - long the bor -

Bb7 Eb

der, (Roy) the pals of the gol - den west.

We ride a lone - some

Fm

trail with on - ly a song for com - pa -

Bb7 F7

ny. (All) Pound - ing leath - er, stick - in' to - geth - er,

Bb7

tired but hap - py as can be. So,

Eb F7

here's to all the boys of law and or -

Bb7 G7

der, the old friends who are the best.

Republic Pictures Page 72
"Pals of the Golden West" Script Revision: #5

CUT TO LONG SHOT BORDER PATROL TRAILER CAMP. DAY.

Pat Brady and the Roy Rogers Riders are singing "Pals of the Golden West" as they begin their day at the border patrol camp. Roy and Pancho with Bullet, Roy's dog, ride in and Roy sings along with the men.

SLUMBER TRAIL

(As sung by Roy Rogers, Dale Evans, Pat Brady, and the Roy Rogers Riders at the border patrol camp)

transcribed by
SCOTT HOMAN
ERIC VAN HAMERSVELD

words & music by
JACK ELLIOTT

C
wail. (Roy/Dale) Pack your dreams, (Riders) Pack you dreams.
Cdim
(Roy/Dale) Time to go, (Riders) Time to go. (All) A
C G7 C
head - in' down the slum - ber trail. (Roy/Dale) Some -
F F#dim C Adim
where up there be - yond the blue, two
G7 C
lov - ing eyes are watch - ing you. A
F F#dim C Adim
ve - ry spe - cial an - gel who will
G7 D7 G7
bless and keep you all night through. So,
Cdim
close your eyes. (Riders) Close your eyes. (Roy/Dale) Lit - tle one.
C G7
(Riders) Lit - tle one. And (All) lis - ten to the sand - man's
C
tale. (Roy/Dale) Night - y night. (Riders) Night - y night.
Cdim C
(Roy/Dale) Sleep - y one. (Riders) Sleep - y one. (All) I'll meet you on the
G7 C F
slum - ber trail. (Roy/Dale in Spanish) Qui - za u -

Republic Pictures
"Pals of the Golden West"

Page 98
Script Revision: #4

CROSS DISSOLVE TO BORDER PATROL CAMP. NIGHT.

Roy and Cathy arrive at the border patrol camp just in time to sing "Slumber Trail" to Pancho along with Pat Brady and the Roy Rogers Riders.

P.S. My hope is that this is just THE BEGINNING.
That these songs will live again for future
generations of both big and little buckaroos.

-Eric

IT WAS ALWAYS THE MUSIC. . .

Len Sly, Bill "Slumber" Nichols, and Bob Nolan working on a new song.

Roy singing with the Whippoorwills.

Roy at home recording a scratch track.

Roy and Dale at home rehearsing.

Dale singing on NBC radio at the Sherman Hotel in Chicago.

A family songfest.

Roy and the Cactus Cowboys entertaining at the Walter Reed Army Hospital.

. . . AND IT STILL IS!

Young Dusty gets a singing lesson from dad.

Dusty's now all grown up and a seasoned entertainer.

Rob Johnson, one of Roy and Dale's grandsons, with Mary Briseno and Linda Johnson performing at the Northern California Outdoor Music Festival.

Rob Johnson and his group, "Heritage", singing his composition, "Hero" in honor of his grandfather, Roy.

Roy and Dale's granddaughters, Candie Halberg, Mindy Petersen, and Julie Ashley performing as the "Rogers Legacy".

THE HAPPY TRAILS CHILDREN'S FOUNDATION

By purchasing this book you not only own a unique celebration of Western Americana, but you have also helped Roy and Dale's continuing efforts on the part of abused children. The author and publisher have made arrangements to have part of the sale of this book donated to **The Happy Trails Children's Foundation.**

Roy and Trigger entertaining kids in a hospital.

Roy and Dale devoted a lifetime to supporting children in need. They entertained at hospitals and orphanages all over the country, and even put rubber boots on Trigger's hoofs so they could take him right into the rooms with the kids. They were also actively involved in the 4-H Clubs and were strong advocates for many school safety programs.

In 1982 the community of Victorville, California, near where Roy and Dale lived, formed the Victor Valley Child Abuse Task Force to stem the rising tide of child abuse, neglect, abandonment, and death in the High Desert. Roy and Dale began supporting the organization's efforts and, in 1992, the organization's name was changed to **The Happy Trails Children's Foundation**.

Along the way, many generous folks pitched in to establish a safe haven for the more severely abused and neglected children. A generous bequest from the estate of George Harold Cooper provided the financial base for a permanent home.

Then Dr. and Mrs. Philip Marsden donated a house which was moved to a 40 acre site in Apple Valley, California that had been donated by Tom and Lynn Hrubik. The house, known as the **Cooper Home**, was remodeled to become the Foundation's offices. Two cottages were constructed to house the children.

Today the Cooper Home consists of two pleasant cottages and out-buildings, and well-manicured play areas, all surrounded by snow-capped mountains and natural desert terrain under healthy, smog-free skies. This setting provides a peaceful, serene environment in which the children, ages 7 to 15, can begin their healing process.

Presently, the home is operating at a maximum capacity with a waiting list. Our goal is to increase the facilities to provide services for up to 120 children.

To accomplish this we need funding for four additional cottages. We will also need a much larger laundry, a larger maintenance facility, and more storage area for the kids' personal belongings and supplies. We also want to increase services for entire families, including a family counseling center that would double as a gym. Finally, our kids are special and they have special educational needs. Our plan is to provide on-site classrooms for them.

We want to expand the recreational activities which are an integral part of the program. During their stay at the Cooper Home, the kids go through many changes in their young lives. In addition to being away from home for extended periods, they are trying to understand and resolve difficult personal issues. Often they are lonely and frustrated. Adequate recreational facilities would give them an opportunity to just have fun.

Since the Cooper Home opened, more than 300 children have received residential care and treatment services. Our current objective is to build a third cottage on campus to

Joel "Dutch" Dortch, Executive Director

A view of the current Cooper Home facility.

increase our capacity to 60 beds. This much needed new building will cost in excess of $750,000.

An organization called the Single Action Shooting Society (SASS), in which both Roy and his son, Dusty, were active members, has designated the foundation as their charity of choice. Enter Joel "Dutch" Dortch. Dutch was at the time, and still is, deeply involved in SASS activities, both as a participant in the sharp shooting contests and the charity efforts. His success with the charity aspects of SASS prompted Dusty to ask him to be the Executive Director of the Happy Trails Children's Foundation. Dutch graciously accepted.

The Cooper Home is under the aegis of Trinity Children and Family Services, a national non-profit childcare organization with more than 30 years experience. They operate children's programs in 28 group homes and foster family agencies.

We invite you to join with us in our ongoing efforts to improve and expand the work of the foundation, either with your tax deductible gifts or through volunteerism.

Our playground for the younger kids.

You can also become a member of our Trailblazers Club and receive a Membership Card, a Membership Certificate suitable for framing, a Happy Trails pin, a quarterly newsletter, and invitations to attend special events for club members. Our goal is to make membership possible for everyone and, of course, all the dues go to support the kids.

A little fun with the hoops.

The Happy Trails Children's Foundation is a non-profit, tax-exempt charitable organization under the Internal Revenue Code, Section 501(c)(3), run by a volunteer board of directors, and a paid and volunteer staff.

For more information, please contact:
The Happy Trails Children's Foundation
10755 Apple Valley Road
Apple Valley, CA 92308
(760) 240-3330
Web site: www.happytrails.org
E-mail: happytrails@happytrails.org

APPENDIX

* (Film No.) Counts the number of the Republic films that Roy Rogers stared in starting with "Under Western Stars". Film number 40 was his first staring roll with Dale Evans.

*Film No.	Film	Song	Writer(s)	Performer(s)
40	The Cowboy and the Senorita (B/W) Released: 5/12/44 77m Prod: #1221	"Cowboy and the Senorita"	Ned Washington, Phil Ohman	Rogers
		"Bunk House Bugle Boy"	Tim Spencer	Rogers, Pioneers
		"What'll I Use for Money"	Ned Washington, Phil Ohman	Rogers, Evans, Lee, Pioneers
		"Besamé Mucho"	Sunny Skylar, Consuelo Velasquez	Evans
		"Round Her Neck She Wears a Yeller Ribbon"	(Traditional)	Lee, Pioneers
		"Enchilada Man"	Ned Washington, Phil Ohman	Rogers, Evans, Lee, Pioneers
41	The Yellow Rose of Texas (B/W) Released: 6/24/44 69m Prod: #1322	"Lucky Me, Unlucky You"	Charles E. Henderson	Rogers
		"The Yellow Rose of Texas"	(Traditional)	Rogers, Evans
		"Song of the Rover"	Bob Nolan	Pioneers
		"Down in the Old Town Hall"	Charles E. Henderson	Rogers, Evans
		"Western Wonderland"	Ken Carson, Guy Savage	Rogers, Pioneers
		"Timber Trail"	Tim Spencer	Pioneers
		"A Two-Seated Saddle and A One-Gaited Horse"	Tim Spencer	Evans
		"Down Mexico Way"	Jule Styne, Eddie Cherkose, Sol Meyer	Janet Martin
		"Take It Easy"	Albert Le Breu, Irving Taylor, Vic Mizzy	Evans
		"Showboat"	Charles E. Henderson	Evans
42	Song of Nevada (B/W) Released: 8/5/44 75m Prod: #1323	"It's Love, Love, Love"	Joan Whitney, Alex Kramer, Mack David	(Not in edited version)
		"There's A New Moon Over Nevada"	Ken Carson	Pioneers
		"Little Joe the Wrangler"	Jack Thorpe	(Not in edited version)
		"The Harum Scarum Baron of the Harmonium"	Charles E. Henderson	(Not in edited version)
		"A Cowboy Has to Yodel in the Morning"	Ken Carson	(Not in edited version)
		"Home On the Range" (Parody)	Dr. Brewster Higley, Roy Rogers Dan Kelley, Smiley Burnette	(Not in edited version)
		"What Are We Gonna to Do About This Rainy Day"	Charles E. Henderson	(Not in TV version)
		"The Wigwam Song"	Glenn Spencer	Lee, Rogers, Pioneers
		"Sweet Betsy From Pike"	(Traditional)	Rogers, Pioneers
		"And Her Golden Hair Was Hanging Down Her Back"	Felix McGlennon, Monroe H. Rosenfeld	Evans, Pioneers
		"Nevada"	Charles E. Henderson	Rogers, Evans, Pioneers
43	San Fernando Valley (B/W) Released: 9/15/44 74m Prod: #1325	"My Hobby Is Love"	Charles E. Henderson	Porter, Pioneers
		"One Thousand Eight Hundred and Forty Nine"	Tim Spencer, Roy Rogers	Pioneers
		"San Fernando Valley"	Gordon Jenkins	Rogers, Evans, Pioneers
		"I Drottled a Drit Drit"	William Lava, A. Walker	Porter, Pioneers
		"They Went That-a-Way"	Tim Spencer	Rogers, Gargon
		"How Could Anyone Be Sweeter Than You"	Charles E. Henderson	Rogers, Evans
		"Over the Rainbow Trail We'll Ride"	Ken Carson	Pioneers
44	Lights of Old Santa Fe (B/W) Released: 11/6/44 78m Prod: #1326	"Amor"	Sunny Skylar. Gabriel Ruiz, Ricardo Lopez Mendez	Evans
		"Cowpoke Polka"	Tim Spencer	Rogers, Pioneers, Gabby
		"I'm Happy In My Levi Britches"	Tim Spencer	Rogers, Pioneers
		"Cowboy Jubilee"	Ken Carson	Rogers, Pioneers
		"The Nerve of Some People"	Jack Elliott	Evans, Rogers
		"Trigger Hasn't Got a Purty Figure"	Tim Spencer	Rogers
		"Ride 'em Cowboy"	Roy Rogers, Tim Spencer	Pioneers
		"Lights of Old Santa Fe"	Jack Elliott	Rogers, Evans, Pioneers, Gabby
45	Utah (B/W) Released: 3/21/45 78m Prod: #1329	"Thank Dixie For Me"	Dave Franklin	Evans
		"Welcome Home Miss Bryant"	Ken Carson, Bob Nolan	Rogers, Pioneers
		"Five Little Miles"	Bob Nolan	Pioneers

Film No.	Film	Song	Writer(s)	Performer(s)
		"Beneath a Utah Sky"	Glenn Spencer	Rogers
		"Wild and Wooly Gals"	Tim Spencer	Rogers
		"Utah"	Charles E. Henderson	Rogers, Evans, Pioneers
		"Lonesome Cowboy Blues"	Tim Spencer	Rogers
46	Bells of Rosarita (B/W) Released: 6/19/45 68m Prod: #1324	"Bugler's Lullaby"	Robert Mitchell Mitchell, Betty Best, Ken Curtis (trumpet0	Boys' Choir
		"Bells of Rosarita"	Jack Elliott	Rogers, Boys' Choir
		"Under a Blanket of Blue"	Marty Symes, Al Neiburg, Jerry Livinston	Evans
		"Singing Down the Road"	Charles Tobias, Raymond Scott	Rogers
		"Gonna Build a Big Fence Around Texas"	Cliff Friend. George Olseu, Katherine Phillips	Rogers, Boys' Choir
		"Michael Finnegan"	(Traditional)	Boys' Choir
		"When the Circus Came to Town"	Jimmy Eaton, Julian Kay, Terry Shand	Pioneers
		"Trail Herdin' Cowboy"	Bob Nolan	Rogers, Pioneers
47	The Man From Oklahoma (B/W) Released: 8/1/45 68m Prod: #1328	"Skies Are Bluer"	Sanford Green, June Carroll	Rogers, Evans, Pioneers
		"We're Gonna Have a Cowboy Wedding When the Sage Is All Abloom"	Milo Allison Sweet, Nathaniel Vincent	Rogers, Pioneers
		"I'm Beginning to See the Light"	Harry James, Duke Ellington, Johnny Hodges, Don George	Evans
		"For You and Me"	Kim Gannon, Walter Kent	Evans
		"Prairie Mary"	Charles Tobias, Abel Baer	(Not in edited version)
		"The Martins and the Coys"	Alan Cameron, Ted Weems	(Not in edited version)
		"Draggin' the Wagon"	Tim Spencer	(Not in edited version)
		"Cheero Cheero Cherokee"	Tim Spencer	Pioneers
48	Sunset in El Dorado (B/W) Released: 9/24/45 66m Prod: #1421	"Go West, Young Man"	Tim Spencer	Pioneers
		"I'm Awfully Glad I Met You"	George Meyers, Jack Drislane	Evans
		"Lady Who Wouldn't Say Yes"	Jack Elliott	Rogers, Evans
		"Be My Little Lady Bug" (Bumblebee)	Henry I. Marshall, Stanley Murphy	(Not in edited version)
		"The Quilting Party"	(Traditional)	(Not in edited version)
		"Belle of the El Dorado"	Jack Elliott	Rogers, Evans
		"It's No Use"	Ken Carson	(Not in edited version)
		"The Call of the Prairie"	Ken Carson	Rogers, Evans
49	Don't Fence Me In (B/W) Released: 10/20/45 71m Prod: #1327	"A Kiss Goodnight"	Floyd Victor, Reba Herman, Freddie Slack	Evans
		"Choo Choo Polka"	Zeke Manners, Mike Shore	Rogers, Pioneers
		"My Little Buckaroo"	M. K. Jerome, Jack Scholl	Rogers
		"Don't Fence Me In"	Cole Porter, Robert H. Fletcher	Rogers, Evans, Pioneers
		"The Last Roundup"	Billy Hill	Pioneers
		"Along the Navajo Trail"	Larry Markes, Dick Charles, Eddie de Lange	Rogers, Pioneers
		"Tumbling Tumbleweeds"	Bob Nolan	Pioneers
50	Along the Navajo Trail (B/W) Released: 12/15/45 66m Prod: #1425	"Free As the Wind"	Jack Elliott	Rogers, Gypsies
		"It's the Gypsy In Me"	Jack Elliott	Rodriguez
		"Saskatoon" (incomplete)	Jack Elliott	Rogers
		"Saving for A Rainy Day"	Jack Elliott	Rogers, Evans
		"Cool Water"	Bob Nalan	Pioneers
		"Along the Navajo Trail"	Larry Markes, Dick Charles Eddie de Lange	Rogers
		"How're Ya Doin' In the Heart Department"	Charles Newman, Arthur Altman	Evans
		"Twenty One Years Is a Mighty Long Time"	Tim Spencer	Rogers, Pioneers

Film No.	Film	Song	Writer(s)	Performer(s)
51	Song of Arizona (B/W) Released: 3/9/46 68m Prod: #1422	"Song of Arizona"	Jack Elliott	Rogers, Pioneers, Boys' Choir
		"Way Out There"	Bob Nolan	Rogers, Gabby, Boys' Choir
		"Half-A-Chance Ranch"	Jack Elliott	Evans
		"Round and Round-the Lariat Song"	Jack Elliott	Rogers, Evans
		"That Feeling in the Moonlight"	James Cavanaugh, Ira Schuster, Larry Stock	
		"Michael O'Leary, O'Brian, O'Toole"	Tim Spencer	Pioneers
		"Will Ya' Be My Darling"	Jack Owens, Mary Ann Owens	Rogers, Evans
		"When Mister Spook Steps Out"	Jack Elliott	Rogers, Evans
52	Rainbow Over Texas (B/W) Released: 5/9/46 65m Prod: #1428	"Lights of Old Santa Fe" (incomplete)	Jack Elliott	Rogers, Evans
		"Texas U.S.A."	Tim Spencer	Rogers, Pioneers
		"Little Senorita"	Jack Elliott	Rogers, Evans
		"Outlaw"	Jack Elliott	Saloon Singer
		"Rainbow Over Texas"	Jack Elliott	Rogers, Evans, Pioneers
		"Cowboy Camp Meeting"	Tim Spencer	Pioneers
53	My Pal Trigger (B/W) Released: 7/10/46 79m Prod: #1427	"Livin' Western Style"	Don Swander, June Hershey	Rogers
		"Harriet"	Abel Baer, Paul Cunningham	Rogers, Evans
		"El Rancho Grande"	Silvano R. Ramos, Emilio Uranga, Bartley Costello	Pioneers
		"Ole Faithful"	Michael Carr, Hamilton Kennedy	Rogers
		"Long, Long Ago"	(Traditional)	Evans
54	Under Nevada Skies (B/W) Released: 8/26/46 69m Prod: #1429	"Ne-Hah-Neé"	Bob Nolan	Rogers, Pioneers
		"I Want to Go West"	Jack Elliott	Evans
		"Under Nevada Skies"	Jack Elliott	Rogers, Evans, Pioneers
		"Sea Goin' Cowboy"	Tim Spencer	Pioneers
		"Anytime That I'm With You"	Jack Elliott	Rogers, Evans
55	Roll On, Texas Moon (B/W) Released: 9/12/46 67m Prod: #1523	"What's Doin' Tonight in Dreamland"	Jack Elliott	Rogers, Pioneers
		"Jumpin' Bean"	Tim Spencer	Pioneers
		"Won't You Be a Friend of Mine?"	Jack Elliott	Rogers, Evans
		"Roll On, Texas Moon"	Jack Elliott	Rogers, Evans
56	Home in Oklahoma (B/W) Released: 11/8/46 72m Prod: #1520	"Home in Oklahoma"	Jack Elliott	Pioneers, Chorus
		"I Wish I Was a Kid Again"	Jack Elliott	Rogers
		"Everlasting Hills of Oklahoma"	Tim Spencer	Pioneers
		"Jailhouse Song" (incomplete)	Jack Elliott	Gabby
		"Breakfast Club Song"	Jack Elliott	Rogers, Evans, Gabby, Pioneers, Breakfast Club
		"Cowboy Ham & Eggs"	Tim Spencer	Rogers, Pioneers
		"Miguelito"	Jack Elliott	Rogers, Evans
		"Hereford Heaven"	Roy Turner	Flying L Ranch Quartet
57	Heldorado (B/W) Released: 12/15/46 70m Prod: #1534	"Silver Stars, Purple Sage, Eyes of Blue"	Denver Daling	Rogers
		"Heldorado"	Jack Elliott	Rogers, Evans, Pioneers
		"My Saddle Pals and I"	Roy Rogers	Rogers, Pioneers
		"Good Neighbor"	Jack Elliott	Rogers, Evans
		"You Ain't Heard Nothin' 'Till You Hear Him Roar"	Bob Nolan	Brady, Pioneers
58	Apache Rose (Trucolor) Released: 2/15/47 75m Prod: #1526	"Ride Vaqueros"	Jack Elliott	Rogers, Vaqueros
		"José"	Tim Spencer, Glenn Spencer	Pioneers, Evans
		"Wishing Well"	Jack Elliott	Rogers, Pioneers
		"There's Nothing Like Coffee in the Morning"	Jack Elliott	Evans
		"Apache Rose"	Jack Elliott	Pioneers

Film No.	Film	Song	Writer(s)	Performer(s)
59	Bells of San Angelo (Trucolor) Released: 5/15/47 78m Prod: #1525	"Bells of San Angelo" "Hot Lead" "A Cowboy's Dream of Heaven" "I Love the West" "Early in the Morning" "Lazy Days"	Jack Elliott, Arron Gonzalez Tim Spencer Jack Elliott Jack Elliott Jack Elliott Tim Spencer	Rogers, Pioneers Brady, Pioneers Rogers, Pioneers Evans, Pioneers Rogers, Evans Pioneers
68	Susanna Pass (Trucolor) Released: 4/29/49 67m Prod: #1627	"Two-Gun Rita" "Susanna Pass" "A Good, Good Morning" "Brush Those Tears From Your Eyes"	Jack Elliott Jack Elliott Foy Willing, Sid Robin Albert Trace, Jimmy Lee Oakey Haldeman	Rodriguez Rogers, Evans, Riders Rogers, Evans, Riders Rogers, Riders
69	Down Dakota Way (Trucolor) Released: 9/9/49 67m Prod: #1628	"Alphabet Song" "Cowboy's Dream" "Candy Kisses"	Dale Butts, Sloan Nibley (Traditional) George Morgan	Rogers, Brady, Riders Rogers, Evans, Riders Evans, Riders
70	The Golden Stallion (Trucolor) Released: 11/15/49 67m Prod: #1830	"There's Always Time For A Song" "Golden Stallion" "Down Mexico Way" "Night On the Prairie"	Foy Willing, Sid Robin Foy Willing, Sid Robin Jule Styne, Eddie Cherkose, Sol Meyer Nathan Gluck, Anne Parentean	Evans Rogers, Evans, Riders Rodriguez Rogers, Evans, Riders, Brady, Rodriguez
71	Bells of Coronado (B/W) Released: 1/8/50 67m Prod: #1629	"Got No Time for the Blues" "Bells of Coronado" "Save A Smile (for a Rainy Day)"	Foy Willing, Sid Robin Foy Willing, Sid Robin Foy Willing, Sid Robin	Evans, Riders Rogers, Evans, Riders Rogers, Evans, Brady
72	Twilight in the Sierras (Trucolor) Released: 3/22/50 67m Prod: #1831	"Rootin', Tootin' Cowboy" "Pancho's Rancho" "It's One Wonderful Day" "Twilight in the Sierras"	Foy Willing, Sid Robin Foy Willing, Sid Robin Foy Willing, Sid Robin Foy Willing, Sid Robin	Rogers, Riders Brady, Rodriguez, Riders Rogers, Evans, Brady Riders Rogers, Riders
73	Trigger, Jr. (Trucolor) Released: 6/30/50 68m Prod: #1834	"The Big Rodeo" "May the Good Lord Take a Likin' to You" "Stampede"	Foy Willing, Sid Robin Roy Rogers, Peter Tinturin Foy Willing, Darol Rice	Rogers, Brady, Riders Rogers, Evans, Riders Rogers, Riders
80	South of Caliente (B/W) Released: 10/15/51 67m Prod: #1840	"My Home is Over Yonder" "Gypsy Trail" "Yasha the Gypsy" "Won't You Be A Friend of Mine"	Jack Elliott Jack Elliott Lee Wainer Jack Elliott	Rogers, Evans, Brady R/R Riders Rodriguez, Rogers, Evans Pinky Lee Rogers, Pinky Lee
81	Pals of the Golden West (B/W) Released: 12/15/51 68m Prod: #1841	"You Never Know When Love May Come Along" "Pals of the Golden West" "Slumber Trail"	Jack Elliott Jack Elliott Jack Elliott	Pinky Lee, Rodriguez Rogers, R/R Riders, Brady Rogers, Evans, R/R Riders

ABOUT THE AUTHOR

With a BA Degree in Television & Film Production from TCU, for over 30 years Eric van Hamersveld has been involved in all creative, technical and business phases of the entertainment industry. He has been an on-the-air director for a CBS affiliate and an animator for Warners Bros., J. Ward Productions, and Hanna Barbara Studios. His credits include: *"The Pink Panther"; "Road Runner"; "Speedy Gonzalez"; "George of the Jungle"; "Yogi Bear"; "Huckleberry Hound"; "Capt'n Crunch"; "Star Kist-Charlie The Tuna"; "MCA Universal Studios"* movie title; *"How the Grinch Stole Christmas", James Thurber's: My World and Welcome to It",* and, for the Walt Disney Company, he produced visual special effects for the EPCOT, Disneyland, and Tokyo Disneyland theme park projects.

Currently, he is the illustrator for a series of childrens' books for Digital Imagination and also a computer multimedia graphics director with credits that include: *"Teen Health", "Physical Sciences",* and *"Children's Bible Stories",* for McGraw Hill Publishing; *"Fractions Pizza"* for Panasonic; and training courses for Ford, Chrysler, and GM.

Because of his love for the golden era of B-Western motion picture production, and having grown up in Fort Worth, Texas, "Where The West Begins", years ago he began a serious effort to collect and document information about this genre. His library contains over 25 volumes written about this topic, boxes of clippings and correspondence, and a collection of hundreds of films.

Eric lives with his wife, Sue, and their parrot, Paco, in Carlsbad, California.